TOMBS, GRAVES
AND MUMMIES

TOMBS, GRAVES
AND MUMMIES

EDITOR: PAUL G. BAHN

Weidenfeld & Nicolson
London

Compilation © Paul Bahn

First published in Great Britain in 1996 by
George Weidenfeld & Nicolson Ltd
The Orion Publishing Group
5 Upper St Martin's Lane
London WC2H 9EA

British Library Cataloguing-in-Publication Data
A catalogue for this book is available from the British
Library

ISBN 0 297 83628 5

Picture researcher: Joanne King
Designed by Bradbury and Williams
Designer: Bob Burroughs
Maps by Mountain High Maps ®
Copyright © 1996 Digital Wisdom, Inc.
Printed in Italy

TITLE PAGE: The Treasury of Atreus at Mycenae.

LIST OF CONTRIBUTORS

PAUL G. BAHN, General Editor and contributor, Hull, England (Early periods, Western Europe)

CAROLINE BIRD, School of Archaeology, La Trobe University, Melbourne, Australia (Australasia)

PETER BOGUCKI, School of Engineering and Applied Science, Princeton University, USA (Later Periods, Central and Eastern Europe and ex-USSR)

CONNIE CORTEZ, Department of Art History, University of California, Santa Cruz, USA (Mesoamerica)

PHILIP DUKE, Department of Anthropology, Fort Lewis College, Durango, USA (North America)

CHRISTOPHER EDENS, Philadelphia, USA (Near East, Central Asia)

DAVID GILL, Department of Classics and Ancient History, University College, Swansea, Wales (Classical Archaeology)

JOHN HOFFECKER, Argonne National Laboratory, Illinois, USA (Early periods, Central and Eastern Europe and ex-USSR)

MARK HUDSON, Department of History and Culture, Okayama University, Japan (Far East)

SIMON KANER, Department of Archaeology, University of Cambridge, England (Late periods, Western Europe)

KATHARINA SCHREIBER, Department of Anthropology, University of California, Santa Barbara, USA (South America)

STEVEN SNAPE, School of Archaeology, Classics and Oriental Studies, University of Liverpool, England (Egypt and the Levant)

LOUISE STEEL, Department of Archaeology, University of Edinburgh, Scotland (The Aegean)

ANNE THACKERAY, Department of Archaeology, University of the Witwatersrand, South Africa (Africa)

CONTENTS

PREFACE *10*

BONES

1. LUCY: OUR MOST FAMOUS RELATIVE *14*
by Anne Thackeray

2. THE TURKANA BOY *18*
by Anne Thackeray

3. BEFORE THE NEANDERTHALS:
THE FIRST EUROPEANS *20*
by John Hoffecker and Paul G. Bahn

4. PEKING AND JAVA MAN: EARLY
HUMANS IN EASTERN ASIA *22*
by Mark Hudson

5. EARLIEST AUSTRALIANS *26*
by Caroline Bird

6. HUMAN SACRIFICE AT
ARCHANES-ANEMOSPILIA *30*
by Louise Steel

GRAVES

7. THE PUZZLE
OF NEANDERTHAL BURIAL *34*
by John Hoffecker

8. LATE ICE AGE BURIALS OF EURASIA *38*
by John Hoffecker

9. JERICHO SKULLS *42*
by Christopher Edens

10. LA CHAUSSÉE-TIRANCOURT *46*
by Simon Kaner

11. THE TALHEIM NEOLITHIC MASS BURIAL *48*
by Peter Bogucki

12. MASS BURIALS IN NORTH AMERICA *50*
by Philip Duke

13. MASS GRAVES: VISBY AND EAST SMITHFIELD *52*
by Simon Kaner

14. THE TRAGIC END OF THE ROMANOVS *56*
by Paul G. Bahn

CEMETERIES

15. SCANDINAVIAN MESOLITHIC BURIALS *62*
by Peter Bogucki

16. MURRAY VALLEY CEMETERIES *66*
by Caroline Bird

17. THE ROYAL CEMETERY AT UR *68*
by Christopher Edens

18. THE CEMETERY AT KHOK PHANOM DI *72*
by Mark Hudson

19. BATTLE CEMETERIES *74*
by David Gill and Simon Kaner

20. THE PARACAS NECROPOLIS *78*
by Katharina Schreiber

21. THE TEMPLE OF QUETZALCOATL
AT TEOTIHUACÁN *82*
by Connie Cortez

22. INGOMBE ILEDE *86*
by Anne Thackeray

23. VOICES OF THE SEVENTH CAVALRY *88*
by Philip Duke

TOMBS

24. THE SHAFT GRAVES OF MYCENAE *92*
by Louise Steel

25. DANISH BRONZE AGE
LOG COFFIN BURIALS *96*
by Simon Kaner

26. TOMBS IN THE PERSIAN GULF *100*
by Christopher Edens

27. KLASIES RIVER MOUTH CAVE 5 *104*
by Anne Thackeray

28. HOCHDORF *106*
by Peter Bogucki

29. PHILIP OF MACEDON *110*
by David Gill

30. ROYAL BURIALS
OF EARLY IMPERIAL CHINA *114*
by Mark Hudson

31. THE LORDS OF SIPÁN *118*
by Katharina Schreiber

32. MONTE ALBÁN, TOMB 7 *122*
by Connie Cortez

33. THE TOMB OF PACAL AT PALENQUE *126*
by Connie Cortez

34. IGBO-UKWU *130*
by Anne Thackeray

35. EARLY PACIFIC ISLANDERS *132*
by Caroline Bird

CORPSES

36. DISCOVERING THE ORIGINS
OF NEW WORLD HUMANS *138*
by Philip Duke

37. THE ICEMAN *140*
by Paul G. Bahn

38. PAZYRYK AND THE UKOK PRINCESS *146*
by Peter Bogucki

39. LOST CAUCASOIDS OF THE TARIM BASIN *152*
by Mark Hudson

40. HERCULANEUM AND POMPEII *154*
by David Gill

41. INKA MOUNTAIN SACRIFICES *160*
by Katharina Schreiber

42. BOG BODIES OF BRITAIN AND DENMARK *164*
by Simon Kaner

43. THE FRANKLIN EXPEDITION *170*
by Philip Duke

44. MUMMIES IN THE FAR NORTH *174*
by Philip Duke

MUMMIES

45. CHINCHORRO – THE OLDEST MUMMIES
IN THE WORLD *180*
by Katharina Schreiber

46. MAKING MUMMIES *182*
by Steven Snape

47. MUMMIES AND MEDICINE *186*
by Steven Snape

48. THE DEIR EL-BAHRI CACHE *188*
by Steven Snape

49. THE FAMILY OF TUTANKHAMEN *192*
by Steven Snape

50. THE MUMMIES OF
THE NORTHERN FUJIWARA *198*
by Mark Hudson

Maps *200*
Bibliography *204*
Index *208*
Acknowledgments *213*

PREFACE

Since archaeology is the study of the material remains of the human past, there can be few experiences more vivid and emotional for an archaeologist than to come face to face with the very people who produced those remains — especially if the bodies are well preserved, or are those of particular rulers or others whose names and deeds are known to us. The vast majority of human remains that survive from the past, especially the remote past, are in the form of skeletons or cremated bones; but there are also surprisingly large numbers of bodies that have come down to us with soft tissue intact, preserved through aridity, extreme cold, waterlogging or deliberate mummification. In addition, there are "imprints" left by bodies that have long since disappeared — footprints and handprints in cave floors (especially in Ice Age France); painted handprints and stencils in caves and rock-shelters around the world; fingerprints on potsherds; and of course the famous hollows left by the dead of Pompeii (p. 154).

Human remains and burials have been of major importance in the history of archaeology, although they are only a small part of what archaeologists study; the archaeologist has traditionally been most interested in a grave's layout and the accompanying objects or clothing rather than the body. It is physical anthropologists who tend to study and curate human remains — few archaeologists ever bothered to analyse bodies or skeletons, and very little is taught on archaeology courses about human remains (as opposed to animal bones, for example).

So it was a considerable shock to the archaeological world when, in the late 1970s, it came under vehement attack by native peoples in North America and Australia, and by ultra-orthodox Jews in Israel, who objected vociferously to the disturbance, analysis and display of "ancestral human remains", and who demanded the return of their ancestors for reburial. Most archaeologists — and physical anthropologists — had never given any

thought to this: they had always felt free to investigate whatever and wherever they wished, with only warfare, natural hazards or economic difficulties (lack of equipment, funds or personnel) to set limits to their activities. Nothing was to be found in either textbooks or lectures concerning the ethics of the discipline or respect for the wishes of indigenous people.

Where the dead were concerned, there were numerous accounts in print about how to excavate graves or skeletons, with an intense concentration on funerary rites, orientation of the grave or body, the presence, absence or type of grave goods — but not a word about whether one had the right to disturb the dead in this way, let alone any suggestion of sounding out the indigenous people's feelings on the matter. When asked about disturbing the dead, in a 1973 television interview, Sir Mortimer Wheeler merely claimed this was a sentimental tradition, and the excavation of graves did no harm.

In the above-mentioned countries, however, the 1980s saw a radical transformation of the situation. Special committees were set up by archaeological and anthropological associations and by museums to discuss the issue, and to thrash out policies that would go some way towards settling the demands of the objectors while limiting the damage to existing collections and the threat to future excavation and research.

Inevitably, it was the extremists whose views were heard most often, because they were the most active and vociferous, and because the press is far more interested in conflicts than in agreements. On the one hand there were those academics who opposed any interference with their work, any return of skeletal material, any reburial. On the other, there were indigenous groups, often self-appointed representatives for entire nations, who insisted on the return and reburial of all such material, regardless of its age or provenance, and who used the issue as a political football, since skeletons and museum collections are a highly visible symbol of past oppression and of current struggles for rights of all kinds. Human remains are an emotive issue, and it was all too easy to cast the academics as unfeeling racists or patronizing colonists who treated the remains as mere data. Some American Indians have recently carried their claims to such extremes that they even demand the return of naturally shed strands of human hair recovered from archaeological sites.

It should, however, be remembered that by no means all past disturbance of the dead was carried out by archaeologists (tomb-robbing has been called the world's second oldest profession, and was already rife in ancient Egypt, nor was it limited to the remains of foreign native peoples. Moreover, relatively little research excavation for burials occurs today, and most archaeological encounters with the dead now come accidentally or through salvage excavations.

Few archaeologists, other than extremists, had great objections to the return of recent skeletal remains, or those collected under horrific circumstances (such as some Tasmanian remains); but there has been, and still is, considerable alarm at the actual or proposed reburial of ancient bones that display important clues to cultural behaviour — such as artificial deformation during infancy.

Anthropologists also point out that no analysis of human remains is ever definite, since new techniques are constantly arising that enable new questions to be asked and help to improve the information already acquired. New methods proliferate today, with isotopic analysis of bones and genetic studies offering remarkable and unexpected breakthroughs. Even in the most sensitive areas such as America (p.51) and Australia (p.28), indigenous views on the reburial issue vary widely, and a growing number of local communities are in favour of some analysis of remains, provided that their permission is sought and that the resulting information is explained to them.

Mutual respect is the key to future understanding in this area, and it is highly probable that increasing numbers of indigenous communities will cooperate and even encourage archaeological endeavours once they come to perceive the benefits of the knowledge that can be obtained in this way. However, it is hard to see how compromise will be reached with those ultra-orthodox Jews who see the opening of a tomb, of whatever age, for study as a totally unacceptable violation of privacy which is contrary to their particular interpretation of Jewish law, and which they see as the moral equivalent of subjecting a living person to a scientific experiment.

Archaeologists, however, would argue that the study of the dead brings enormous and worthwhile benefit in terms of knowledge. In the following pages we have attempted to show the incredible variety of human remains that survive in the archaeological record, and of the information that they can give us about the past — parasites and pathologies, X-rays and scans, blood groups and DNA, faces and physiology, genealogies and ethnicity. There are so many amazing specimens from all over the world that it was very difficult to narrow our selection down to fifty. Since the book's title was originally planned to be "Lost Bodies", we were able to use the concept of human remains being "lost" as a criterion of selection — in other words, we have focused primarily on bodies that have truly been discovered. It is hoped that this book's contents — presented soberly and with the utmost respect for the deceased individuals and for the feelings of living peoples — will, in a sense, enable the dead to live again, to speak to us and tell us something of their lives and their cultures. ∎

PAUL G. BAHN

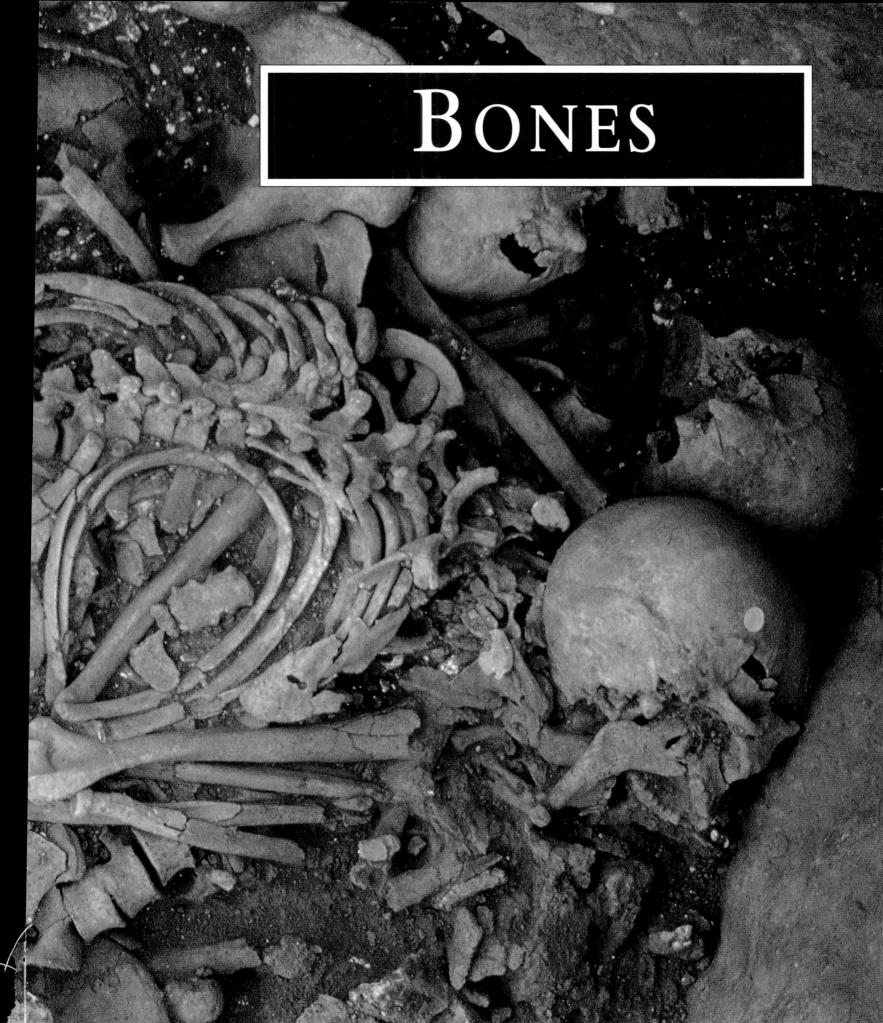

BONES

LUCY: OUR MOST FAMOUS RELATIVE

The 30th of November 1974 dawned as yet another scorching day at Hadar in the centre of the Afar Desert in northeastern Ethiopia when Donald ("Don") C. Johanson (then Curator of Physical Anthropology at the Cleveland Museum of Natural History and currently Director of the Institute of Human Origins in California) and Tom Gray (then an American graduate student) set out to record geological information and search for fossils in an area where they had found an australopithecine knee joint the previous year. As the morning wore on and temperatures approached 43°C (110°F), Johanson and Gray were about to return to camp when Johanson noticed a piece of elbow bone on a rocky slope. Closer examination revealed more bits of bone of an australopithecine. As Johanson later recalled:

"'I can't believe it,' I said. 'I just can't believe it.' 'By God, you'd better believe it!' shouted Gray. 'Here it is. Right here.' His voice went up into a howl. I joined him. In that 110-degree heat we began jumping up and down. With nobody to share our feelings, we hugged each other, sweaty and smelly, howling and hugging in the heat-shimmering gravel, the small brown remains of what now seemed almost certain to be parts of a single hominid [a member of the *Hominidae,* the biological grouping or fam-

Early members of the human family were known mainly from small fragments of bone until the 1974 discovery of Lucy's 40% complete 3.18-million-year-old skeleton in an Ethiopian wasteland. Lucy was a kind of australopithecine. These were small-brained ape-like creatures, which lived from before four million to just after one million years ago, and which took the first steps on the road to modern people by standing, walking and running on two legs.

ily to which humans belong] skeleton lying all around us." Meticulous excavation of the area produced several hundred pieces of bone which made up about 40% of a female australopithecine skeleton. It was officially catalogued as the AL 288-1 Partial Skeleton and in 1978 was assigned the scientific name *Australopithecus afarensis.* It is known to the world as Lucy, from the Beatles' song *Lucy in the sky with diamonds,* which rocked the African bush from a tape-player in the expedition camp on the night of the discovery.

A little ape-like creature that walked

Lucy would not have looked like a person, no matter what clothes she was dressed in, as she had a mixture of ape and human features. She was only 1.1 m (3 ft 7 in) tall, equivalent to the height of a modern six-year-old, but was fully grown and probably in her late teens or early twenties when she died, as her wisdom teeth were fully erupted and had been exposed to several years of wear. Deformation of her back bones indicates that she was beginning to experience a bone disease like arthritis. The shape of her hip-bone and birth canal through it suggest that she was almost certainly female.

Other *A. afarensis* remains, particularly those of a three-million-year-old skull and arm bone found at Hadar in 1992, are larger than those of Lucy. Some researchers have suggested that *A. afarensis* fossils represent two differently sized species, while others consider that there was one species, in which males were much taller and heavier than females, as is the case with modern gorillas. Very little of Lucy's skull was preserved, but the 1992 skull indicates that *A. afarensis* had an ape-like head with a for-

Lower jaw of specimen Sts 52 and cranium of Sts 5, from Sterkfontein, South Africa. These specimens represent *Australopithecus africanus*, considered by some to be ancestral to all modern humans.

The 40% complete skeleton of Lucy, perhaps the best known remains of *Australopithecus afarensis*. This upright-walking, small-brained ape-like creature lived in East Africa just over three million years ago and is one of the earliest known members of the human family.

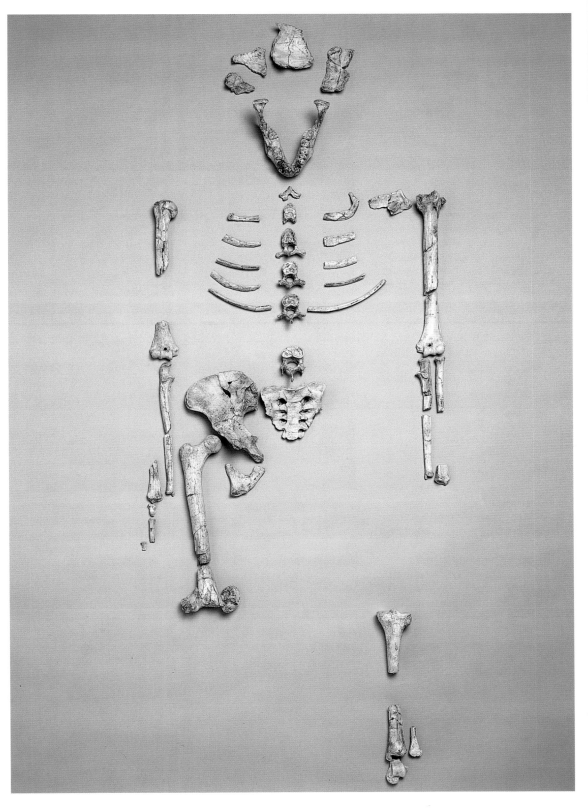

ward-jutting jaw, heavy brow ridges, flaring cheeks, strong muscles, and an ape-like brain size only a third as big as that of modern humans.

However, despite having an ape-like appearance, Lucy's leg bones indicate that she walked on two legs, though with slightly bent legs and not a fully modern human gait. Footprints left by at least two *A. afarensis* individuals some 3.7 million years ago in damp volcanic ash, which later hardened, at Laetoli in Tanzania, indicate that these creatures had a two-legged walk with weight distribution like ours. The big toes do not splay out from the rest of the foot as they do in apes like chimpanzees, which rarely walk upright. Some researchers suggest that a curvature in Lucy's finger and toe bones resembles that found in tree-dwelling apes. It is possible that Lucy and her kind also climbed trees to forage for fruits and nuts, or to escape predators.

Fossil pollen and animal bones show that, 3 million years ago, Hadar was a mixture of habitats ranging from open grassland to woodland with evergreen conifers and olive trees. Damage to *A. afarensis* teeth indicates that these creatures ate mostly fibrous foods, and perhaps fruit and nuts, although they may sometimes also have eaten small animals like termites and lizards.

Lucy's death

There is archaeological evidence for disposal of the dead around 200,000 years ago at Atapuerca (see p. 20), for deliberate burial of the dead only after about 100,000 years ago, and widespread un- questionable examples of purposeful burial only after about 35,000 years ago. The discovery of a partial skeleton as complete as that of Lucy from an age that was millions of years before intentional burial is extremely rare, because the destructive actions of scavengers and nature generally ensured that little or nothing was left of any bones lying on the ground before they became

Lucy's South African relative

A lesser known, but also inform-
ative, partial skeleton of a female australopithecine of a
roughly similar age and size to
Lucy was found in 1947 at
Sterkfontein in South Africa by
Robert Broom, a palaeontologist
at the Transvaal Museum in Pre-
toria. Sts 14 comprises hip,
leg, back and rib bones assigned to a female australopithecine of a different species
from Lucy, *Australopithecus
africanus*. Comparison between
the kinds of animals found with
her and those from dated East
African sites indicates that Sts

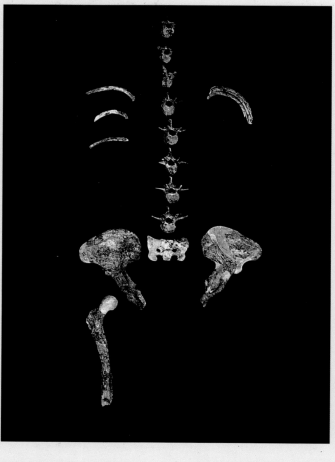

ABOVE: Robert Broom holds the
block of breccia (calcified cave
sediment) containing the Sts 14
partial skeleton (shown also
above) in comparison with a
modern human hip bone.

14 is at least 2.5 million years
old. Like Lucy, she moved along
on two short legs, but without
the striding gait of modern humans. Some researchers consider that *A. africanus* was directly ancestral to the line from
which modern humans developed, while others assign this
role to *A. afarensis*.

Sterkfontein is a complex of
now-eroding ancient cave fillings once mined for lime. Many
of the australopithecine remains
found there are thought to have
been the prey of large cats, and
probably also hyenas. Leo-
pards would have dragged their
prey into trees which typically
grow at the entrances of
dolomite caves like Sterkfontein, from where bones
dropped into the cave.

being presented with a skull
and brain cast of a young child
that had been blasted from a
lime quarry near Taung, in
north-central South Africa. In
1925 Dart named these re-
mains *Australopithecus africanus*
("southern ape of Africa"),
and considered this creature to
be intermediate between apes
and humans. This interpretation did not win general acceptance until several decades
later, when the discovery of
many more remains of several
kinds of australopithecines
from other South African as
well as East African sites confirmed that these creatures
were indeed early members of
the human family.

At the time of her discovery,
Lucy was the oldest and most
complete hominid ever found.
Initial estimates of her age
ranged between 3.6 to 2.8
million years ago. However,
recent advances in the potas-
sium-argon dating technique,
which was used to date the
layers of volcanic ash between
which Lucy was found, indicate that she lived 3.18 million
years ago (plus or minus
10,000 years).

However, Lucy is no longer
the oldest known member of
the human family tree. Since
her discovery, Johanson and his
colleagues have found more
than 320 *A. afarensis* fossils
dating to between 3.4 and 3
million years ago at Hadar, including, in 1975, a collection

covered with sediment. Lucy did not die savagely at the hands of
a predator: there were no tooth marks on her bones and the
bones were not splintered or crushed. It is possible that she died
from illness or drowning at the edge of a lake or stream, where
her remains were covered by sand or mud, which subsequently
hardened into rock. There she lay for millions of years until rains
exposed her natural grave. If Johanson and Gray had not happened on her elbow that morning in 1974, the next rains would
have washed away and scattered her bones forever.

Who was Lucy?

Australopithecine fossils were first recognized in South Africa in
1924 by Raymond Dart, then newly appointed Professor of
Anatomy at the University of Witwatersrand in Johannesburg, on

of bones of at least 13 individuals nicknamed "The First Family".
In the late 1970s, 3.7- to 3.5-million-year-old australopithecine
footprints were discovered at Laetoli in Tanzania, while a 3.9-mil-
lion-year-old skull fragment found in 1981 at a site south of
Hadar may also belong to *A. afarensis*.

More recently, in 1994-5, Meave Leakey of the National Museums of Kenya and an American colleague, Alan Walker, working
at Kanapoi near Lake Turkana in northern Kenya, found pieces of
a 4.1-million-year-old upright walking hominid named *Australopithecus anamensis* (*anam* is the Turkana word for "lake"). These
remains have many features in common with Lucy and her kind,
but have more primitive and ape-like teeth.

In late 1994 even older possible hominid remains, comprising
skull and teeth fragments dating to 4.4 million years ago, were

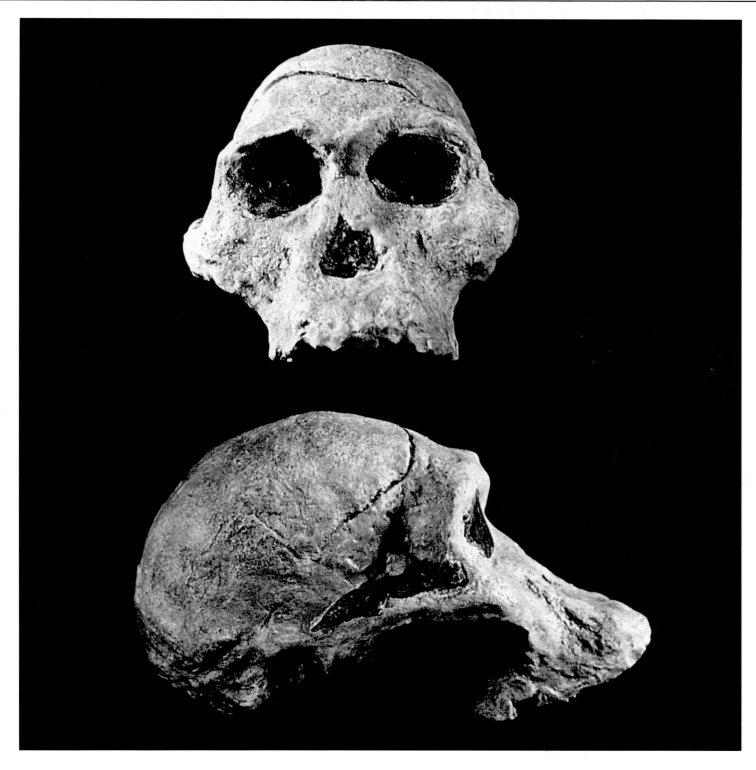

Front and side views of "Mrs Ples", Sts 5, found in 1947 at Sterkfontein by Robert Broom and John Robinson. It is one of the best preserved crania of *Australopithecus africanus*, missing only the teeth.

found at Aramis in Ethiopia by a team led by Tim White of the University of California at Berkeley. Their chimpanzee-like features led White to propose a new genus name for these remains: *Ardipithecus ramidus* (*ardi* means "ground" or "floor", while *ramidus* refers to "root" in the Afar language). Further study is needed to determine whether or not this creature is indeed a member of the human family tree.

Even if Lucy's claim to fame as our oldest known human relative has been usurped by continuing discoveries, she and her kind show that the road to humanity began with two-legged walking, long before large brains or stone tools appeared. These would develop only half a million years or more after this little ape-like creature lived. ∎

THE TURKANA BOY

"*Tumepata kichwa! We've found the skull!*" This utterance from an excavation team led by Richard Leakey of the National Museums of Kenya and Alan Walker, an American colleague, heralded one of the truly great palaeoanthropological discoveries of all time. Since the establishment of a research project on the east side of Lake Turkana in 1968, the bones of more than 200 early humans had been found, but detailed investigation of sediments

The most complete early human skeleton ever found is that of a youth excavated from 1.5-million-year-old sediments near the Nariokotome sand river on the western shores of Lake Turkana in northern Kenya in 1984-8. Only the feet and a few other pieces are missing, which is extremely rare in human remains from before times of deliberate burial. The skeleton is an early *Homo erectus*, a species intermediate between the first upright-walking members of the human family tree and modern people. Its discovery has changed the story of our evolution.

on the west side of the lake began only in 1984. In August of that year, a legendary Kenyan fossil-hunter, Kamoya Kimeu, was taking a walk on a rest day when he noticed a small piece of hominid skull lying on the pebbles of a small tributary of the Nariokotome sand river, some 5 km (3 miles) inland from Lake Turkana at a site called Nariokotome III or NK3. Subsequent excavation in five seasons until 1988 resulted in the discovery of almost all the body parts of a young male skeleton, catalogued as KNM-WT 15000, and provisionally classified as *Homo erectus*.

The age of the skeleton has been determined by its position between dated layers of volcanic ash as being between 1.56 and 1.51 million years ago, or 1.53 plus or minus 0.05 million years. (Previous estimates ranging from 1.65 to 1.55 million years were slightly too old.)

A strapping lad

One of the biggest surprises was the long length of the limb bones of the skeleton, whose second molars had only just erupted and whose milk canines were still in place, indicating a developmental stage equivalent to a modern eleven-year-old. It is esti-

mated that he would have been about 1.82 m (6 ft 1 in) tall and weighed some 68 kg (150 lb) had he survived to maturity. Initial considerations that he was a rare tall individual were dispelled when re-examination of other East African *Homo erectus* remains confirmed that these early humans were much taller than ever imagined. This contradicted a widely held belief that humans have gradually grown taller through time. Rather, we seem to have reached our present general height at least 1.5 million years ago.

The completeness of the skeleton also permitted the first study of the physiological consequences of early human body proportions. Apart from an upward-tapering chest, the body proportions of the Turkana boy are modern. Indeed, the tall Dinka people, who today live about 200 km (124 miles) west of Nariokotome, have trunk and body proportions almost identical to those of KNM-WT 15000. The Dinka are, however, not more closely linked genetically to early African *Homo erectus* populations than any other modern humans, and this resemblance is physiological in origin. Studies of sediments as well as fossil pollen and animal bones indicate that the Lake Turkana region has had the same climate as today for about 1.5 million years. The stature, weight and body proportion information for the Turkana boy suggest that he was adapted to the high mean annual temperatures of 30.8°C (87°F). Early African *Homo erectus* individuals thus had limb proportions like those of modern African people who live in

Excavations of the "Turkana boy" NK3 site at the Nariokotome sand river on the western shores of Lake Turkana.

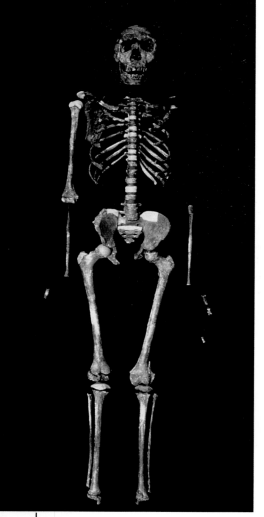

The remarkably preserved 1.5-million-year-old skeleton of the long-limbed "Turkana boy" found at Nariokotome in northern Kenya in 1984-8.

Cranium and lower jaw of the strikingly modern-looking 1.5-million-year-old "Turkana boy" (specimens KNM-WT 15000 A and B).

A marshy final resting place

At 1.5 million years ago, the Nariokotome area had one or more shallow lakes or ponds and small perennial channels of permanent water from the Omo River to the north. This availability of water would have supported lush floodplain grassland and, in belts along the river channels, forest. Such an environment would have been home to many kinds of herbivores, as well as their attendant predators and scavengers.

The only suggestion of how the Turkana boy died is a periodontal lesion on the right side of his jawbone, indicating inflammatory gum disease. It seems likely this was linked to the loss of his deciduous second molar, which occurred not long before he died. Death from septicaemia caused by gum disease was common before the availability of antibiotics, and this could well have been the cause of his demise.

The state of preservation of the bones do not suggest he died in the jaws of a predator. When he died, his body either fell into a marsh or was washed into it by floodwaters. It floated face down while decomposing, bits were washed back and forth, kicked by large herbivores, sucked by catfish, and chewed by turtles, until they came to rest in a shallow part of the swamp, where they were rapidly covered by mud and volcanic ash. There they remained for 1.5 million years until erosion of the sediments exposed the fragment of skull that caught the keen eye of Kamoya Kimeu in 1984.

An early human

Until the 1960s, the earliest known member of our genus, *Homo*, was *Homo erectus*, discovered in Asia in 1891 by Eugene Dubois. Even after australopithecines (see p. 16) were identified in Africa from 1925 onwards, and the distinction of being the earliest member of the genus *Homo* was transferred to *Homo habilis* from East Africa in 1964, Asia continued to be regarded as the place where true people that looked like us developed. However, the discovery of *Homo erectus* remains dating from some 1.5 million years ago in Africa from the 1970s onwards, of which the Turkana boy is perhaps the most remarkable, suggested that Africa was not only the cradle of early humanity, but also of humankind that resembled us quite closely in many ways. The relationship between the African and Asian *Homo erectus* fossils nevertheless continues to be the subject of debate.

The completeness of the Turkana boy skeleton has made it much easier to know which other African early *Homo erectus* fossil fragments belong to this species and which do not. Presently available comparisons between early human fossils of the relevant time period from Africa and Asia suggest to Alan Walker that the Turkana boy is *Homo erectus*, although more detailed study might indicate differences that would assign it to a new species of *Homo*. The Turkana boy jawbone is strikingly similar to remains from East Turkana labelled *Homo ergaster* by some researchers. Further study might therefore result in labelling fossils like the Turkana Boy *Homo ergaster* instead of *Homo erectus*.

Whatever scientific name is attached to it, the "humanness" of this 1.5-million-year-old skeleton shows that there were rapid, major evolutionary changes in our lineage after 1.8 million years ago, which led to the appearance of the first ancestral humans rather like us. ■

hot, dry places, were shaped as they were for efficient cooling, and were dependent on water and possibly also salt.

Despite the overall similarity between KNM-WT 15000 and modern human skeletons, there are differences, and perhaps the most striking of these is the size and shape of the brain case. Brain capacity is estimated at only 900 cc (about two-thirds that of modern humans). This necessarily implies differences in behaviour between *Homo erectus* and *Homo sapiens sapiens* and nullifies modelling the behaviour of *Homo erectus* on that of historically or ethnographically known hunter-gatherers.

African *Homo erectus* made stone tools, including sharp flakes used for cutting and scraping, as well as hand-held tools shaped on both sides, called "bifaces". Pointed or pear-shaped bifaces are called "handaxes", while examples with a broad axe-like cutting edge are known as "cleavers". Despite the existence of large collections of these tools, their use is unclear. Studies of microscopically visible damage suggest they were used on a wide variety of materials, including plants, meat and wood. This tool-making tradition is known as the Acheulean, after the St Acheul site in France, where handaxes were first recognized in the 1830s. The Acheulean lasted from about 1.5 million years until about 150,000 years ago, and is the longest-lasting technology the world has seen.

There is no indubitable evidence as to whether *Homo erectus* could make fire, speak a language, or hunt big game regularly, though it seems they did consume meat, probably from scavenging.

BEFORE THE NEANDERTHALS: THE FIRST EUROPEANS

Were the first Europeans primitive forms of the genus *Homo* similar to the hominids who lived in Africa over a million years ago, or did they have a more modern appearance — perhaps already reflecting the larger brains needed to cope with the cooler landscapes of the northern hemisphere? Were they skilled hunters of large mammals, or did they subsist primarily on plant foods and occasionally scavenge meat from a frozen carcass? Archaeologists are still struggling with these questions, which they are forced to answer with the few fossil bones and simple stone tools that have been dated to half a million years or more in Europe.

The first skeletal remains of an ancient hominid to come to light in Europe were discovered in Germany at the beginning of the century. For more than twenty years, the noted palaeontologist Otto Schoentensack had predicted that human bones would be found in the sandpits along the Neckar River near Heidelberg, Germany, which had yielded the fossil remains of many extinct animals. In 1907 workmen uncovered a jawbone in one of these pits, although the exact position and dating of the find have never been certain. The jaw is massive and primitive, and bears a striking similarity to the early forms of the genus *Homo* that appeared in Africa two million years ago and subsequently migrated into the Near East in Asia. Schoentensack and his successors at the University of Heidelberg continued to search for fossils over a period of decades, but no further remains of "Heidelberg Man"

Although Europe is the birthplace of archaeology and the study of human fossils, its early prehistoric settlement remains obscure. Who were the first Europeans — the predecessors of the Neanderthals — and when and why did they venture into this part of the world?

were found. Although some fragments of stone and animal bone recovered from the sandpits were thought to represent crude tools, none was an incontestable humanly made artefact. Today the Heidelberg jaw is believed to date to roughly half a million years ago, and is still one of the oldest human fossils known in Europe.

Many years were to pass before another European human fossil of comparable antiquity was discovered, reflecting the extreme rarity of datable finds from this period. By contrast, numerous skeletons of later Ice Age peoples — Neanderthals and Cro-Magnons — were found in various parts of the continent. But in 1962 a Hungarian geologist discovered an important archaeological site at Vértesszöllös, near the city of Budapest. Excavations yielded simple stone tools, many of which were difficult to distinguish from naturally fractured rocks, and concentrations of burned bones, buried in spring and loess deposits thought to be at least 350,000 years old. The burned bone concentrations may represent the earliest evidence for the use of fire in Europe. Vértesszöllös also produced some isolated skeletal remains of its inhabitants, including a fragment of the back of the skull that reflected the primitive appearance of the Heidelberg find but also revealed a large brain.

During the following decade the remains of another early European were discovered in a quarry at Bilzingsleben in East Germany. Isolated teeth and skull fragments were excavated from spring deposits located near an ancient lake, which have been dated to between 200,000 and 400,000 years ago. The skull fragments — all of which may be derived from the same individual — suggest an extremely archaic-looking human with a massive brow-ridge and a small brain. Bilzingsleben also yielded large quantities of stone tools, fragments of animal bone representing possible food debris, and traces of hearths. Many of the archaeological finds seem to be relatively undisturbed, providing a rare glimpse of an encampment from this ancient period.

In 1994 archaeologists in northern Spain made an astounding discovery that dramatically altered the picture of early settlement in Europe. A team of scientists led by Juan Luis Arsuaga and Eudald Carbonell found stone tools and human skeletal remains in deeply buried cave deposits that apparently date to more than three-quarters of a million years ago. The site is located among a large complex of caverns and natural passageways within the Sierra de Atapuerca near the city of Burgos. Caves of such antiquity are rare — most of them gradually erode away within a few hundred thousand years — which is undoubtedly one reason why

The Heidelberg jaw, a large broken human mandible with small teeth and receding chin, was found in a sandpit at Mauer, south Germany, in 1907.

human fossils older than half a million years are scarce. Approximately 100 bone fragments and teeth representing five or six individuals were found. In addition to the human skeletal remains, crude stone tools chipped from river pebbles and flints and large mammal bones were recovered. Although analysis of the finds is at an early stage, it is clear that the human remains possess some primitive and unique features that may require the establishment of a new human fossil species — an evolutionary predecessor of "Heidelberg Man".

The Atapuerca discoveries indicate that humans probably occupied Europe much earlier than previously thought — perhaps almost a million years

The Pit of the Bones

On present evidence, the deliberate burial of human remains began with the Neanderthals (see p. 35), but there are earlier indications of rudimentary funerary practices. At Atapuerca, northern Spain, a limestone cave known as the Sima de los Huesos (Pit of the Bones) is producing huge quantities of bones of an archaic *Homo sapiens* (a form transitional between *Homo erectus* and Neanderthals). At the bottom of a 12 m (39 ft) shaft, layers dating to more than 200,000 years ago have so far yielded over 1600 bones from at least 32 individuals (and possibly as many as 50). The bones are mixed up, with no anatomical connections, but all parts of the body are present. They come mostly from adolescents and young adults of both sexes. The most plausible explanation for their presence here is that the bodies were placed in the shaft, over several generations at least, in a form of mortuary ritual that may point to some embryonic religious belief. The lack of bones of herbivores (food animals) shows that they were not accumulated in the shaft by carnivores, and the absence of stone tools suggests that the cave was not an occupation site.

Human skulls, jaws and limb bones in the Pit of the Bones.

ago. The recent dating of an early *Homo* jaw from Dmanisi in the Caucasus region provides supporting evidence for this conclusion by documenting a human presence at latitudes comparable to those of Southern Europe at an even earlier time, perhaps 1.5 million years ago. However, it appears likely that the first populations to colonize Europe did so only during the warmer intervals of the Ice Age. Not until after 200,000 years ago — following the appearance of the Neanderthals — were humans able to cope with full glacial conditions. Moreover, the colder and drier parts of Europe such as the Russian plain do not seem to have been occupied at all until the Neanderthal epoch.

These observed limitations on the types of environments successfully colonized by the first Europeans provide some possible clues to their way of life, which otherwise remains poorly understood. Most archaeologists now suspect that the pre-Neanderthal inhabitants of Europe did not rely heavily on the hunting of large Ice Age mammals such as elephant, horse and bison. This may explain their inability to occupy regions poor in available plant foods. A microscopic analysis of the teeth in the Heidelberg jaw revealed the severe wear associated with a heavy consumption of plants. However, some meat may have been obtained by scavenging carcasses, which could account for the presence of large mammal bones at some living sites; early human populations in Europe may have used their tools and control of fire to exploit frozen carcasses during winter months that were inaccessible to non-human scavengers. Overall, the technology of these populations seems to have been quite primitive, and their absence in colder regions probably reflects limited ability in the production of winter clothing and construction of shelters. Nevertheless, the gradual increase in human brain size that took place during this phase of expansion into higher latitudes may be primarily due to the adaptive challenge presented by these new environments. ■

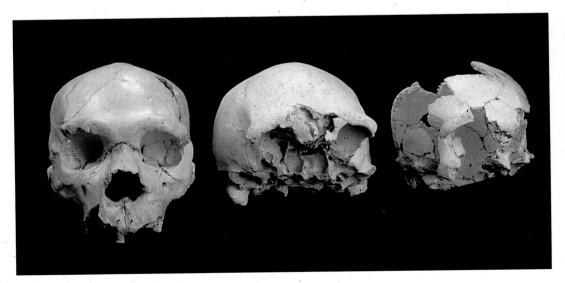

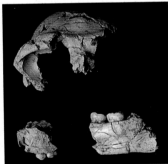

LEFT: Skulls 5, 4 and 6 from Atapuerca's Pit of the Bones.

ABOVE: Skull and jaw fragments from Gran Dolina, Atapuerca.

PEKING AND JAVA MAN: EARLY HUMANS IN EASTERN ASIA

Dubois was fascinated by the possibility of finding Darwin's "missing link" between apes and humans in the tropical regions of Southeast Asia. In 1887 he gave up his teaching post at the University of Amsterdam and joined the medical corps of the Dutch East Indian army, sailing to Indonesia with his wife and new baby. Despite extensive searches, however, it took four years before Dubois finally found what he had been hoping for — the

The groups of _Homo erectus_ fossils known collectively as Peking and Java Man have played a crucial role in the study of human evolution. Java Man was first discovered by the Dutch anatomist Eugene Dubois in 1891.

skull cap and a tooth of a primitive hominid which he named _Pithecanthropus erectus_ or "upright ape man".

Dubois' original finds were made at Trinil on the Solo River in central Java. The Solo River has produced abundant fossil material from both animals and humans, and over the past century there have been a number of other finds of the species now known as _Homo erectus_. Some 40 individuals — a third of all the _Homo erectus_ fossils discovered worldwide — have come from Java. Unfortunately, none of these Javan fossils has yet been found associated with stone tools or other archaeological remains. We therefore know almost nothing about the lifestyle of Java Man, although it has been suggested that the widespread use of bamboo tools may explain the lack of an extensive stone toolkit such as that used by _Homo erectus_ in Africa, Europe and China.

After Dubois' discovery of early human fossils from Asia, other Western scholars also became interested in the possibility that the origins of humankind were to be found in the East. One such scholar was the notable Canadian anatomist Davidson Black who, after unsuccessful excavations in Thailand and elsewhere in north China, found financial support for work at the Zhoukoudian cave complex near Peking in 1928. A few years earlier, a Swedish geologist had already found a tooth at Zhoukoudian which Black had assigned to the species

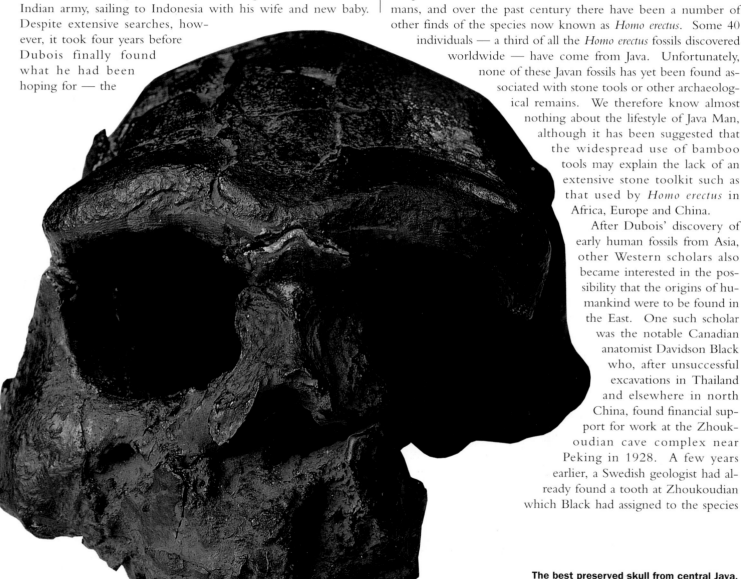

The best preserved skull from central Java, Sangiran 17, was found in 1969, and is the only specimen with the face preserved.

OPPOSITE: Reconstruction of Peking Man's skull by Franz Weidenreich, a German anatomist.

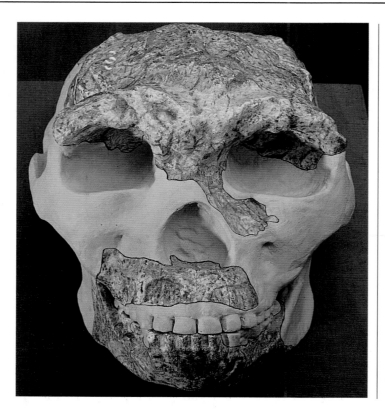

"Peking Man". Excavations at the site continued until the Japanese occupation in 1937, and the remains of over 40 human skeletons were unearthed. There was now clear evidence that between 500,000 and 250,000 years ago Zhoukoudian was occupied by *Homo erectus* people anatomically similar to those in Java.

In contrast to those in Java, however, the Zhoukoudian fossils are associated with abundant cultural evidence: tens of thousands of quartz stone tools, animal bones (some of which were probably the remains of the meals of Peking Man), and extensive layers of ash which suggest that *Homo erectus* already made use of fire. Archaeological interpretation of Zhoukoudian is complicated by the great length of time during which the caves were visited by Peking Man. Hyenas, rodents and owls are likely to have been responsible for most of the faunal remains accumulated in the caves. The fact that the Peking Man skulls all have the facial parts

LEFT: The reconstructed skull and jaw of Lantian Man, found at two localities in Shaanxi province, China, in the 1960s. Slightly more primitive than the Peking and Java specimens, it has a particularly robust brow-edge and a thicker cranial wall.

BELOW: The Sangiran 17 skull from Java. This adult had extremely robust teeth, which became sharpened through a diet of fruit and seeds. The left side of the face has been remodelled as a mirror-image of the right.

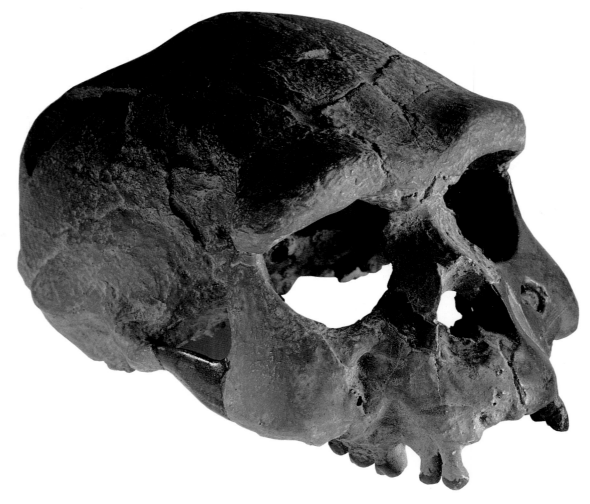

Reconstruction of the Java Man found in Trinil in 1891.

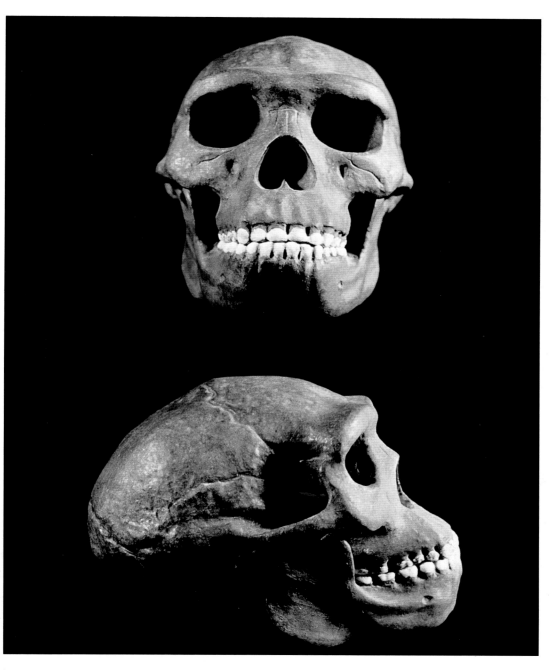

missing led some earlier scholars to propose that cannibalism may have been practised at Zhoukoudian, but gnawing of the skulls by hyenas now seems a more likely explanation.

The discoveries of Java and Peking Man demonstrated that Asia played a significant role in the story of human evolution. However, after the Second World War — when the Chinese fossils went missing — the focus of interest shifted back to Africa. It became accepted that *Homo erectus* had originated in Africa and then spread to Eurasia, the first hominid to leave its African homeland. In recent years perhaps *the* most controversial problem in the study of human evolution has been the degree to which these early *erectus* colonists passed on their genes to the modern inhabitants of Asia and Australia, or whether in fact they became extinct with the spread of *Homo sapiens* after about 100,000 years ago.

No consensus has yet been reached on this problem, but debate has been thrown wide open over the last couple of years by new dates from both China and Indonesia. In 1994 American scientists published new analyses of geological samples from Sangiran and Mojokerto, Javan sites which have produced *Homo erectus* fossils. Their results were extraordinary — the dates of 1.66 and 1.81 million years ago are almost double the original estimates of the age of Java Man. A year later, equally surprising dates were reported from Longgupo Cave which is located just south of the Yangzi River in central China. Various scientific dating techniques and the presence of the fossilized bones of a giant panda and other extinct fauna point to a date of between 1.78 and 1.96 million years ago for the stone artefacts and hominid remains from Longgupo. Not all experts agree that these dates can be taken at face value. In the Javan case, for example, we cannot be completely sure of the link between the excavated fossils and the geological material which was analyzed. However, the fact that two Asian sites have inde-

pendently produced evidence suggesting hominid occupation around two million years ago does represent quite strong circumstantial evidence. The possibility that our ancestors moved out of Africa much earlier than was once thought has to be taken seriously.

The hominid remains from Longgupo Cave are sparse, consisting only of a tooth and a fragment of a jaw bone, but they are enough for some anthropologists to argue that they belong to a more primitive species than *Homo erectus* — possibly *Homo habilis* or *Homo ergaster*. On the basis of these preliminary results it has already been argued that *Homo erectus*, including Peking and Java Man, may in fact have evolved in Asia and then spread back to Africa. Much more work is needed before the likelihood of this can be determined, but the importance of the pioneering finds of Java and Peking Man remains secure for the foreseeable future. ∎

EARLIEST AUSTRALIANS

Humans could not have evolved separately in Australia, so the earliest Australians must have migrated from Asia. They must have come by sea, since Australia has never been linked by land to mainland Southeast Asia

The origins of the Australian Aborigines have interested western scholars ever since European explorers first set foot on the Australian continent. All fossil humans known from Australia are fully modern people or *Homo sapiens sapiens*. Aborigines themselves say that they have always been there, although some oral traditions tell of Dreamtime ancestors who came across the sea.

were increasingly challenged.

In 1967 the physical anthropologist Alan Thorne had noticed some robust and archaic-looking skull fragments in the Museum of Victoria in Melbourne. He managed to trace the remains back to the

at any time during the last three million years, even at times when sea levels have been much lower than today.

Until the late 1960s very few fossil human remains had been found in Australia. The first human skull was found in 1884 at Talgai in southern Queensland. It had belonged to a fifteen-year-old boy who had died as a result of a blow to the head. Although, like all fossil human remains found in Australia, he clearly belonged to *Homo sapiens sapiens*, he was very large and robust and rather archaic in appearance. Discoveries of further robust and archaic-looking skulls at Mossgiel in the Riverina and Cohuna in Victoria prompted comparison with *Homo erectus* fossil material from Southeast Asia, and led the pioneering Australian physical anthropologist N. W. G. Macintosh to declare that they all bore the "mark of ancient Java". Another important fossil skull found in 1940 by a quarry worker at Keilor in suburban Melbourne is much more delicate and gracile, and was generally believed to be more recent. However, after several important finds of fossil material from the late 1960s onwards, these ideas

eastern shore of Kow Swamp in northern Victoria, not far from Cohuna where an archaic skull had been found in the 1920s. Excavation began in 1968, and more skeletons with robust and

0 1 2 3 4 5 cm

This robust skull has a sloping forehead and thick skull bones. It was found at Cossack, Western Australia, and is about 6500 years old.

rugged features were unearthed. At least forty individuals, including men, women and children, were discovered. Most were buried between about 13,000 and 9500 years ago.

At about the same time the geomorphologist Jim Bowler was studying the climatic history of the Willandra Lakes. These are a series of interconnected lake basins in the arid far west of New South Wales. They have been dry now for about 15,000 years, but at various earlier periods they were full of fresh water. In 1968 Bowler noticed some burnt bones encrusted with carbonate protruding out of the large crescent-shaped dune on the eastern shore of Lake Mungo. A team of archaeologists removed the remains in a large block, and Alan Thorne excavated it in the laboratory. This proved to be the world's oldest known ritual cremation. It turned out to be the remains of a young woman who had been buried about 25,000 years ago. Her body had been burnt and the bones smashed into tiny fragments. These were then collected and buried in a small depression. In 1974 an even older and more complete skeleton was discovered. This was an inhumation rather than a cremation, and dated back about 30,000 years. An adult male had been buried lying on his side and sprinkled with red ochre. Since then, the remains of more than 100 individuals have been found, although many are very fragmentary.

Archaeological sites around the Willandra Lakes provide a rich picture of the lives of the people who camped there when the lakes were full. They ate fish and frogs, freshwater mussels and crayfish from the lakes. They also hunted animals such as wallaby, wombat and native cat, as well as a wide range of small animals like rat kangaroos and lizards.

These were remarkable finds. The first definite evidence that Aborigines had lived in Australia during the last Ice Age had only come in 1962, from Kenniff Cave in Queensland, but the Mungo finds pushed the occupation of Australia back to 30,000 years. They gave a picture of a complex way of life that included a glimpse of the rich ceremonial domain that is such an important feature of Aboriginal culture. Moreover, the fossil material itself was a surprise. Older fossil human remains tend to be more robust than more recent ones. However, instead of being even more archaic and rugged in appearance than the Kow Swamp material, the Mungo remains were very delicate and gracile.

Alan Thorne proposed a theory to explain this. He suggested that there had been at least two separate migrations to Australia from different parts of Southeast Asia. The robust Kow Swamp people were similar to more ancient fossils from Java, while the more gracile Mungo people more closely resembled Chinese finds. The mingling of the two groups then produced modern Australian Aborigines. Thorne's ideas remain contro-

Wind erosion at Lake Mungo, western New South Wales, has uncovered the remains of more than a hundred individuals.

Aborigines and fossil human remains

Over the last few decades Australian Aborigines, like other indigenous peoples in former colonies, have been increasingly asserting their rights to self-determination and control of their cultural heritage. They have been very critical of anthropologists and archaeologists. The study of human remains has been an extremely bitter area of dispute, and Aborigines have campaigned vigorously for the return and reburial of skeletal re-

mains now in museums. Aborigines do not see any difference between recent burials and very ancient ones, and often see scientific excavation as grave-robbing. As a result, archaeologists and anthropologists have had to reconsider their relationships with Aboriginal people and how they conduct scientific research. Many have supported Aboriginal campaigns for reburial of recent remains, especially those of known individuals, but

have opposed the return of more ancient remains such as those from Kow Swamp. These were handed back to the local Aboriginal community in 1990 and have been reburied. More recently, human remains from Lake Mungo were voluntarily returned to the custody of the Aborigines of the Mungo area.

In 1992 Alan Thorne returned human remains to Aboriginal elders at Lake Mungo.

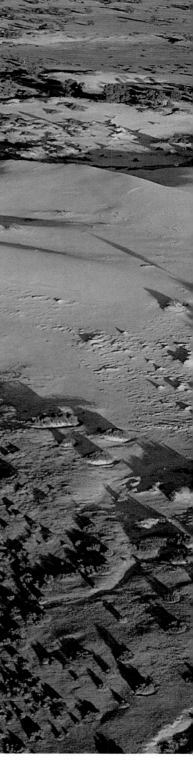

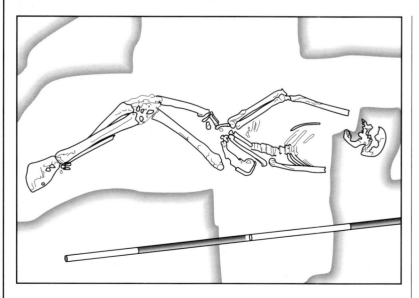

30,000-year-old burial of an adult male from Lake Mungo. The corpse was sprinkled with red ochre during the burial.

versial. Other scholars feel that the differences have been exaggerated and stress the diversity of Aboriginal physical features. Peter Brown has suggested that the long sloping foreheads of the Kow Swamp and Cohuna skulls have been artificially flattened and deformed. The practice of deforming children's heads by binding or pressing with the hands is known from several parts of the world, but is rare in Australia. The discovery of an extremely robust fossil skull at Lake Garnpung, near Lake Mungo, in 1980 seemed at first to lend weight to Thorne's ideas. Willandra Lakes Hominid (WLH) 50, as it is known, is not very well dated, but some estimates put it at well over 30,000 years old. This would make WLH 50 older than the more delicate and gracile remains from Mungo, and thus provide support for the idea of an early migration of robust individuals from Indonesia.

An aerial view of the "Walls of China", the large crescent-shaped dune bordering Lake Mungo.

However, Steve Webb, a physical anthropologist who has made a special study of disease in prehistoric Australian populations, believes that the thickening of the skull bones is a pathological condition, resulting from a blood disorder.

There are two main theories about the origin of modern humans. Some anthropologists believe that *Homo sapiens sapiens* originated in Africa and spread out from there, replacing earlier human types. Others argue for continuity in regional physical characteristics and prefer to see local evolution. The fossil evidence from Australia is important for choosing between these two alternatives. ■

HUMAN SACRIFICE AT ARCHANES-ANEMOSPILIA

The shrine at Anemospilia is the only known example of a Minoan freestanding shrine. It is a rectangular building within an enclosure wall (*peribolos*), and consists of three non-connecting rooms on a north-south alignment, which open onto a narrow corridor (*prothalamos*) running the full width of the north side of the building. The corridor was accessed through three doorways opposite the entrances to the rooms. There was a fourth, wider entrance at the east end of the corridor. A monumental pair of limestone horns was found on the surface above the corridor, which would originally have crowned the façade of the shrine. Vast quantities of pottery were found inside the shrine, including more than 400 examples of the palatial Kamares ware, and there were also portable altars or offering tables. Along the back wall of the east room there was a stepped stone bench on which numerous clay vases, including specialized cult vessels or *rhyta*, were found. The excavators interpreted these as offerings to the deity worshipped at the shrine. The central room appears to have housed the cult

In 1979 the Greek archaeologists Yiannis and Evi Sakellarakis made the extraordinary discovery of an apparent human sacrifice in a mountain shrine at Archanes-Anemospilia. The shrine, which is located on the lower northern slopes of Mount Juktas, in northern Crete, was destroyed by earthquake and a massive conflagration around 1700 BC. This same earthquake was also responsible for the destruction of the first Minoan palaces at Knossos, Phaistos and Mallia.

statue of the deity. This was probably made of wood and so has not survived, except for a pair of life-sized clay feet found on a low clay bench. Also in the room were nine large storage jars and a number of smaller pots. Little pottery was found in the west room, but instead there was a fixed stone bench interpreted by the excavators as an altar for blood sacrifices.

Four human skeletons were recovered from the shrine at Anemospilia, three from the west room and one from the corridor. These are of particular importance as they are the first Minoan human remains to be discovered outside a burial context. The most interesting of the skeletons was that of a young male who was found lying on the stone bench in the west room. He was aged around eighteen years and was 1.65 m (5 ft 3 in) tall. The skeleton was lying diagonally across the bench, on its right side. The head was slightly raised, the arms were bent and the hands level with the chest. The left leg was bent back, so that the left heel was almost touching the thigh. The more elevated bones on the left side of the body display greater burning than those on the lower, right side. The anthropologists who studied the skeleton assumed that this was the result of absence of blood in the left part of the body at the time of burning, and concluded that the individual had suffered a dramatic loss of blood shortly before the destruction of the shrine. A large bronze blade, decorated with a boar's head and perhaps the weapon that had been used to kill the young man, was found lying on his abdomen. The assumed loss of blood, the apparent bound position of the skeleton, and the proximity of an apparent sacrificial blade have led archaeologists to identify this skeleton as a victim of human

Reconstructed heads of the priest and priestess from the mountain shrine at Archanes-Anemospilia, Crete.

Model of a shrine.

sacrifice, who was killed shortly before the earthquake which destroyed the shrine.

Two other skeletons were found in the west room: a mature male aged about 38 and a female in her late twenties. Both were lying on the floor by the side of the altar, and were killed by the collapsed roof. The male measured 1.78 m (5 ft 10 in) in height and was lying on his back, to the west of the altar. He was wearing a silver and iron signet ring on the little finger of his left hand, and around his wrist he wore an agate cylinder seal decorated with a man rowing a boat, the prow of which was in the shape of a bird's head. These articles of jewellery are insignia of office, indicating that in life the man had been a priest. His high status allowed the priest access to a better quality diet, and his skeletal remains indicate that he was healthy and well-nourished. The female skeleton was in the southeast corner of the room, lying face down with her arms bent level with her face, as though to protect her head from the falling masonry. She was about 1.54 m (5 ft) tall and appears to have suffered from thalassaemia, a condition common to malarial areas, though otherwise she appears to have been healthy and well-nourished. The excavators have interpreted her as a priestess of the cult practised at the sanctuary. The medical forensic team responsible for the facial reconstructions of the skull of Philip II from Vergina (see p. 113) and the Mycenaean warriors from Grave Circle B (see p. 94) have also attempted the faces of the priest and priestess from Archanes-Anemospilia. The other two skeletons were too badly preserved to allow their faces to be reconstructed. These reconstructions are important as they give us the first real indication of the actual appearance of the Minoans, which we can compare with their own impressions in fresco paintings.

The fragmentary remains of the fourth skeleton were found in the corridor, lying prone on the ground in front of the entrance to the central room. The skeleton was too badly preserved to be properly identified. The bones were very badly burned and in the intensity of the fire many had been completely incinerated and had disappeared. Scattered among the fragmentary remains were pieces of a polychrome bucket-shaped vase with ornamental depiction of a bull. A similar vase is depicted on the Late Minoan III sarcophagus from Ayia Triadha, as part of the cult equipment used in bull sacrifice. It is believed that these vases were used to collect the blood from sacrificial victims, usually bulls. The excavators suggested that the individual in the corridor was an acolyte attached to the shrine at Anemospilia.

Despite the many destruction levels at numerous Minoan sites caused by earthquake, these are the only human remains yet to have been found in destruction levels. This is all the more remarkable considering the extensive earthquake damage at the major palace centres contemporary with the destruction of the shrine at Archanes, and implies that the Minoans probably had some warning of the impending disaster, such as earth tremors. The exceptional discovery at Anemospilia bears all the hallmarks of a human sacrifice, probably in an attempt to propitiate the gods and avert disaster. This is not a unique example from the ancient world. Ancient peoples often resorted to exceptional means to appease the gods and so to escape imminent disaster in times of great distress, such as plague and other natural catastrophes or war. This appears to have been the case at Anemospilia. The four bodies represent three temple officials — the priest and priestess who carried out the sacrifice and the temple acolyte in the corridor carrying away the victim's blood in the sacrificial basin, as well as the victim himself. Unfortunately for the temple officials their sacrifice failed to appease the gods, and they were trapped in the shrine during the earthquake and killed by collapsing masonry. They lay undisturbed here for some 3500 years until they were discovered by archaeologists. ∎

General view of Archanes-Anemospilia.

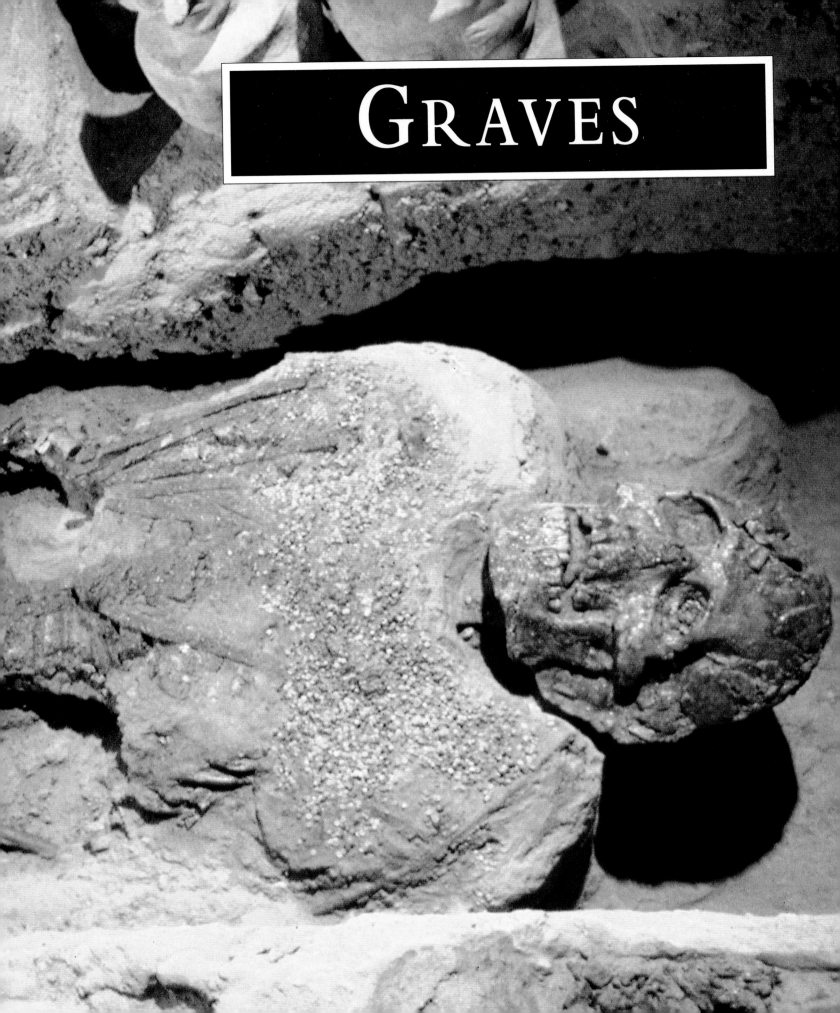

GRAVES

THE PUZZLE OF NEANDERTHAL BURIAL

Most of the earliest graves are associated with the Neanderthals of Europe and the Near East, who left little evidence of religion and symbolism. It is a classic problem in field archaeology: how is the excavator to distinguish an intentional grave from incidental burial, especially in a cave where animals and people may be killed and buried by falling rocks and rubble? How is the archaeologist to distinguish grave goods from the stone tools and animal bone debris that often lies in the same deposits?

Our more remote ancestors — australopithecines (see p.14) and early forms of the genus *Homo* — are represented by isolated fragments of bone and teeth scattered across the landscape and, in rare instances, by partial skeletons preserved by unusual circumstances

The earliest human graves remain a subject of heated debate. Evidence of intentional burial of the dead reaches back 50,000 to 100,000 years and perhaps earlier, and is inextricably linked to the first stirrings of religious belief in human society. But the interpretation of these graves — some of which are said to contain offerings for the dead and other traces of ancient ritual — has always been controversial.

(e.g. buried by volcanic ash fall). During the late nineteenth century, even after the discovery of the Neanderthal and Cro-Magnon peoples, archaeologists doubted the existence of any intentional burials during the Stone Age. In the spring of 1908, however, the Swiss prehistorian Otto Hauser uncovered a complete Neanderthal skeleton in the cave of Le Moustier in the Dordogne region of France. According to Hauser, the skeleton lay on its side "as if it were sleeping", with the head resting on a bed of flint artefacts and the left hand lying near a beautifully flaked stone hand axe. In order to authenticate the find, Hauser had it twice reburied and "discovered" in the presence of visitors, thus creating subsequent doubts about its position. The impact of this important discovery was probably reduced further by personal animosity and national rivalry directed at Hauser, who later outraged his French colleagues by selling the skeleton to a museum in Berlin.

Nevertheless, in the summer of the same year, two young French priests reported a second Neanderthal burial in a small cave at La Chapelle-aux-Saints. These two brothers, Amédée and Jean Bouyssonie, had discovered another complete skeleton — later made world famous by the anatomist Marcellin Boule as the brutish type-fossil of the Neanderthals — resting in flexed position in a burial pit, accompanied by flint artefacts, animal bones and fragments of red ochre. This discovery was followed by more dramatic finds in the Dordogne region at La Ferrassie, where the noted French archaeologist

Skeletons excavated from La Ferrassie rockshelter before the First World War convinced many scholars that the Neanderthals had intentionally buried their dead.

Denis Peyrony excavated the remains of two adult Neanderthals in 1909-10. In subsequent years, five more burials — all of them Neanderthal children and infants — were reported from this rock-shelter. These discoveries appeared to settle the issue, and by the time of the First World War most prehistorians were willing to accept the conclusion that the Neanderthals had intentionally buried their dead.

In the years following the war, archaeologists reported new Neanderthal burials from other parts of Europe and the Near East, as well as new evidence for rituals associated with treatment of the Neanderthal dead. The Russian archaeologist Alexey Okladnikov found the fragmentary skeleton of a Neanderthal boy in a remote cave in the mountains of southern Uzbekistan in 1938. According to Okladnikov, the skeleton was surrounded by a ring of goat horns, to which he attached religious meaning. Other claims of evidence for rituals associated with animals at Neanderthal sites emerged in these years and later, especially rituals associated with the remains of cave bears. The bear

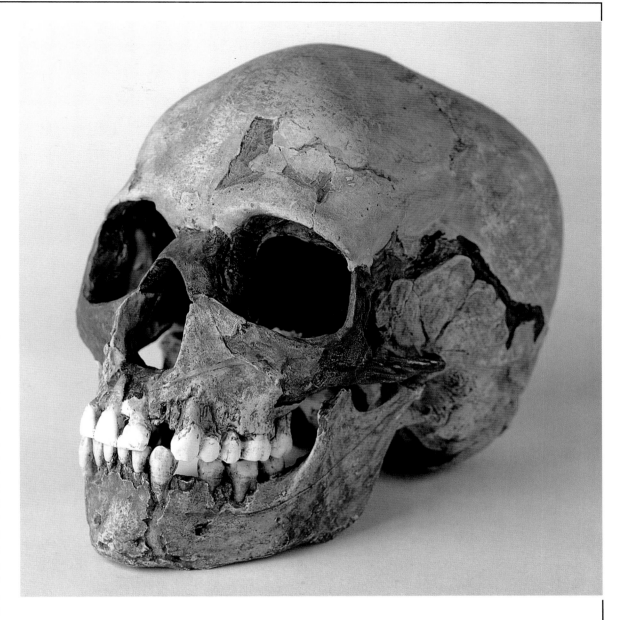

has always played a prominent role in the mythology and religion of hunting and gathering peoples in northern latitudes, and its large Ice Age ancestor must have been a dangerous and formidable neighbour to the European Neanderthals. Archaeologists have reported the deliberate burial of bear skulls in a number of sites, and in at least one instance the burial of a complete bear carcass alongside the grave of a Neanderthal.

An even more sensational find was announced in 1939 from a coastal village in central Italy. In a small cave near Monte Circeo — where Odysseus was said to have been held captive by Circe — the amateur fossil-hunter Alberto Blanc discovered a Neanderthal skull which appeared to have been placed on a circular arrangement of stones on the cave floor. Blanc suggested that the placing of, and damage to, the skull indicated both a violent death ("probably ritual murder") followed by an act of ritual cannibalism. The interpretation of the Monte Circeo find had a profound effect on how prehistorians viewed the Neanderthals, who now seemed to have led a mental and spiritual life comparable to that of modern humans.

The remains of people considered intermediate between the Neanderthals and modern humans were found at Jebel Qafzeh in Israel, and have recently been dated to roughly 90,000 years ago. They provided new evidence of intentional burial and grave goods from this time period.

The resumption of field expeditions after the Second World War produced more reports of Neanderthal burial and ritual, including some remarkable finds from the Near East that further reinforced this view. In 1953 the American archaeologist Ralph Solecki discovered the first of nine Neanderthal skeletons in Shanidar Cave, located in the hills of northern Iraq. Eventually Solecki concluded that five of these individuals had been intentionally buried, while the remainder had been victims of falling rocks. Solecki also suggested that the healed injuries and degenerative disease evident on one of the adult skeletons — who would have required daily care and feeding to survive — revealed an unexpected degree of compassion in Neanderthal society. Even more startling was the suggestion, based on study of pollen recovered from the surrounding cave sediment, that one of the Shanidar skeletons had been buried with flowers. Solecki affectionately referred to the Shanidar Neanderthals as "the first flower people".

In recent years archaeologists have reacquired their scepticism about Neanderthal burial and ritual. Intensive studies of the natural processes that cause the accumulation and modification of bones in caves indicate that many of the finds attributed to ritual behaviour, such as the cave bear remains and the damaged Monte Circeo skull, are more easily explained by these processes. Doubts have been raised about the validity of earlier excavation reports concerning the presence of burial pits and other features. The careful excavation of a Neanderthal skeleton discovered in France during 1979 revealed no evidence of a burial pit. There is now a broad consensus among prehistorians that the remains of the Neanderthals yield few traces of art and symbolism, which has fuelled scepticism about their religious beliefs and rituals. Nevertheless, the body of evidence for Neanderthal burial — accumulated by many people over many years — cannot be dismissed out of hand. It is as much of a mystery today as it was before the First World War, and one that still holds important implications for the origins of society and culture among modern humans. ■

RIGHT: The "Old Man" of La Chapelle-aux-Saints, discovered in 1908, became famous as the type-specimen of Neanderthal burial - but is now considered atypical.

BELOW: One of the Neanderthal skeletons recovered from Shanidar Cave in Iraq in 1953 was thought to have been buried with flowers.

LATE ICE AGE BURIALS
OF EURASIA

Graves dating to the late Ice Age — from roughly 30,000 to 10,000 years ago — have been excavated from caves and rock-shelters in many parts of Western Europe, and from ancient campsites across Central Europe, Russia and Siberia. Some of them contain remarkable examples of ornamentation and art, and suggest a culture rich in materials and beliefs. They provide not only a striking contrast to everything that had preceded them, but in most parts of the world their elaborate character was not to be

If the graves of the Neanderthals remain ambiguous, the populations of modern humans who appeared across Eurasia less than 40,000 years ago left an incontestable record of deliberate burial reflecting the explosion of ritual and symbolism that took place at this point in prehistory.

equalled for thousands of years following the end of the Ice Age.

Archaeologists have found burials associated with the earliest appearance of modern humans in Eurasia. The first of these was discovered in 1823 in Great Britain, many decades before the archaeological record of the late Ice Age became known. Recovered from Goat's Hole Cavern at Paviland, in southern Wales, and christened the "Red Lady of Paviland" by the geologist William Buckland, the skeleton later proved to be that of an

adult male, buried along with ivory bracelets and rods, perforated shells and a liberal sprinkling of red ochre. The presence of artefacts typical of the Aurignacian culture indicates relatively early dating — probably more than 25,000 years ago.

Other Aurignacian burials have been discovered on the continent of Europe, including the robust skeletons discovered in 1868 at the Cro-Magnon rock-shelter in the Dordogne, France, which became the type-specimens for early modern humans. At the Grotte des Enfants on the Italian Riviera, an adult male was found with his head resting on a stone slab covered with red ochre and associated with shell ornaments. In the same cave

BELOW: Skeleton of a male aged between twelve and fourteen found in the cave of Arene Candide, Italy, covered in red ochre. Hundreds of perforated seashells adorn his head, and he has four perforated antler batons with him.

archaeologists excavated a double burial containing the remains of an adult female and a male youth: the head of the youth was found encased in a protective arrangement of stone, and ornaments and red ochre were also recovered from the grave. In northern Spain, at the cave of Cueva Morin, Aurignacian burials included a bizarre example reportedly containing the outline of a headless corpse, whose bones had weathered away, which had apparently been interred with the remains of an animal; the shape of the severed head lay nearby, adjacent to a stone knife.

Graves from this early period, but lacking association with the widespread Aurignacian culture, have also been found in eastern Europe. Russian archaeologists discovered a burial that most probably dates to before 25,000 years ago in one of the many open-air sites located near the village of Kostenki on the Don River. The burial pit contained the tightly flexed skeleton of an adult male, along with some stone artefacts and large quantities of red ochre. Further north, at the open-air site of Sungir, the late Soviet archaeologist Otto Bader excavated several graves of comparable age that remain perhaps the most spectacular of all Ice Age burials. The first of these contained the skeleton of an older male, lying in a pit filled with ochre-saturated earth; a large stone and the skull of a female were found resting on the surface of the grave. The skeleton was partially covered with numerous ornaments, including ivory bracelets and over 3500 ivory beads which were found in long lines across the forehead, chest, knees and ankles,

Human head, in mammoth ivory, from Dolní Vestonice, Moravia.

and along the legs — apparently strung together as necklaces or attached to clothing.

The second burial contained the skeletons of two adolescents — perhaps a male and a female — lying in extended position, head to head. The floor of the grave was saturated with charcoal and the earth filling the grave was enriched with red ochre. Both skeletons were covered with thousands of ivory beads which had apparently been sewn onto the clothing, which seemed to have been fastened over the chest with long pins. The hands and feet were also adorned with ivory bracelets and bead necklaces. Spears made from straightened mammoth tusk lay adjacent to each skeleton, and various other artefacts were found with the remains of the dead. The Sungir burials suggest a previously unimagined degree of complexity in Ice Age dress and ornamentation.

The most impressive examples of Ice Age burial in Central Europe are associated with the younger Gravettian culture, of c. 25-20,000 years ago, which is best known for its evocative "Venus" figurines. In 1894 the noted Czech archaeologist Karel Maska discovered a mass grave at the open-air site of Predmostí in Moravia. The burial pit, which measured 4 by 2.5 m (13 ft by 8 ft 3 in), contained the skeletons of eight adults and twelve children, laid to rest beneath mammoth bones and stones. Unfortunately, many details of this early discovery remain obscure. From another open-air site in Moravia, at Dolní Vestonice, Czech archaeologists uncovered the burial of a woman — again resting beneath mammoth bones — who had apparently suffered from partial facial deformation in life. Incredibly, both an engraved and a sculpted image of this woman were found nearby. In 1986 a triple burial containing two young adult males and, between them, one young adult of indeterminate sex was discovered at the same site. The skeletons lay in extended position, adorned with necklaces of drilled fox teeth and small ivory pendants, and buried with large quantities of red ochre. Although the margins of a grave pit could not be identified, the placing of the skeletons indicated that they had been buried simultaneously.

Gravettian burials have also been found in Western Europe, most notably along the Italian Riviera at the Grimaldi Cave complex. One of these caves yielded another triple burial, containing the remains of an adult male, young male and young female. The skeletons lay in extended position, adorned with various orna-

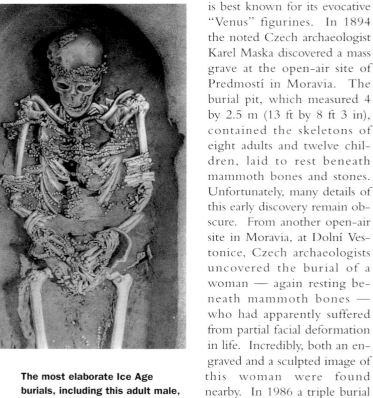

The most elaborate Ice Age burials, including this adult male, were discovered in Russia at the site of Sungir.

ABOVE: A triple burial containing numerous grave goods and large quantities of red ochre was discovered at Dolní Vestonice in 1986.

OPPOSITE: The "Old Man of Menton", from one of the Grimaldi Caves on the Italian Riviera. He was covered in red ochre, and on the head are more than 200 perforated seashells and 22 perforated stag teeth.

ments of shell, bone and teeth, and covered with red ochre. Stone tools were found in the hands of the adult male and the young female. In another cave two infants were found buried side by side on a bed of sea shells.

Thousands of miles to the east, Russian archaeologists discovered a grave of comparable age at the site of Mal'ta near Lake Baikal in Siberia. In 1929 the fragmentary and decomposed skeleton of a child was excavated from a shallow burial pit, partially surrounded by stones. The body had been interred with many ornaments and objects, including one of the most elaborate items of Stone Age jewellery ever found — a pendant and bead necklace of mammoth ivory — placed around the neck of the child. Among other objects were a bracelet, a perforated disc and a small ivory sculpture of a bird.

Curiously, burials dating to the final phase of the Ice Age — typically associated with the Magdalenian culture — are neither especially common nor elaborate. One of the more widely known examples was excavated at St Germain-la-Rivière, in France, where the skeleton of an adult female was found in flexed position within a small stone chamber. The body had been buried with a necklace of drilled deer teeth. ∎

JERICHO SKULLS

The world's first farmers lived in the Near East, near the eastern shores of the Mediterranean Sea (an area also called the Levant). Excavations at Jericho and other sites have exposed hamlets of the Natufian culture (10,500-8500 BC), whose inhabitants experimented with planting wild wheat and barley. These experiments led to the domestication of these and other plants during the following, neolithic period. In the Near East farming began well before the invention of pottery,

Jericho in the Jordan River Valley holds the spectacular remains of a fortified neolithic village, over 5000 years older than the Biblical Joshua, beneath thick remains of Bronze Age cities. The inhabitants of this early village practised a distinctive burial ritual, centred on an ancestor cult that displayed the plastered skulls of dead family members.

tinued to gather wild plants. Most of the meat in the diet came from hunted animals; goat and sheep herding developed in the mountains to the north and appeared in the Levant only during PPNB times. Farming, and storage of surplus crops, allowed

and these early phases are called Pre-Pottery Neolithic A and B, abbreviated to PPNA (8500-7300 BC) and PPNB (7300-6300 BC). The early farmers of the Levant grew several kinds of grains, lentils and other legumes, and flax, but also con-

more people to live together, and settlements grew larger and more sophisticated. Jericho grew from a Natufian hamlet to almost town-size in PPNA times, when the scatter of circular houses covered about ten acres, and a large stone wall, enhanced by a massive solid stone tower, bordered the settlement on at least three sides. In the following PPNB period Jericho developed the multi-room, rectilinear dwellings that later permitted the growth of densely packed villages in the Near East. Other PPNB villages contained the same novel architecture, and some were now much larger than Jericho, topped by Ain Ghazal (near Amman in Jordan) at 12 hectares (30 acres).

The inhabitants of Jericho and other PPN villages buried their dead not in cemeteries, but beneath the floors of their houses or in the spaces between houses. These burials

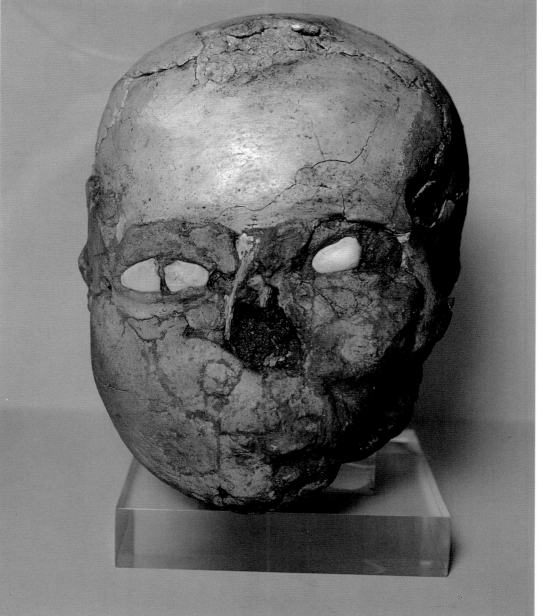

LEFT: The Jericho portrait skulls (seventh millennium BC) represented individuals' features in modelled plaster and depicted the eyes with shell, but left the back of the skull unplastered.

OPPOSITE: This fine Jericho portrait skull is one of the few cases in which the jaw bone was also used to make the plastered visage.

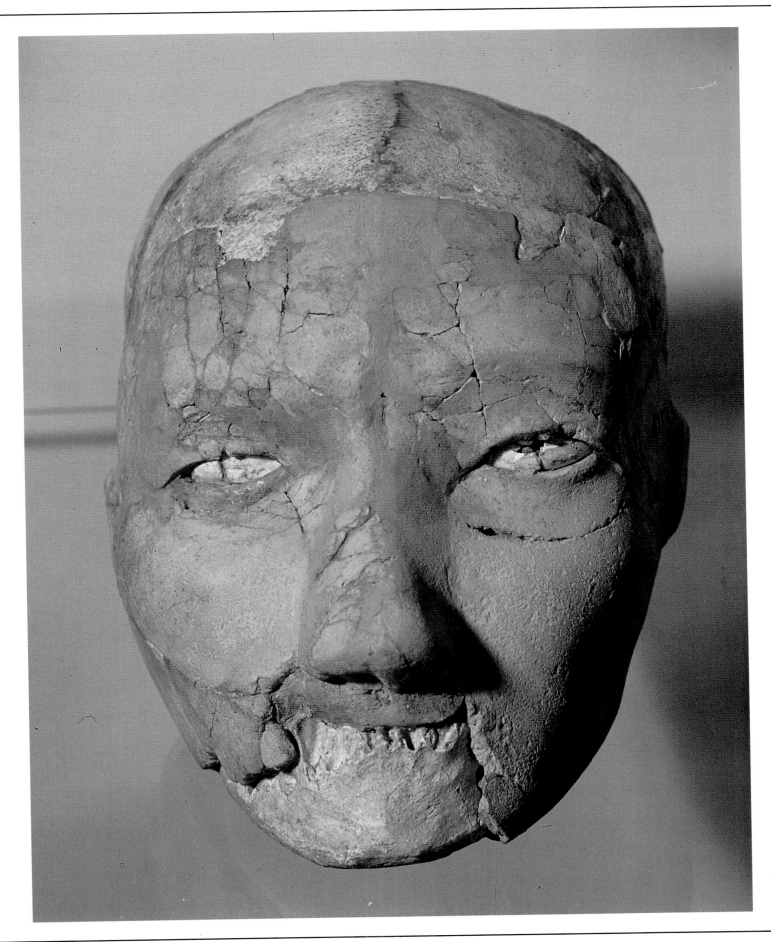

took several different forms. In some cases individual bodies were laid in pits, often in a flexed position, while in others there are several bodies in a single pit. Some burials have red ochre sprinkled over the body, and sometimes the skulls are painted; the bones themselves may be in a state of disarray. But the most striking aspect of these burials is how often the skeletons of adults (though not juveniles) have their skull missing. In one example at Jericho, a jumble of bones within a 1 by 2 m (3 by 6 ft) burial included nine jaw bones but no skulls, and only two articulated skeletons (with the bones in anatomically correct position). In another instance, the bones of over 30 people were mixed up together beneath a plastered floor, some placed in individual pits and others just tumbled together, with few heads; the position of some bones shows that many limbs were still attached by their ligaments when the skeletons were mixed.

The missing heads played a crucial role in rituals of an ancestor cult — the heads were deliberately detached from the body. The jumble of bones at Jericho suggested that the bodies may have been buried temporarily to rot the flesh, and then dug up again in order to find the skulls. The evidence at other sites like Ain Ghazal suggests a similar process even when the skeletons are still articulated. Once acquired, the skulls were given special treatment. Often they were collected together in burial pits that contained only crania. In one case at Jericho, seven skulls were placed in a circle around an eighth within a pit, and in another instance three skulls were buried together. Other sites display similar burial rituals.

Other skulls, usually without the jaw bone, served as the framework for plaster death masks, or portraits. Made only during PPNB times, these portraits modelled the face of the dead, usually leaving the rear of the skull unplastered. Details of the face, like eyebrows and beard, might be rendered in plaster, the eyes set with shell (clam or cowrie), and the hair, moustache and beard indicated by black painted stripes. A finishing coat of fine plaster mixed with iron oxide often gave a pink-tinted, fine finish to the face. A variation on the theme appeared at the Nahal Nemar cave, in the Judean Desert near the Dead Sea, where the backs (not faces) of half a dozen skulls had been coated with asphalt (not plaster) in a net-like pattern. Like the unadorned skulls, the portrait skulls often appear in groups, like the seven skulls together at Jericho, or the dozen cached at Tell Ramad, near Damascus. At Ain Ghazal four skulls were buried in a row beneath a possibly sacrificial double infant burial.

Most archaeologists agree that these peculiar practices — separating heads from bodies, the collective burial of skulls beneath floors, and especially the creation of portrait skulls (mostly from the heads of adult males) — reveal the rituals of an ancestor cult. Indeed, the portrait skulls seem to have been intended, at least some of the time, for display among the living. The Tell Ramad cache came equipped with clay pedestals on which the skulls might be displayed, and the group of seven from Jericho seems originally to have functioned within a house (and only to have been incidentally buried when the house collapsed). Other arte-

facts may also be connected with this cult. Several stone masks, including a painted example from the Nahal Nemar cave, seem to represent old men with beards, rendered in a style similar to the portrait skulls. And nearly life-sized human figures rendered in plaster also present faces painted in a manner very like that of the skulls. Jericho yielded a magnificent example of this art form, and Ain Ghazal contained two caches of these statues, including

The portrait skulls at Jericho dating from Pre-Pottery Neolithic B generally commemorated adults, so the children buried there kept their heads.

at least one female figure.

The emergence of an ancestor cult, at first involving only separate burial of skulls during the PPNA, and then becoming more elaborate during the PPNB period with the portrait skulls and additional ritual artefacts, can be regarded as a symptomatic response to the process of nomadic hunters and gatherers settling down in permanent and increasingly elaborate farming villages.

Besides allowing larger numbers to live together, farming also required people to adopt a different attitude towards the land and its contents. In particular, individual families within a community came to own the soil, and ideas about property and about rights to use land seem to have changed. The ancestor cult proclaimed the enduring links of families to place and way of life, a claim to property and tradition. ∎

LA CHAUSSÉE-TIRANCOURT

The early farmers of Western Europe built elaborate megalithic tombs for their dead. The first tombs appeared in Brittany some 7000 years ago, and gradually spread throughout Western Europe, each region developing different styles.

La Chaussée-Tirancourt is a megalithic tomb (i.e. built of large stones) of the *allée couverte* (gallery grave) type, near Amiens in the Somme region of northeastern France. Between about 4800 and 4100 years ago the remains of more than 360 individuals were buried in its funerary chamber. At some time around 2100 BC the tomb was deliberately sealed, and closed so effectively that it escaped notice until it was discovered by accident in 1967. The tomb was meticulously excavated over ten years by Claude Masset and Jean Leclerc, and their team spent a further decade analyzing what they found.

People in northeastern France in the fifth millennium BC lived in scattered farmsteads and hamlets. One of the ways they maintained social links with each other was for members of different households to be buried in centrally located shared tombs. The evidence from La Chaussée-Tirancourt suggests that members of particular households were buried in specific parts of the tomb, and that this spacing was maintained over a long period of time.

The builders of La Chaussée-Tirancourt first dug a large trench into the limestone bedrock. In this trench, 15 m (50 ft) long, 3.5 m (11 ft 6 in) wide and some 1.7 m (5 ft 7 in) deep, the funerary structure was built, divided into a burial chamber to the west, 11 m (36 ft) long and 3 m (10 ft) wide, and a smaller antechamber to the east. Set in a little way from the sides of the trench, two rows of orthostats, slender standing stones, marked out the sides of the burial chamber. The ends of the chamber were blocked by larger stone slabs. A small hole in the slab at the eastern end acted as the entrance from the antechamber.

The space that was left between the walls of the trench and the burial chamber allowed people to move around the outside of the burial chamber, at least in the early stages of the monument's use.

Behind the slab at the western end of the chamber was a small cell-like space, named in the Picardy dialect the *muche*, reached from the burial chamber by a small gap between the terminal slab and the last orthostat on the south side. The function of this space is unclear, but it is a feature shared by a number of megalithic tombs. However, unlike many megalithic tombs, the funerary structure at La Chaussée-Tirancourt was not covered by large capstones. Instead it seems that the whole monument was roofed with wood and earth, possibly thatched with straw.

Little remains of the earliest burials at La Chaussée-Tirancourt, interred in the tomb about 4800 years ago. Some time after their bones had become covered by layers of accumulated sediment, some changes were made to the structure of the burial chamber. For some reason long lost, the two orthostats at the northern end of the burial chamber were removed, heralding a new phase of burial activity. Within a relatively short time of each other, the bodies of some 60 individuals were buried in succession in the chamber, earlier inhumations being moved to make way for new arrivals.

These burials seem to have formed three groupings, distinguished by genetic abnormalities that can be seen on the bones. One group, clustered at the western end of the chamber, exhibited an unusually high frequency of "hypotrochanterian fossae" (a feature at the end of the thigh-bone), and was further distinguished by the rarity of a characteristic that was fairly common in the other burials of this phase, the presence of a third trochanter, a muscle attachment, on the femur. The two clusters of burials in the southern part of the chamber formed a second distinct group, distinguished by a high incidence of incrustation on the humeral trochlea, part of the articulation of the shorter arm bone. The third group was made up of a cluster of burials on the northern side of the chamber. These genetic abnormalities were inherited and suggest that people from particular households were being buried in distinct parts of the tomb.

There followed another lull in the use of the tomb, during which time a 15 cm (6 in) thick layer of deposits built up over the bones of the dead. The start of the next phase of activity was marked by some redesigning of the entrance to the burial chamber. One of the orthostats on the right hand side of the entrance was removed, and a ramp constructed which made entry to the burial chamber much easier.

Following these changes, the largest number of individuals from any phase was interred in the tomb. Over 300 bodies were deposited in a series of eight burial compartments. These compartments were probably originally wooden cases, but by the time they were excavated the wood had long since perished, leaving only the clustering of the bones. A number of disarticulated

More than 360 people were buried over 700 years in the megalithic tomb of La Chaussée-Tirancourt, northeastern France, a focal point for surrounding neolithic farmsteads and hamlets.

bones were found in the upper parts of these clusters. These may have fallen out of the cases into the spaces between, and subsequently have been replaced on top of the other bodies, disturbing the upper layers of bones.

Careful analysis of the bones from this layer led to an extraordinary discovery. Just as certain distinctive features on the bones in the lower layer allowed the archaeologists to suggest kin-based groupings of burials within the chamber, so too in this upper layer two or three such groupings could be discerned. Tibias from the case at the northwestern end of the tomb often had an additional articular facet. The three cases in the southeastern part of the chamber formed a second grouping, characterized by an absence of olecranian perforation (a feature in the arm bone) in females, and the common presence of hypotrochanterian fossae. Remarkably, the humeri from the westernmost of those three cases exhibited a relatively high incidence of incrustation of the humeral trochlea, the very same abnormality as was witnessed in the southeastern grouping of burials from the lower level. These fascinating discoveries, based on the painstaking analysis of bones, has advanced our understanding of the burial practices of the early farmers in this part of France far beyond the notion that they were simply buried together in communal tombs, and points the way forward to the possibility of appreciating the social relations within their communities.

Very few artefacts were found within the burial chamber itself, just two bone awls, an adze and two copper beads. The antechamber, however, contained the remains of funerary rituals and offerings: a small pot of the Seine-Oise-Marne culture, three perforated axe sleeves, one of which was polished, a perforated shell and a greenstone axe-shaped pendant. The placing of these objects in the antechamber and the absence of objects in the burial chamber itself suggest that these grave goods were for collective use rather than for the benefit of deceased individuals. Within the tomb, however, some distinctions were being made between children and adults. The bones of six children were found

Bone analysis revealed sets of shared anomalous genetic traits indicating that particular families were probably buried close together in the long communal tomb of La Chaussée-Tirancourt.

grouped together in a niche, separated from the adult burials. The numbers of children were, in fact, exceptionally low, supporting the hypothesis that not all members of the community served by La Chaussée-Tirancourt were buried within its confines.

Shortly before 2100 BC the grave was closed. The chambers, *muche* and passages were filled in and sealed with a thick layer of loam. Fierce fires were lit above the tomb, destroying the roof and the tops of the orthostats, covering the whole monument in a thick layer of ash. Subsequent inundation by alluvium hid La Chaussée-Tirancourt, preserving its fascinating secrets for posterity. ■

THE TALHEIM NEOLITHIC MASS BURIAL

Originating in the Hungarian Plain near Budapest, these early farmers spread west and north until they reached eastern France and northern Poland. They are known as the "Linear Pottery Culture" from the incised lines on their pottery. Evidence from bones and charred seeds indicates that they kept domestic cattle, sheep, goats and pigs and grew different types of wheat and barley. Their houses were long, timber-framed structures, clustered into settlements in the valleys of streams. In 1983 a man digging in his garden at Talheim came across human bones and promptly notified local authorities. It was clear that the human bones were in their proper anatomical articulation, so complete skeletons were represented. A week-long rescue excavation was organized in 1983, and after the significance of the find was clear, a fuller two-week excavation of the surrounding area took place the following year.

The first farmers of Central Europe have generally been considered to have been peaceful folk who colonized the major river valleys between 5500 and 5000 BC. Artists' reconstructions of their settlements generally depict bucolic rural scenes of farming families tending their fields and livestock, building houses and making pottery. This idyllic image was shattered by the discovery and excavation in 1983-4 of a mass grave at Talheim, in southwestern Germany.

The excavations exposed a concentration of skeletal remains about 2.9 m (9 ft 6 in) in length, up to 1.5 m (5 ft) wide and 25 cm (10 in) thick, lying in a pit slightly larger than the mass of bones. Bones lay chaotically across, over and under each other. They were very well preserved and complete, indicating that these were the remains of complete bodies which had been piled in a pit and buried. Among the bones were fragments of Linear Pottery vessels, and radiocarbon dating of the bones indicated that they were 7000 years old, in agreement with the ceramic finds.

Analysis of the bones indicated that the grave contained the remains of at least 34 individuals. More than half were lying on their stomachs, with their arms and legs splayed in various directions. Others were lying on their sides or backs. Among the 34 individuals were 16 children and adolescents and 18 adults. Infants were totally absent. Most of the adults were in their 20s, al-

though several were over 50 and one over 60. Of the adults, nine could be identified as male and seven as female, based on anatomical characteristics of the skull and pelvis. The average height of the grown Talheim men was 1.69 m (5 ft 6 in), and of the women 1.56 m (5 ft 2 in). Some of the bones showed signs of healed fractures, but in general these people seemed to have been in good health.

Any thoughts that the 34 individuals in the Talheim burial had died a natural death were dispelled by the finding of profound indications of trauma on many of the skeletons. Over half had received blows to the skull. Many of these blows were so severe as to have produced actual holes in the skull which clearly would have been lethal. The holes are generally ovate in shape, several centimetres long and and 2-3 cm (1 in) wide. Other skulls had signs of blows with blunt objects which produced depressions and deformations several centimetres in diameter. Finally, two crania, including that of the 60-year-old, had traces of the impact of a flint arrowhead. The traumatic injuries clearly occurred while the individuals were still alive and are severe enough to have been

The trauma on this skull from Talheim was caused by an object corresponding in cross-section to a typical neolithic stone axe.

The densely compacted deposit of human bones at Talheim contained the remains of at least 34 men, women and children.

Further remains from Talheim. Many of the skeletons were lying face down with arms and legs splayed.

slaughtered with forceful blows. We can only guess what the dispute was about: territory? livestock? mates? Or was it simply to demonstrate the power and might of one group of farmers over another?

The violent scene at Talheim is reflected in the increasing number of fortifications discovered at Linear Pottery settlements in many parts of Europe. Ditches and palisades surrounding settlements at sites like Darion, Oleye and Longchamps in Belgium and Vaihingen/Enz in southwestern Germany (not far from Talheim) are clearly defensive in character. Some researchers have proposed that the primary purpose of these defences was protection against indigenous foragers who found themselves displaced by the agriculturalists. While this may have been the case, it is clear from the Talheim evidence that the Linear Pottery colonists also had to fear other farmers like themselves.

Archaeologists tend to idealize the prehistoric people they study and often paint a picture of harmony and equilibrium. The mass burial at Talheim reminds us that prehistoric life had a dark side which could be violent and brutal. The 34 victims who were thrown into the pit vividly depict this stark reality. ∎

the cause of their deaths.

The outlines of the holes and of the depressions in the skulls correspond very closely to the cross-sections of the polished stone axes used by the Linear Pottery farmers. The sorry conclusion is that these individuals were killed by blows from such axes, concentrated on the skulls. They were then thrown without ceremony into the large pit, where they landed in all sorts of positions. The slaughter appears to have happened all at once, for the intertwining of the bodies indicates that the victims were all tossed into the pit at the same time. The chaotic arrangement of the skeletons indicates that whoever threw them in was not interested in following a burial rite. Graves in Linear Pottery cemeteries, by contrast, are very carefully arranged, with one crouched body to each small grave pit. The absence of any grave goods also indicates that the Talheim burial occurred without ritual.

Perhaps the most shocking aspect of the Talheim burial was that the killers seem also to have been Linear Pottery farmers rather than rogue hunter-gatherers who might have lived in the woods nearby. For whatever reason, two groups of farmers came into conflict, and one group lost decisively. The brutality with which its members were killed is vividly seen in the damage to the skulls. Men, women and children were indiscriminately

The bones at Talheim are stark testimony to an extremely violent episode.

MASS BURIALS
IN NORTH AMERICA

Many Native American tribes traditionally exposed their dead to the natural elements so that they could be reclaimed by nature. Therefore, prehistoric human remains are found by North American archaeologists relatively rarely. Even rarer are mass burials, in which hundreds of humans were interred. Such mass burials can be either catastrophic, in which a large number of people died in one event and were buried together, or they can be attritional, representing the natural mortality rates of a society over a longer period of time.

Prehistoric archaeology in North America is currently undergoing a major transformation as old ways of doing things are re-evaluated and new techniques and theories are introduced. Nowhere is this transformation more dramatic than in the reclaiming of human remains found in archaeological sites by their Native American descendants. The debate surrounding this "repatriation" involves the value of science, contemporary politics and ultimately who can claim "ownership" of the past.

Catastrophic burials give scientists a "snapshot" of a population at a particular point in time, allowing them to reconstruct the age ranges of individual groups and their individual health profiles. A good example of such a burial comes from the Crow Creek site in South Dakota. This site, occupied in the fourteenth century by Plains Indian farmers, was protected by a ditch 380 m (1250 ft)

Mass grave sites such as this provide archaeologists with a snapshot of the biology of an individual society.

long, and at some time during that century the village was attacked and over 500 individuals killed. The bodies were then thrown into one end of the fortification ditch and covered with a layer of river clay.

When archaeologists investigated this portion of the site they found the remains of a bone bed up to 1 m (3 ft) deep and about 6.50 m (20 ft) across, and the resulting analysis of such a large number of bodies allowed archaeologists to shed remarkable light on these people before they were reinterred permanently.

The researchers found relatively few women aged between twelve and nineteen, and few young children. Were these taken as captives, perhaps? The bodies of the dead were mutilated, their hands and feet being cut off and their heads scalped. Scalping must have been common, for one individual showed evidence of having recovered from an earlier scalping before being killed at Crow Creek.

By looking at the individual bones, scientists have been able to determine that at the time of death many individuals were malnourished. The bones of the tops of the eye-sockets, for example, were pitted, as were the bones of the skull. Also, Harris lines were seen on long-bones — these coloured lines result from the natural bone growth rate having been temporarily stopped through lack of adequate nutrition. Scientists also determined that the people at Crow Creek suffered from such ailments as arthritis, sinus infections, dental abscesses, hip displacements and bone fractures. Very little evidence of cancer or dental caries was found. That these people cared for the infirm was reflected in the number of individuals with evidence of physical handicaps.

Using a computer simulation model, which took into account such variables as resource availability, climate and population levels, Larry Zimmerman, the archaeologist who excavated the Crow Creek site, was able to suggest that overpopulation, combined with an unstable climate, had resulted in competition between different Indian groups for land, and this may have been the cause of the massacre.

Attritional burials represent the dead of a society over several centuries or even longer, and these sites give scientists the opportunity to look at the changes in health, age range, sex range and other features of a society over a period of time. They also allow for the recreation of social status and changes to social organization over time.

Indian Knoll, Kentucky, is an Archaic-period archaeological site that dates to the third millennium BC. Excavations have revealed that the people at Indian Knoll survived by the hunting of deer, the gathering of hickory nuts and acorns, and the collecting of

The arrangement of bones suggests that these burials were made hurriedly.

shellfish from the nearby Green River. However, what makes Indian Knoll really exciting is that it contained over 1000 burials. Rarely do archaeologists get the chance to look at such a large population.

The Indian Knoll population had a life expectancy of just over eighteen years, and about one in ten of them had evidence of healed fractures, which suggests that they lived fairly hard and robust lives. The burials also gave very interesting clues to this group's prehistoric social organization. Both males and females had funerary goods, the male bodies being found with axes, woodworking tools, awls and fish hooks, and the women with bone beads, and tools for preparing nuts. A small number of the bodies had "exotic" goods, objects made from distant materials, like Great Lakes copper or shells from the Gulf of Mexico. Even adolescent burials had exotic materials. Such "ascribed-status" burials indicate that young people were probably honoured for the family they belonged to, and this suggests a well-established social ranking system in Indian Knoll society. Archaeologists also talk of an "achieved status", whereby social standing is achieved only by adults in the course of their individual lifetimes.

Other communal burial sites afford archaeologists similar insights into prehistoric life. The Woodruff Ossuary is located on the Plains of northwestern Kansas and dates to the middle of the first millennium AD. The ossuary consists of a set of at least 14 pits up to 1.8 m (6 ft) deep, the tops of many of which were then removed by the excavation of a large basin. The pits and the basin contained at least 60 individuals, both male and female, young and old. All the skeletal remains were disarticulated with the exception of one adolescent who was accompanied by a large number of strung shell beads.

The Dickson Mound site in Illinois was in use between AD 1100 and 1250, and contained the remains of about 250 individuals. The mound is approximately 60 by 30 m (200 by 100 ft) in size (it has been greatly levelled over the centuries and so its original height is unknown). The burial mound was associated with three separate village areas, all of them occupied for short periods of time. Dickson fell out of use at about the same time as the decline of Cahokia, a huge urban and religious centre, located just east of the present-day city of St Louis. Some researchers have suggested that the decline of Cahokia resulted not so much from warfare or climatic change as from epidemic disease. Interestingly, in regard to this, the last burial area used at Dickson had a high number of mass graves.

From a strictly scientific point of view, the excavation and analysis of prehistoric human remains provide unique opportunities to understand further the human biology and social organization of prehistoric populations. However, over the past twenty years, in keeping with aboriginal groups elsewhere in the world, Native Americans have complained bitterly about what they consider to be the desecration of their ancestors' remains. They ardently believe that removing their ancestors from their place of rest, analyzing their bones (sometimes to the point of destroying them) and them leaving them to gather dust on a laboratory shelf is a gross violation of their religious and civil rights.

In response to these legitimate concerns, the United States government in 1989 passed the Native American Graves Protection and Repatriation Act (NAGPRA). This act requires all museums, universities and colleges that have received federal funds to consult with the appropriate Indian tribes to determine, where possible, the tribal affiliation of human remains in their possession, as well as the affiliation of certain objects such as grave goods and artefacts that may be of cultural or historical importance to individual tribes. These human remains and objects must then be given back to the particular Indian tribes, so that their descendants can rebury or otherwise dispose of them with the correct cultural sensitivity. Also, restrictions were placed on how much analysis could be performed on archaeologically recovered human remains.

Archaeologists who study such burials must show them the great respect all human remains deserve.

At first the involvement of Native Americans in archaeology caused great polarity. Many archaeologists felt that this would spell the end of scientific archaeology, while many Native Americans felt that archaeology could tell them absolutely nothing about their own pasts. However, as NAGPRA has worked itself through the discipline, both "sides" seem to be working towards a new spirit of compromise. Archaeologists increasingly acknowledge that they cannot ignore the wishes of Native American groups in the name of science, and Native Americans increasingly realize that archaeology, used appropriately, can contribute to a greater understanding of individual tribal histories. ∎

MASS GRAVES: VISBY AND EAST SMITHFIELD

Sometimes the investigation of a mass grave can alter our views about how people dealt with disaster, views that often have their origins in emotionally charged historical records written by people close to the event. Such is the case at the fourteenth-century Black Death cemetery at East Smithfield in London. Only thirteen years separate the East Smithfield burials from the chaotic dumping of bodies in the battle cemetery before the gates of Visby on the Baltic island of Gotland, where the archaeological evidence supports and embellishes the horrors of the historical accounts.

Mass graves are stark but eloquent memorials to some of the more terrible disasters, plagues and battles that have afflicted humankind throughout history. Their investigation presents particular problems for the archaeologist but also very special opportunities for gaining greater knowledge about larger samples of populations from any one time than is normal.

The battle cemetery at Visby

On 27 July 1361 a battle took place outside the gates of the walled city of Visby. From the thirteenth century onward, this city had become wealthy on the profits of the flourishing Baltic trade which linked Germany, Scandinavia and new Russian markets. The rich urban merchant class pushed for more and more independence from the increasingly weak-willed Swedish kingdom of which Gotland was a part. At the same time the city became estranged from the wealthy rural peasant-merchants who inhabited the surrounding countryside of Gotland. In 1340 Waldemar Atterdag became King of Denmark, and began a programme of national rejuvenation and expansion, reclaiming a series of provinces that had been lost to Sweden. After success in Scania, he turned his attention to the wealthy and strategically important Gotland.

Waldemar set out from Denmark in midsummer 1361. First he captured the island of Oland and its fortress at Borgholm. The armada landed on Gotland on 22 July, probably at Vastergarn, 24 km (15 miles) south of Visby, the best harbour on the island. Three battles are recorded as having taken place, one of them at Fjale Marsh where the Gotland peasantry were defeated. The last defence of Gotland took place before the gates of Visby. The remnants of the defeated rural peasants bore the brunt of the fighting, as the defenders of the city itself were not used to fighting, and were none too enthusiastic about helping their rural compatriots. About 1800 Gotlanders fell at the hands of the Danish army that fateful day. Their blood is recorded as having flooded the streets of the city down to the sea.

Visby capitulated at once, and its wall was breached to allow the victorious army to enter. Unlike the countrymen, however, whose manors were systematically pillaged, the burghers of Visby bought their way out of danger. The peasant-merchants buried hoards all over the island in a futile attempt to save something from the ravaging Danes. Waldemar Atterdag

Mass grave from the battlefield at Visby.

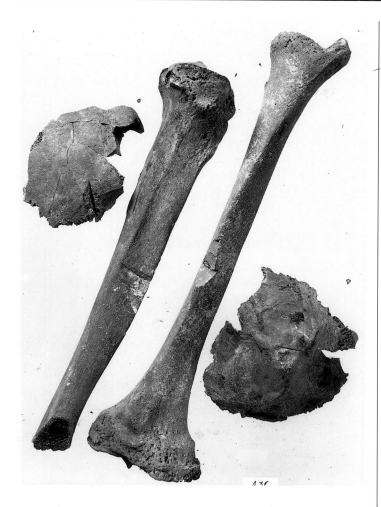

ABOVE: Skull and limb bones of the massacred Gotland army showing grievous injuries inflicted by the Danish onslaught.

RIGHT: Most bodies were stripped by plunderers before being thrown into the grave pits. Some vestiges of armour survived, however, such as this chainmail coif, still attached to the head it was supposed to protect.

left Gotland on 28 August. By an act of fate, the ship carrying the booty was sunk on the way back to Denmark.

After the battle the dead were interred in a series of hastily dug grave-pits where they lay undisturbed until the early twentieth century, when new prosperity resulted in urban expansion outside the walls of Visby. In 1905 the first of four common or mass graves was discovered and excavated by Oscar Wennersten and Nils Lithberg. The 300 skeletons they meticulously excavated caused a sensation in the world's press. The bones formed a metre-thick deposit, described as looking like a coral reef. The bones lay in a tangle of disarray, the bodies having been flung into the pit after the battle, many of them stripped beforehand by plunderers. Some still wore vestiges of armour, notably two heads enveloped in chainmail coifs. Many of the bones bore horrific injuries.

Between 1909 and 1928 two more mass graves were investigated by Bengt Thordeman and Poul Nørlund. In the course of these excavations, the bones of a total of 1185 individuals were recovered, many of them showing signs of the grisliest injuries.

Two or three more common graves were located, but left largely uninvestigated. Comparing their size with the three excavated graves, Thordeman was able to suggest a total of nearly 1600 bodies buried in front of the gates of Visby, not far short of the 1800 dead described in the fifteenth-century Gotlandic chronicles.

The results of the archaeological investigation of the mass graves, in particular the study of the gruesome injuries inflicted on the brave but hopelessly overpowered Gotland army, create a detailed picture of the nature of the battle. Injuries were divided into three types. Some 456 wounds were inflicted by cutting weapons (swords and axes), and 126 injuries resulted from piercing weapons (arrows, lances and "morning stars", wooden balls studded with square or hexagonal spikes and attached by a chain to a handle, used to hit the enemy on the head). An indeterminate number of fatalities were caused by crushing weapons, such as maces and war-hammers.

Cuts were divided into superficial (those that did not penetrate beyond the compacta of the bone), deep (those that penetrated the medullary cavity), and those that severed the bone. Blows that severed bones are relatively rare (29 in total), and occur in equal number on the tibia and fibula. These were very often single, well-aimed blows that would have been inflicted with very great force. The weapon had to cut through armour, clothing and flesh before reaching a bone, sometimes passing through another bone too. One man had his legs cut off in a single mighty blow which struck the right tibia from below on the ventral side before cutting through the left tibia from the inside. Many crania bear signs of very heavy cutting blows: one had had a large part of the left side struck off. One almost toothless old man had received a blow to the lower maxilla, and was missing a large piece of the jaw. Other bones show evidence of more of a struggle, with several lighter cuts being inflicted before the final devastating blow.

Most warriors held their swords in their right hand and carried their shield on their left arm. The left foot was usually placed just before the right. The attacker normally leaped forward to deliver the first blow, trying to bring his sword straight down onto his opponent's head, or make a sweeping cut to the right side. The opponent normally deflected this first onslaught with his shield, at the same time bringing the sword arm of the attacker to the opponent's left. Seizing this opportunity, the attacker aimed a second oblique blow downwards to the left, often going for the legs. This blow was more difficult to parry, explaining the higher proportion of injuries on the left-hand side of the body. The shield seemed to protect the upper part of the body much more effectively than the lower: only 15% of all injuries were sustained on the arms, of which the vast majority were inflicted on the humerus. Tibias show 65% of all injuries to the lower body, probably because they were the least protected part of the body, either by armour or flesh. Hands, feet, fingers and toes show few injuries, because they could be easily moved out of the way, and

The second longest burial trench at East Smithfield, containing 242 carefully laid out bodies in layers up to five bodies deep.

Skulls often bore the brunt of the worst injuries, inflicted by spiked "morning stars", war hammers, maces, arrows and lances.

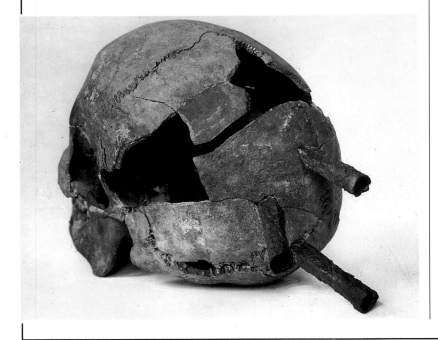

because feet were protected by shoes, hands by gauntlets.

The ramshackle nature of the peasant army is well shown by the fact that over one-third of those buried on the field were boys and old men, including a large number of cripples and lame people. They were equipped with antiquated armour, no different from that used by their Viking forebears. All in all, the tangled bodies of the fallen are testimony to the brutality before the gates of Visby, bearing out its reputation in the historical records.

East Smithfield

Between June 1986 and June 1988 the Department of Greater London Archaeology of the Museum of London excavated a cemetery at East Smithfield which was known to be the location of mass burials resulting from the Black Death that raged in the capital city from 1348 to 1350 and remained endemic until 1665. The results of the excavation suggest that the disposal of plague victims took place in a much more orderly and controlled fashion than is indicated in historical accounts that describe the dead being tipped into deep pits with no order at all.

Some 2400 burials were investigated, just over 400 of which were interred in four mass burial facilities, the others in individual graves indistinguishable from normal medieval burials. The cemetery was large and could have held many more burials, indicating a high degree of planning for disposal of the dead.

The mass burial trenches were probably used only when the rate of mortality was very high; it would doubtless have fluctuated over time. The longest burial trench was 125 m (410 ft) in length and contained 105 burials, all carefully packed in. The second was 67 m (220 ft) long, 2 m (6 ft 6 in) wide and had a surviving depth of 1.25 m (just over 4 ft). Some 242 bodies were recovered from the northern half of this trench. They had been carefully placed in it, packed very densely up to five bodies deep. There were no signs of bodies being tossed into the trench in a panic. The shortest trench had a stepped base, for ease of access, the deeper southern part being filled first. This trench contained 50 bodies, again carefully packed up to five deep.

Some 230 bodies were buried in coffins. It is quite likely that

the original number was higher, but different preservation factors across the site, in particular the effects of effluents from the Royal Mint that later occupied the site, mean that in many cases no traces survived. Some of the bodies were still wrapped in shrouds while others had traces of ash. Various historical sources refer to the practice of packing coffins with ash, possibly to absorb the fluids produced in the course of putrefaction, suggesting a delay between death and burial in some cases.

The burials may have been arranged according to criteria such as age. The central part of the western area of the site contained a high concentration of children, although the numbers of children from the cemetery as a whole were surprisingly small. The cemetery was divided into eastern and western areas, possibly resulting from earlier land boundaries or the deliberate zoning of burials according to some presently unknown criteria. No markers survive to indicate the position of the graves or the boundary of the cemetery. Beyond a few coins, which date the graves to some time after 1343, there is no evidence to date the sequence of burial. And yet East Smithfield is proof that, even at the height of the Black Death, London disposed of her dead under controlled conditions and with dignity. ∎

ABOVE: The burial of plague victims at Tournai (fourteenth-century manuscript). The East Smithfield cemetery shows how orderly such burial was in London, even at the height of the plague.

BELOW: The shortest of the four mass burial trenches at East Smithfield was 9.5 m (31 ft) long and contained 50 burials.

THE TRAGIC END OF THE ROMANOVS

Against a background of armed uprisings, strikes and demonstrations, Nicholas had been forced to abdicate in March 1917, and was subsequently arrested. In July the Romanovs were taken to Tobol'sk in Siberia, where they lived in the governor's house. In April the following year the family was moved to the Bolshevik centre of Yekaterinburg, where they were imprisoned in what was called "The House of Special Purpose". We know exactly what happened on that fateful July night from the executioners' own written testimony, which has become available from

During the night of 16-17 July 1918, in the house of the engineer Ipatiev, in the centre of Yekaterinburg in the Urals, eleven people were shot. This episode came to symbolize that bloody era of mass terror, as the victims were the Romanovs: Tsar Nicholas II of Russia, his wife Alexandra, their thirteen-year-old haemophiliac son Alexey, and their four daughters — Olga, Tatyana, Marie and Anastasia (aged twenty-three to seventeen) — together with the family doctor, a maid, a cook and a manservant.

Soviet archives in recent years. Acting on direct orders from Lenin, a twelve-man execution squad fired revolvers at the eleven prisoners who, on a pretext of unrest in the town, had been woken up and led down to "safety" in the cellar, a small room measuring little more than 4 by 5 m (14 by 17 ft). The Tsar was killed by the first bullet; the women ran about the room screaming. The daughters endured particularly gruesome deaths, since the jewels hidden in their underclothes protected them from the hail of bullets, and they had to be finished off by bayonets and clubbing. Alexey too

г. Свердловск.
Дом. где в 1918 г. казнены Романовы.

was still groaning at the end, and was shot two or three more times at point blank range by Yurovsky, the leader of the squad.

The dead were carried out one at a time on makeshift stretchers and loaded onto the back of a truck. They were driven into the forest, to an old mineshaft. Here the corpses were stripped naked, and the girls' "diamond bullet-proof vests" were discovered — Alexandra too was wearing a belt made of several pearl necklaces. In all there were 8 kg (17½ lb) of hidden jewellery. The valuables were removed, everything else from the bodies was burned, and the corpses were thrown into the shaft followed by hand grenades. However, it was then decided to transfer the bodies to deeper shafts filled with water. They were loaded again onto a truck during the night of 18-19 July, but en route to the deep shafts the vehicle became bogged down on the forest track and could go no further. So the men dug a grave-pit. At the same time they tried to burn two of the bodies nearby — they thought these were Alexey and his mother, but it seems that instead of the latter they burnt one of his sisters by mistake, since the corpses must already have been in a dreadful state.

Portrait photographs of Nicholas and Alexandra with skulls from the pit at Yekaterinburg superimposed on them by computer, showing the precision of the fit.

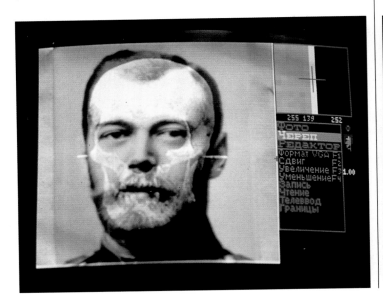

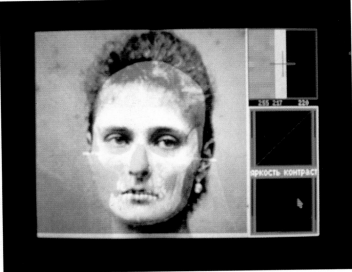

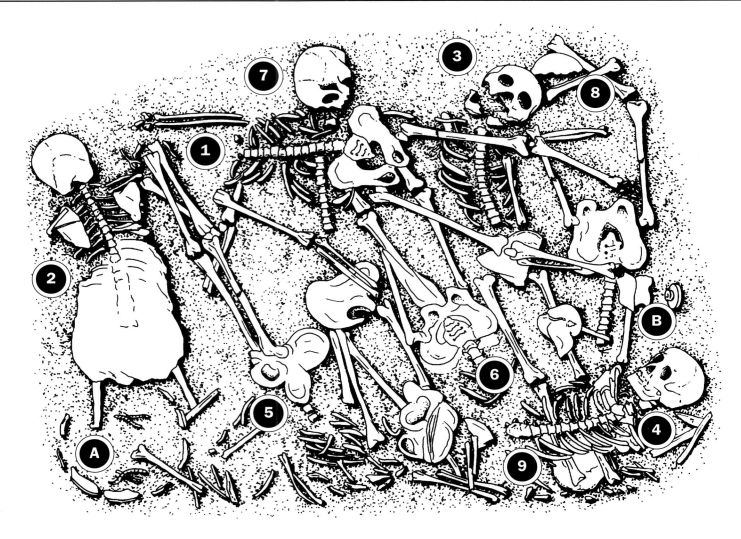

The pit: A and B, remnants of the crushed acid jars; 1, bones of Nicholas II (his skull had already been removed); 2, Dr Botkin; 3, 4 and 6, Grand Duchesses, with bayonet marks on bones; 5 and 9, male servants, one still bound with rope; 7, Alexandra; 8, Demidova, the maid, first into the pit and worst damaged, probably through lying in acid.

The pit was dug and the remaining nine corpses were laid in it. Sulphuric acid was poured over the faces and the whole body to hinder identification and to prevent the stench of decomposition. The pit was then filled with earth and brushwood, railway sleepers were laid over the top, and the truck was driven backwards and forwards over it several times to mask all signs of digging. There the Romanovs remained — in a pit in a boggy forest, so far from the gilded palaces of their heyday — for over 70 years.

Shortly afterwards, investigations by White Russians recovered at least 30 bullets from the walls and floor of the cellar; and around the mineshaft various grisly items were found — bullets, fragments of clothing and footwear, spectacle lenses, the doctor's dentures, the body of Anastasia's dog, and a finger. All bore the traces of fire. The investigators assumed that the corpses had been dismembered here, burned, and the remains destroyed with acid. So they never sought the actual burial place: it is known from photographs in their report that they went to that spot in the forest, but they never dreamed what was beneath their feet.

As one Bolshevik commissar is said to have boasted, "The world will never know what we did with them."

It was only in 1979 that Aleksandr Avdonin, a Yekaterinburg geophysicist, and his associate Geli Ryabov, a former policeman, made a systematic search of the area and came upon the railway sleepers, under which they found human bones. At that time, however, it was necessary to keep the discovery a secret or risk a visit from the KGB. They removed some skulls and bones and then reburied them in the same spot, packed in a box, in July 1980. They were able to inform the authorities only in 1991, and President Boris Yeltsin — ironically the very man who had ordered the bulldozing of the Ipatyiev House in 1977 on Moscow's orders when he was party boss in the region — then gave permission for excavations. On 9 July the Yekaterinburg archaeologist Ludmila Koryakova was asked by the authorities to excavate a "burial from the Soviet period". She guessed what was involved and agreed to help.

The group of investigators included police colonels, detectives, KGB, forensic experts, epidemiologists, and policemen with sub-machine guns. The site in the forest was surrounded by a high fence, with two large army tents inside. Eventually the pit was located, and beneath the sleepers, two feet down, they found Avdonin's box containing isolated bones and three skulls. One skull had a hole, 7.5 cm (3 in) in diameter, in the left temple. A sec-

ond skull had an exquisitely made gold bridge in the molars of its lower jaw. The facial bones of the third were missing.

In the layers below, the diggers found scattered bones with increasing frequency, and fragments of thick ceramic jars with screw-on lids. The soil within the jars was black and "greasy", as if burned, and it was obvious that these were the vessels that had contained the sulphuric acid to destroy the corpses.

The pit was almost square, about 1.5 by 2.2 m (5 by 7 ft) and a little over 1 m (3 ft) deep with an uneven floor — the shallowness was caused by bedrock being close to the ground surface here. The skeletons lay in disorder, literally one on top of the other. The dark damp bones were barely discernible from the dark sticky clay. Some soft tissue was preserved here and there, but very little hair — it had probably mostly been destroyed by fire or acid. Several leg bones had traces of thick rope around them. All the skeletons showed traces of violence, such as circular apertures caused by bullets (revolver and pistol bullets were found in the bones and tissues) and traces of blows from bayonets.

In terms of sex and age, these nine persons corresponded exactly to the nine members of the Romanov household known to have been buried (since Alexey and one sister were burned elsewhere): i.e. Nicholas and Alexandra, three daughters, the doctor (whose skeleton is toothless, since his dentures remained at the mine), the maid Demidova and the two male domestics — Kharitonov the cook and Trupp the manservant. The skulls of

The skull of Nicholas II - identified from the sophisticated dental work, and from a mark left by a sabre blow inflicted during a visit to Japan in 1891.

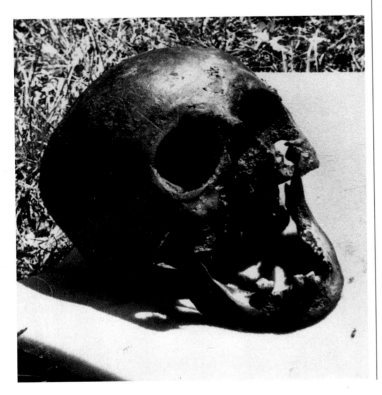

Nicholas and Alexandra had gold and platinum dental fillings of particularly fine work and porcelain crowns, whereas the servants had old and decayed teeth.

Despite all the evidence, and the close correspondence between the excavated finds and the executioners' written accounts, many people around the world voiced strong doubts about the identity of the remains — some clung to complex conspiracy theories in which some or all of the Romanovs escaped execution; others believed it was a hoax, or that the Bolsheviks had deliberately killed and buried a different set of people of the same age and sex to throw investigators off the scent; and of course, innumerable people still believed that Anastasia, the youngest daughter, had escaped death and lived to a ripe old age as the eccentric and enigmatic Anna Anderson, who died in the USA in 1984, still persisting in her claims to be a Romanov.

However, all these doubts were to be dispelled by the superimposition of photographs on some of the skulls; by facial reconstructions from the skulls; and above all by a whole series of DNA tests comparing genetic material recovered from the remains with that of the Tsar's deceased brother and of living relatives of the family, including the Duke of Edinburgh. There is no longer the slightest uncertainty: these are definitely the remains of that tragic family, while Anna Anderson has been proved to be an impostor, a Polish woman who maintained an amazing façade for decades.

The last hope of the "Anastasia survived" theorists is that one sister is not in the pit and thus still missing, but some Russian experts have asserted from photo-superimposition that Anastasia is indeed one of those in the pit, and that the missing sister is Marie. Some American specialists assert equally vigorously that Anastasia is the missing girl. But even if she is, it is clear from the archaeological testimony that the executioners' reports were accurate in their essentials; and all of them were adamant that everyone was shot. There were no survivors on that terrible night. ∎

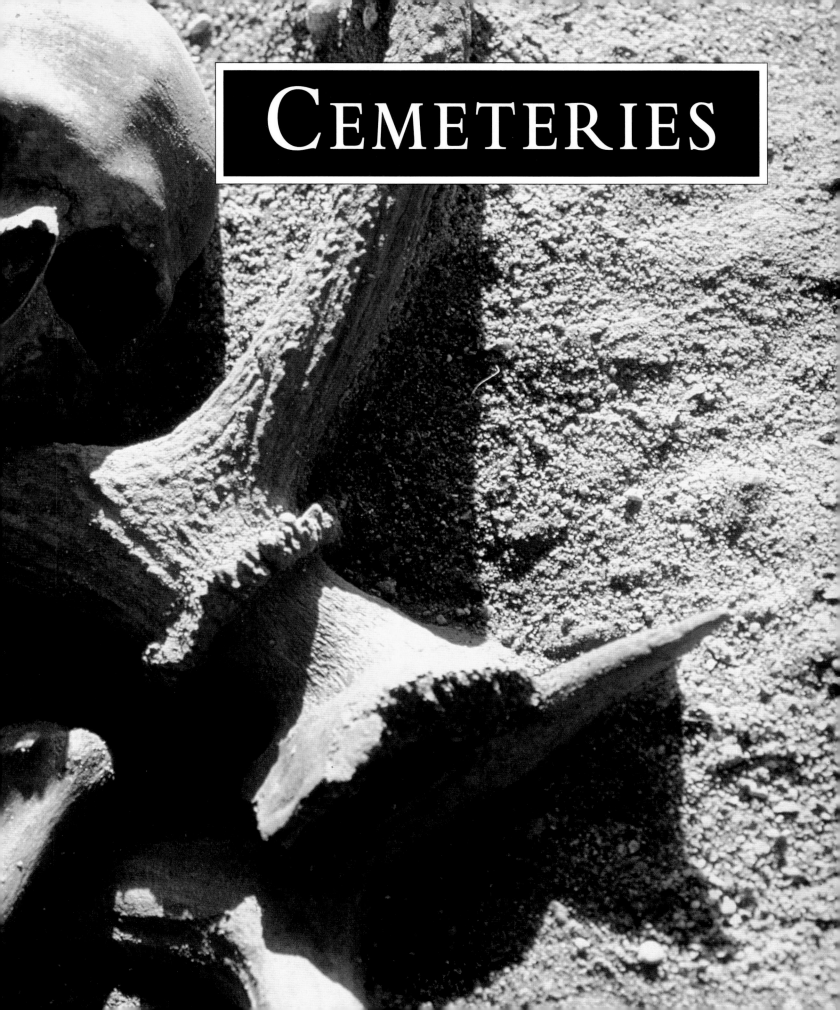

CEMETERIES

SCANDINAVIAN MESOLITHIC BURIALS

Burials from Scandinavia provide a detailed glimpse into the lives of hunter-gatherers who inhabited this area after the Ice Age. They include what must be one of the oldest known boat burials in the world.

After the glaciers retreated from Northern Europe at the end of the Ice Age, forests were soon established across the lowlands of northern Germany, Poland, southern Sweden and Denmark. These forests were inhabited by hunter-gatherers who took advantage of the numerous game animals and the rich plant life found in the woodlands. Along coastlines, especially along the bays and island coasts of southern Scandinavia, large settlements arose. Their inhabitants made use of the rich marine resources such as fish, shellfish, whales and seals. In fact, seafood was so plentiful that the forest foods only appear to have been supplements. We know this from the carbon isotope ratios found in the bones of these foragers.

These hunter-gatherers, known as the "Ertebølle culture", did not have to journey far in the course of a year to find their food. Instead, it appears that they spent long periods in one location, in settlements occupied over several seasons or even years. Inevitably, people died at these settlements, and they were buried in cemeteries. These hunter-gatherer graveyards tell us much about the lives of the Ertebølle people, but they were almost unknown prior to the mid-1970s.

In 1975 a new school was being constructed in the town of Vedbaek, north of Copenhagen. The earth-moving associated with this construction revealed burials which archaeologists quickly recognized as being from the Ertebølle period. The cemetery was very close to the shoreline of what had been an in-

let of the sea six thousand years ago. Although some graves were destroyed by the construction, systematic investigation by archaeologists exposed 18 graves with at least 22 individuals of various ages. In many of the graves a large amount of red ochre (iron oxide) was sprinkled over the deceased. Red deer antlers were included in the graves of older individuals.

Almost all the Vedbaek burials were in an extended position, with one exception in a crouching position. One particularly moving burial at Vedbaek was that of a young woman and a new-born infant. Beneath the mother's head had been a cushion of some perishable material ornamented with snail shells and deer teeth. The baby's body had been placed on the wing of a swan. Somewhat more disturbing was the triple burial of a man, a woman and a child: the man had a bone point in his neck, suggesting a violent death.

The Vedbaek burials caused quite a sensation at the time, and in the next few years several more Ertebølle cemeteries came to light. In the early 1980s the Swedish archaeologist Lars Larsson of the University of Lund began excavations at sites at Skateholm in southern Sweden. The sites at Skateholm were along the shore of a prehistoric lagoon and are now about 500 m (550 yards) inland from the Baltic coast. Skateholm I and II were both cemeteries. Skateholm I yielded 65 burials, while 22 graves were found at Skateholm II. Several of the burials contained the skeletons of dogs, about which more will be said below.

The Skateholm burials, like Vedbaek, provide a detailed glimpse into the lives of the Ertebølle hunter-gatherers. Within the excavated area at Skateholm I, where most of the burials occurred, smaller clusters of graves suggest groups in which members of a family were buried close to each other. Three general categories of graves could be identified, based on the position of the skeleton: supine (extended), crouching and seated. In some graves certain anatomical elements are missing, such as a hand or a foot (and in one case a full lower arm and a thigh bone), suggesting deliberate removal of certain body parts. The maritime diet of these individuals is indicated by the fish bones found in the area of the stomach in many of the skeletons.

The artefacts that accompanied the Skateholm burials were similar to those found at Vedbaek. Men had flint knives and axes,

LEFT: Skeleton of a young woman at Skateholm in Sweden, buried in a seated position. Numerous perforated animal teeth adorned a belt around her pelvis.

RIGHT: At Vedbaek, a 20-year-old woman was buried with a new-born child on a swan's wing at her shoulder. The flint blade on the infant's waist suggests that it is a boy.

grave often contains the remains of animal bones, apparently the remains of a meal eaten before the earth was put back into the pit.

The dog burials at Skateholm are particularly fascinating in that the animals are treated exactly as the human dead are. For example, a dog at Skateholm II had a red deer antler laid along its spine, a decorated antler hammer on its chest, and three flint blades in the hip region alongside, in exactly the same position as is found in male human graves. Red ochre was strewn over the dog's corpse. The decorated antler hammer is unique at Skateholm, suggesting that this was a very special dog indeed. At Skateholm I six dog burials are found in a small area, suggesting that they were also distinct in some way.

Since the Skateholm excavations, more Ertebølle burials have been found in southern Scandinavia. Near Vedbaek more graves were found along the prehistoric inlet, including one in which several children had been laid on a wooden tray. At Strøby Egede

LEFT: Two Skateholm burials. The upper one is a woman; the lower, later one contains an old man holding a child in front of him.

BELOW: Burial of a young male at Skateholm with antlers of several deer placed over his lower legs.

while women had belts and necklaces ornamented with animal teeth. Red ochre often covers parts of the deceased, such as the head or the waist. Antlers of red deer also form a major element in the Skateholm burials. In one grave a young man had a large rack of antlers placed over his legs, while in another burial, a young woman was found in a sitting position on top of antlers. In general, older men and young women received the greatest numbers of grave goods.

In some cases, artefacts which were not specific grave offerings were found in the Skateholm burials. The flint arrowhead lodged in the pelvic bone of one man was the weapon with which he was killed. In another grave a man was found lying on his stomach, with several arrowheads in the grave fill. Larsson suggests that these were shot into the grave. It also appears that there was a degree of ceremony associated with the burial. Traces of wooden structures raised over the grave and then burned down prior to the filling of the pit have been found. The fill of the

a grave with eight individuals was discovered. On the island of Gotland in the Baltic Sea, three individuals were found on a sandy slope where they were buried 8000 years ago.

In 1990-91 a submerged hunter-gatherer settlement site was found just off the coast of an island in southern Denmark at a locality called Møllegabet. During the excavation of the sediments, the remains of a dugout canoe were excavated. Dugout canoes are known from a number of Danish and other northern European sites of this period. The Møllegabet dugout was made from a single trunk of a linden tree at least 60 cm (24 in) in diameter. In excavating around the boat, some human bones were found. After the dugout had been taken out of the water to the laboratory, additional human bones were found in the fill inside it. A return to the site revealed additional human remains which are believed to have washed out of the canoe in the immediate vicinity of where it was found.

All evidence indicates that the Møllegabet dugout contained the remains of a single male individual about 25 years of age. The skull fragment shows the remains of a healed wound, probably the result of an axe-blow. The body appears to have been covered in sheets of bark. In the boat an arrowhead was found which may have been shot into the corpse, as Larsson has suggested was the case in one of the Skateholm graves. Antlers found nearby may also have belonged to the burial. The Møllegabet find suggests that the Nordic tradition of boat burials, so vividly manifested during the Viking age several thousand years later, may have considerable antiquity.

The Ertebølle burials from southern Scandinavia reflect a hunter-gatherer population which had a complex set of rituals associated with death. Although these people did not adopt agriculture until almost a thousand years later, they defy the stereotype of hunter-gatherers as being simple people with uncomplicated beliefs. Instead, individuals (even sometimes dogs) had distinct social identities and were carefully treated in death. ■

MURRAY VALLEY CEMETERIES

The Murray-Darling Basin covers more than a million square kilometres (nearly 400,000 square miles) of the south-eastern corner of Australia. The Murray and Darling Rivers and their tributaries rise in the Great Dividing Range, but for most of their long sinuous courses flow through semi-arid inland plains. The rivers form narrow corridors where there is water, and food resources are plentiful in contrast to the surrounding arid plains. In the most arid continent on earth these great rivers could support relatively large and dense populations. At the time of the European invasion the Murray-Darling Basin was the most densely populated part of Aboriginal Australia.

The archaeologist Colin Pardoe has argued convincingly that a number of sites along the Murray River qualify as cemeteries. The oldest of these is the well-known site of Kow Swamp, where the earliest burials are perhaps 13,000 years old. Coobool Creek,

Cemeteries — defined areas used exclusively for burials — are not often thought of in connection with hunter-gatherer communities. Rather, they are seen as the result of the more settled life of farmers. In Australia, however, Aboriginal people began burying their dead in cemeteries along the Murray Valley about 10,000 years ago and perhaps even earlier.

also on the Upper Murray, is probably about the same age. From about 7000 years ago, the practice of burying the dead in special areas steadily increased and the custom spread downstream along the Murray River. Sites that had previously been used as general camp sites often became exclusively devoted to mortuary rites.

Pardoe explains this remarkable development in terms of social change in response ultimately to the far-reaching environmental changes at the end of the last Ice Age. These saw the development of the complex and extraordinarily rich environments of the present Murray River corridor. Pardoe notes that, where large and dense populations inhabit an area of rich and predictable resources, groups tend to occupy well-defined territories. Cemeteries where only group members are buried become territorial markers.

The people of the Murray Valley were unusual in other ways too. Steve Webb, who has made a special study of the pathology of skeletal remains from the Murray Valley and elsewhere in Australia, found that Murray Valley people suffered from a range of diseases that are more usually found in settled communities. This seems to confirm the notion that there were large numbers of people living in dense communities. This is in sharp contrast to the small mobile groups typical of most of Australia.

Aboriginal burial practices varied widely over the continent. They commonly involved complex rituals, which might be held in several stages. Bones of relatives could be carried around for months before final interment. Simple inhumation, either in an extended or in a crouched position, was a common practice. Some individuals were cremated and their remains either buried or placed in log coffins

Grave goods: Lake Nitchie

Grave goods are sometimes found in the Murray-Darling Basin. Often these are the normal equipment of everyday life, such as stone artefacts. Sometimes necklaces or headbands are also found. Burials may also contain freshwater mussel shells, and one of the Kow Swamp individuals seems to have been laid on a bed of mussel shells. Ochre is common, and its use in burial rituals clearly dates back more than 30,000 years.

One of the most spectacular burials is at Lake Nitchie on the Lower Darling in western New South Wales. Here a man was buried wearing a spectacular necklace of 178 pierced Tasmanian devil teeth. These came from at least 47 animals. The Tasmanian devil is a carnivore that is now extinct in mainland Australia. The Lake Nitchie man was buried nearly 7000 years

ago in a sitting position and crammed into a small shaft-like pit. Ochre pellets were also found in the grave. The man lacked two of his upper front teeth. This is evidence of tooth avulsion, the widespread practice of knocking out one or two of the incisors as part

of initiation rites.

Until recently the Lake Nitchie necklace was a unique find. However, another man was buried with a similar necklace about 7000 years ago on Walpolla Island close to the Murray-Darling junction, some 160 km (100 miles) away.

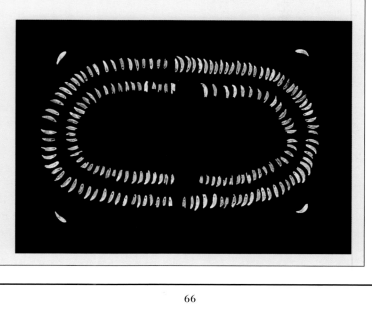

Roonka Flat

Roonka Flat in the Lower Murray Valley was first used for camping about 18,000 years ago. Several hearths associated with oven features and freshwater mussel shells have been excavated. Between about 7000 and 4000 years ago, however, the area seems to have been used exclusively as a cemetery. During the last 4000 years the site was again used for camping, although burials continued.

The burials at Roonka are extraordinarily varied. Mortuary practices include flexed and extended inhumations in either shallow trenches or pits. Fires seem to have been lit in some graves, perhaps as part of mortuary rituals, but there are no cremations. Many individuals were buried with grave goods. In some cases the position of bone pins suggests that bodies were wrapped in skin cloaks. Stone and bone tools and food remains are also found in some graves. The most elaborate burial is of an adult male accompanied by a small child. The bodies were placed in a small chamber hollowed out from the bottom of a shaft. The man wore a headband of two parallel strands of wallaby teeth, and a second headband was also found. He wore a skin cloak fastened with bone pins, and arranged so that the feet remaining on the skins fell over his left shoulder. A band of bird bones suggests that the cloak was fringed with bird feathers. The child's feet were stained with ochre, and it wore a bird skull pendant and a necklace of reptile vertebrae.

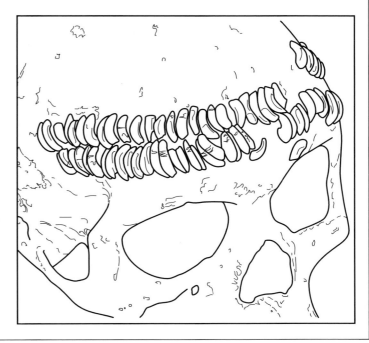

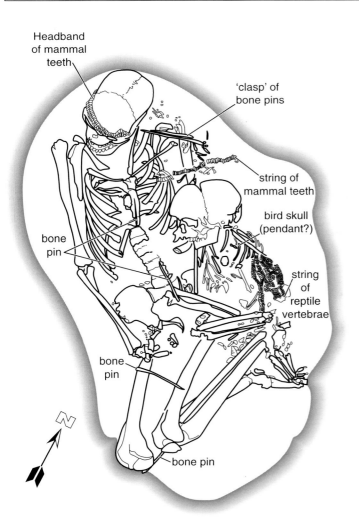

Headband of mammal teeth

'clasp' of bone pins

string of mammal teeth

bird skull (pendant?)

bone pin

string of reptile vertebrae

bone pin

bone pin

N

ABOVE: This man was buried wearing a headband made of wallaby teeth at Roonka Flat.

LEFT: Burial of a man and small child in a small chamber at Roonka Flat, around 2000 BC.

or hollow trees. Bodies were also dried out or exposed on platforms or in trees. The bones might be collected later and buried.

Extended or flexed inhumation and cremation have been practised in the Murray-Darling Basin for about 30,000 years. Secondary burials, where bodies have been exposed and the remains later collected into a bundle and then buried, seem to be more recent. Pardoe suggests that clan members who died elsewhere might have been brought back to the clan territory for burial.

Regularities in the orientation of burials suggests both long-term continuity over time in burial practices and cultural links between different communities along the river. Colin Pardoe has shown that burials in the Murray Valley cemeteries at Roonka, Lindsay Island and Wamba Yadu were most commonly orientated broadly to the south-west, with a slight second preference for the north-east. Roonka is over 500 km (300 miles) downstream from Wamba Yadu, and Lindsay Island is about 135 km (80 miles) downstream from Wamba Yadu. By contrast, the cemeteries of Jeraly and Toongimbie on the eastern riverine plain, more than 500 km upstream from Wamba Yadu, show a quite different pattern, in which easterly orientations were preferred. There are also differences along the Murray River in the proportions of men, women and children buried. Downstream from the junction with the Darling River, more men were buried than women. On the eastern riverine plains the proportions of men and women are more nearly equal. Men tended to be buried in different ways and different directions from women and children. ■

THE ROYAL CEMETERY
AT UR

The Sumerians formed multiple small states which divided the land into competitive territories, each centred on a capital city. These squabbling city-states kept a rough balance of power by alternating wars with alliances, thus keeping any one from gaining too much control for very long. This state of affairs culminated in the middle centuries of the 3rd millennium BC, which archaeologists call the Early Dynastic period, when the various rulers began leaving inscriptions that glorified their own deeds. Among these city-states figured Ur, in the deep south of

The Sumerians of southern Mesopotamia created the world's first civilization when they invented writing and bureaucratic government, built massive and elaborate temples, and began residing in cities around 3500 BC.

the Mesopotamian alluvial plain. Excavations by the British archaeologist Sir Leonard Woolley at Ur during the 1920s and '30s uncovered some of the most important information about the Sumerians available to scholars today. The most spectacular of these discoveries was the Royal Cemetery, where members of Ur's ruling family were buried along with an incredible array of precious and finely crafted objects, and vivid indications of human sacrifice.

The residents of Ur had been dumping their trash near the city ziggurat (a stepped tower with a cult room on top) for many centuries. Around 2500 BC this area was converted to a cemetery that stayed in use over the next five centuries. In the beginning, the dead of élite families as well as more common folk were placed in the cemetery, but after several centuries the graves belonged more uniformly to commoners. Woolley found some 2500 graves in the cemetery. Most were simple affairs, the body wrapped in matting and placed in a simple hole along with a clay pot or two at most. Other graves contained more wealth, such as mirrors, razors, or axes made of copper, sometimes inlaid with silver or gold, jewellery made from precious metals and lapis lazuli, vessels carved from alabaster or soapstone, and the like, along with the pottery. This interred wealth was all the more significant because the Mesopotamian alluvium

LEFT: Looking eastward towards Woolley's dig house across the Royal Cemetery, which lay at the edge of the later sacred precinct at Ur.

OPPOSITE: Meskalamdug's electrum helmet, found on the dead prince's head, is in typical early Mesopotamian royal style.

lacks most raw materials, including metals and stones. Thus all these mortuary goods were made from imported materials, some brought from great distances, like the lapis lazuli which had to travel 2400 km (1500 miles) overland from northeastern Afghanistan and the copper which moved nearly 1500 km (900 miles) by sea from Oman.

However splendid this wealth was, however, the riches of the sixteen royal graves overshadowed it all. These tombs were underground chambers with vaulted roofs, made of brick and stone, and entered along a sloped ramp or through a pit. The graves are tightly clustered together, and seem to have formed the early core of the cemetery; Woolley thought that above-ground funerary chapels marked the graves, thus attracting later interments to this

The rich adornments of sacrificed attendants were formed of masses of beads and precious metal ribbons, all crushed around the wearers' heads.

hallowed ground of royalty. The cuneiform inscriptions that mark some objects identify some of the deceased as the kings Meskalamdug and Akalamdug and the queen Pu-abi, members of the Early Dynastic royal house of Ur.

The wealth in these tombs, which remains unparalleled in Mesopotamian archaeology, included some of the most celebrated pieces of Sumerian art that now grace the halls of the British Museum and the University of Pennsylvania Museum (the institutions that sponsored Woolley's work). The so-called Standard of Ur presents scenes, inlaid with nacre and lapis lazuli, of victorious warfare and ritual celebration on each side of a wooden panel. Lyres, three-dimensional figures of a ram caught in a thicket, and gaming boards were also created in wood and ornamented with geometric designs and figured scenes executed with inlaid mother-of-pearl, carnelian and lapis lazuli. On one lyre the decorative scene of an orchestra of animals playing their instruments made a self-referential visual joke. The electrum (a mixture of

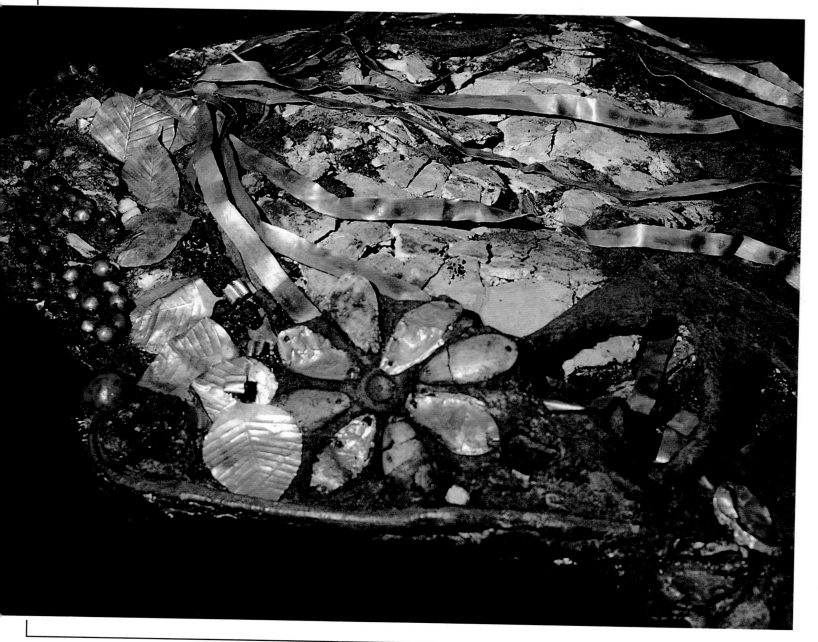

By careful excavation Woolley
was able to reconstruct the court
fashions of female courtiers
whose bodies filled the Great
Death Pit.

gold and silver) helmet of Meskalamdug expresses a mastery of the smith's craft just as much as the tangible wealth of Ur's kings. The myriad common objects, like gold and silver jewellery and vessels, ostrich eggs inlaid with asphalt, cylinder seals of semiprecious stones, cosmetic containers and other goods merely punctuated the message of riches and power.

These material goods were not the only burial offerings left in the royal tombs — the remains of wagons and oxen and the skeletons of many court attendants accompanied the dead king or queen into the afterlife. Woolley described the macabre scene in one grave in these words:

"The burial of the kings was accompanied by human sacrifice on a lavish scale, the bottom of the grave pit being crowded with the bodies of men and women who seemed to have been brought down here and butchered where they stood. In one grave the soldiers of the guard, wearing copper helmets and carrying spears, lie at the foot of the steep ramp that led down into the grave; against the end of the tomb chamber are nine ladies of the court with elaborate golden head-dresses; in front of the entrance are drawn up two heavy four-wheeled carts with three bullocks harnessed to each other, and the driver's bones lie in the carts and grooms are by the heads of the animals.

"In another instance 68 female and six male attendants lay in serried ranks, their court finery still ornamenting their bones, in what Woolley called the 'death pit'."

These graves convey the impression of the immense wealth and the awesome power that the early kings of Ur controlled. Similar burials, though looted and less well preserved, from other Mesopotamian city-states of the same period show that Ur was not unique. Indeed, the massed wealth interred at Ur and the ritual slaughter of subordinate human beings for the sake of the dead ruler are both commonly found at the beginning of many civilizations, like archaic Egypt and Shang China. These ostentatious displays of wealth and power, perhaps necessary to the solidarity and welfare of the kingdom, certainly helped to identify the royals as different from the ordinary folk of Ur. ■

THE CEMETERY AT KHOK PHANOM DI

The success of excavations by a joint Thai-New Zealand team can in part be attributed to a very practical decision to build a roof of steel over this site. A roof provides essential protection against the scorching tropical sun, but previous roofs made of traditional bamboo and thatch had not been strong enough to cover the wider area of excavation essential to understand the complete plan of a settlement or cemetery. With one large 10-square-metre (110-square-foot) pit uncovered, Khok Phanom Di produced one of the most important prehistoric cemeteries anywhere in the world.

Khok Phanom Di is a prehistoric settlement mound in southern Thailand. Though now over 20 km (12½ miles) from the Gulf of Siam, it was once located in a rich mangrove coastal environment at the mouth of an estuary. Excavations in 1985 have produced a uniquely detailed prehistoric family tree.

The full significance of the Khok Phanom Di cemetery was not realized until several months after the end of excavations. Long-awaited radiocarbon dates showed that the site was occupied between approximately 2000 and 1500 BC, a much shorter length of time than had been expected. These dates suggested the possibility that the cemetery might represent a continuous record of the successive burials of the inhabitants of the site over 500 years. Might it be feasible to produce a skeletal "family tree" for prehistoric Khok Phanom Di? Various means of testing this bold hypothesis were quickly devised.

The excavations uncovered 154 burials. All were interred in simple rectangular pits, but considerable variation was present in the associated grave goods. The richest burial was that of a female dubbed "the Princess of Khok Phanom Di". Her grave contained nearly 122,000 shell beads as well as earthenware vessels and tools for pottery-making. Two other female burials were found inside the remains of a clay platform that may originally have been the foundation for some sort of wooden roofed structure. Elsewhere a woman who had died in her mid-40s was found with a mass of fish bones and scales in her pelvic area — almost certainly the remains of her last meal. The problem now was how to arrange all these different burials into some sort of coherent, overall pattern.

The first stage was to sex and age all the skeletons. At the same time nine separate clusters of graves, termed A to I, were identi-fied within the seven chronological mortuary phases. These clusters appeared to represent consistent associations of burials, presumably members of some kind of family or kinship group. Evidence for the clusters first appeared in Mortuary Phase 2. Remains of small circular postholes found around some of the burials in this and later phases may represent the foundations of wooden structures covering the graves. In the tropics such posts decay very rapidly, leaving sparse archaeological traces which are consequently notoriously difficult to interpret. In Mortuary Phase 3, however, the accumulation of a shell-midden in well-defined areas between the burial clusters lent further support to the existence of some sort of fence or enclosure around the graves which prevented the shell-midden from encroaching onto the cemetery proper. In Mortuary Phase 4 grave goods became noticeably fewer and burial pits did not overlap within the clusters as they had previously. Phase 5 saw a break in the pattern of burial clusters, with only four graves present, although these were all wealthy and included the Princess. Phase 6 saw a twofold division into burials within the clay platform and those arranged in a line in front of it. The final Phase 7 contained only four burials at the edge of the excavated trench.

With the basic data of the Khok Phanom Di cemetery in front of them, the excavators could begin the difficult process of trying

LEFT: The female at far left, burial 47, died in her early twenties and was buried with a newly born child at her side.

BELOW: Burial 36 was interred with a stone adze as a funerary offering.

to establish links between the individual burials. An immediate problem presented itself with respect to certain female burials in their mid- to late-teens: had they already borne children before their deaths? The presence or absence of the pelvic bone scarring that is associated with pregnancy provided a way of approaching this question. Other specialist anatomical studies proved equally invaluable. Non-metric skeletal traits — features such as tiny accretions of bone or holes for nerves that are possessed by some people but not by others — were particularly useful since they tend to be determined by genetic rather than environmental factors. In other words, they provide a useful way of testing possible genetic relationships between individual skeletons. In one example from Mortuary Phase 3, a man and a woman each had several distinctive but individual cranial features whereas the child buried with them combined

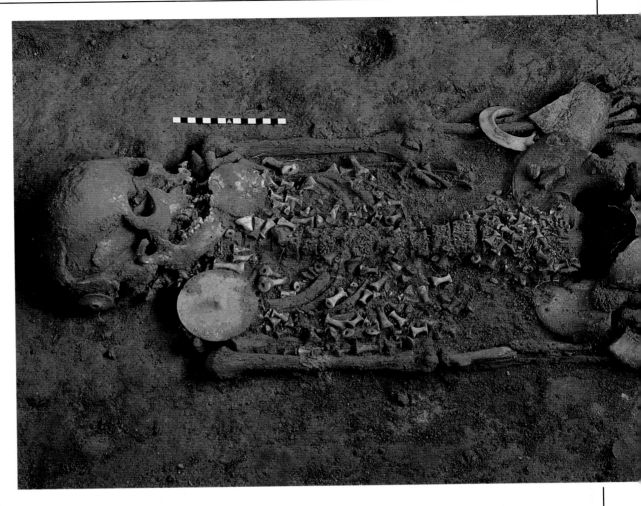

most of the traits found in the adults. This is very good evidence that these three skeletons were father, mother and child.

Using these techniques in association with detailed plans of the cemetery, it was possible to propose genealogies for several of the burial clusters at Khok Phanom Di. In particular, Clusters C and F were traced through Mortuary Phases 2 to 6. The fact that both of these clusters contained about sixteen generations during this same timespan is seen as further support for the reconstructed family tree. As in all aspects of archaeology, it is impossible to be certain that the reconstructed genealogies are correct. All that can be done is to devise new methods of testing the hypothesis, making sure that the results of those tests do not contradict previous conclusions.

A detailed prehistoric family tree of the type devised for Khok Phanom Di is extremely rare and is especially significant in Southeast Asia where climatic conditions mean that well preserved ancient burials of any sort are unusual. The family tree is not, however, an end in itself, but is a prelude to understanding the perhaps even more interesting question of how to explain the historical background behind the various changes in burial structure and ceremony. Evidence for a major shift in environmental conditions between Mortuary Phases 3 and 4 provided a useful clue here. It seems that at the end of Phase 3, the river that had flowed near Khok Phanom Di burst its banks and established a new course some distance away. This disaster, together with the gradual depositing of silt at the river mouth, meant that Khok

The richest tomb at the site, burial 15, was a female nicknamed "the Princess of Khok Phanom Di" by the excavators. Almost 122,000 shell beads were found in her grave.

Phanom Di was now a long way from its traditional source of shellfish. The shell ornaments that had been so common in Phases 1 to 3 became rare in Phase 4. At the same time, the male skeletons became much less robust, particularly in the upper arms — a change that is interpreted as reflecting a decline in male participation in shell-collecting activities that would have involved canoeing on the open sea. One way in which the population of Khok Phanom Di dealt with this crisis becomes apparent with the rich female burials and elaborate pottery of Mortuary Phase 5. The excavators of the site suggest that women gained greater status through the production of fine ceramics which were exchanged with other villages for ready-made shell jewellery. Men may consequently have played a less prominent role in the affairs of the village than they had in the past.

The history of Khok Phanom Di summarized here will no doubt change as new research is conducted. It is an archaeological account that many historians will find too simple and perhaps too reliant on environmental factors. Nevertheless, it is a history which far exceeds what is possible at most archaeological sites. While the people of Khok Phanom Di can no longer tell their own story, their bodies can do the next best thing. ∎

BATTLE CEMETERIES

The Maiden Castle bodies were laid out in a variety of positions, crouched, extended, supine, lying on their side, even sitting up. They were accompanied by grave goods, including pottery vessels and personal accoutrements. Two individuals were buried with legs of lamb.

Some of the male skeletons, interpreted by Wheeler as the battle-scarred bones of warriors, display a number of horrific injuries. Ten had extensive cuts to the skull. The skull of one bore sharp cracks inflicted by a sword that must have caused instant

Amid the spectacular hornwork defences at the eastern entrance of Maiden Castle, the greatest Iron Age hillfort in Britain, 38 bodies were discovered by the famous archaeologist Mortimer Wheeler during his excavation campaign of the 1930s. They were buried in 28 rough-cut graves, and 23 were identified as men, 11 as women.

death. Another man's head had been pierced by a spear, leaving a clear impression on the skull. A third was found with the Roman spearhead that had killed him embedded in his backbone. The spear had entered his body from the front below the heart and the unfortunate warrior was finished off with a blow to the head.

For Wheeler, this "War Cemetery" was direct evidence of the military crushing of resistance by the Romans following their invasion of Britain in AD 43. When the Romans invaded Britain in the centuries either side of the birth of Christ, they encoun-

RIGHT: Reconstruction of part of
the Iron Age Settlement on
Maiden Castle.

BELOW RIGHT: Roman spearhead in
the spine of a young defender of
Maiden Castle.

tered a warlike society whose warriors were well practised in the arts of armed conflict. The Roman commander of the Claudian invasion, Vespasian, is recorded as subduing over 20 defended hill-fort settlements in order to establish the rule of Rome throughout the western part of England. One of the greatest of these strongholds was Maiden Castle, in the south-central part of England, in the territory of the Durotriges tribe. Nearly 2000 years after the subjugation of the warlords of Maiden Castle by the Roman army, Wheeler was convinced that he had discovered the remains of some of the Celtic warriors who may have taken part in the last stand against the invader.

Between 1985 and 1986, however, a limited excavation was undertaken at Maiden Castle, directed by Niall Sharples. In the 50 years since Wheeler's campaign, ideas about Iron Age society have changed a great deal. Although Sharples did not reinvestigate the War Cemetery, he was able to reassess the evidence for the end of the occupation of Maiden Castle.

Sharples noted that only 14 out of a total of 52 burials showed any sign of a violent death, and that they were in a normal cemetery that contained some 100 graves overall. It was known by then that formal cemeteries had appeared in the region around Maiden Castle in the Late Iron Age, replacing the excarnation (exposure) that was the preferred funeral rite of the Middle Iron Age. In addition, Sharples thought that the position and orientation in the grave of most of the bodies appear to have been carefully prescribed, disputing Wheeler's assertion that they had been buried without following any such formal rules. Wheeler had discussed the grave goods, which he regarded as indicating that these warriors had been buried by their friends, who had crept back to the battlefield to bury the dead. Sharples countered this by noting that considerable effort must have been spent collecting together their belongings, as well as in the preparation of the legs of lamb with which two of the inhumations were accompanied into the afterlife. Lastly, of the 14 battle-scarred skulls, four had wounds that had partially healed, as evidenced by the regrowth of bone, suggesting that even if they had ultimately died of their injuries, they did not die immediately. Sharples suggested that, rather than this being the site of the War Cemetery for the battle of Maiden Castle, it was quite possible that the deceased young men were brought to this cemetery from elsewhere, to be buried according to the funerary customs of this Late

Iron Age society. Whether the warriors died defending Maiden Castle or in skirmishes elsewhere, as always in archaeology, new interpretation is only possible thanks to the care taken in the original excavation.

Greek and Roman battles

The topographical study of Greece has often been linked to the search for the great battlefields of the Persian Wars. In particular, the site of the battle of Marathon in Attica has inspired numerous travellers to Greece. Although the surroundings have changed considerably since the defeat of the Persian army in 490 BC, visitors can still see the large mound (or *soros*) erected to commemorate the 192 Athenian dead in the battle, including one of the generals, Kallimachos. Indeed, in the second century AD the Roman travel writer Pausanias drew attention to the mound of the Athenians, and another containing the dead from the Plataian contingent who fought alongside their allies the Athenians. The mound itself has attracted several excavations, notably by Heinrich Schliemann, the excavator of Troy, who discovered prehistoric debris in the mound and presumed that it belonged to a much earlier period; subsequent Greek excavations by Stais in 1890 and 1891 found what appears to have been the platform, 26 by 6 m (85 by 20 ft), on which the bodies were cremated along

At the site of Philip II's great victory at Chaironeia over the Greek coalition forces, mass graves for the Macedonian and Theban dead have been uncovered.

with Athenian pottery of the early decades of the fifth century BC. Nearby, Marinatos excavated a second mound containing eleven bodies, but only two had been cremated. This change in ritual has suggested to some that the inhumations were the bodies of slaves. This mound has been popularly linked to the mound of the dead Plataians.

In Athens itself a mass grave was found in the Kerameikos, with an inscription which identified the dead as Thibrakos and Chairon, as well as a third whose name was lost. This appeared to be the grave of the Lakedaimonians killed in 403 BC — after the end of the Peloponnesian War in which Athens had been defeated — during an engagement between the Spartan force under their king, Pausanias, and the people of the harbour town of Peiraieus, and which was described by the Greek historian Xenophon. The excavation discovered thirteen skeletons. The head of a spear was found within the ribs of one of the dead, while another had been hit in the leg by two separate arrowheads.

Other mounds and monuments mark the site of those fallen in battle. The Polyandrion (a burial of "many men") at Thespiai in Boeotia probably represents the dead from the battle of Delion in 424 BC. Nearby were found a line of nine inscribed stelai which carried 101 names. Two tumuli have been excavated at Chaironeia; this was the site of the Macedonian victory by Philip II and his son Alexander in 338 BC over the combined Greek army of 30,000 men from Athens, Thebes, Megara and Corinth. The burial mound for the Theban contingent was described by the Roman writer Pausanias in the second century AD. The lion

The *soros* or mound at Marathon still dominates the plain where the invading Persians were defeated in 490 BC. Underneath were found the cremated remains of the Athenian dead.

marker was discovered in the early nineteenth century, only to be blown up by the Greek hero Odysseus Androutsos in his search for hidden treasure! The tomb itself was excavated in 1879 and was found to contain a large pit containing 254 skeletons laid in seven rows. A second mound was excavated in 1902/3 which has been identified, thanks to a mention by Plutarch, writing in the first century AD, as the mound of the Macedonians. This included a cremation mound, with human ashes and remains of Macedonian weapons.

Excavations during the 1930s at the site of Hannibal's great victory over the Romans at Cannae in 216 BC showed that, although some of the dead had been placed in carefully prepared cist graves, the remaining thousands of corpses had been thrown down with very little order. The ancient historians Polybius and Livy put the Roman casualties in the range of 70,000 and 50,000 respectively, compared to some 8000 on Hannibal's side. The site of another of Rome's major defeats has recently been identified in Germany. In AD 9 the legate Varus with three legions was ambushed in the Teutoburger Forest, and the force was destroyed. Although there is no evidence of bodies, remains of armour and other debris have now suggested the location. ∎

THE PARACAS NECROPOLIS

In the late nineteenth and early twentieth centuries, various spectacular examples of embroidered textiles appeared in private collections and for sale on the international art market. No one knew where these textiles came from, and the looters who were digging them out of prehistoric graves tried to confuse all those who came looking for the source. But in June 1925 the American anthropologist Alfred Kroeber was shown a cemetery area on the Paracas Peninsula that eventually proved to be the location of the graves that were producing the amazing textiles. In a series of excavations organized by the Peruvian archaeologist Julio C. Tello, and directed mostly by his assistant, Toribio Mejia Xesspe, several distinct cemeteries were identified. Excavation began in August 1925 and continued through 1928. Often excavations had to be conducted at night, to avoid the storms.

The so-called Paracas cemeteries actually fall into three separate groups. The first and earliest is a cemetery located near the summit of a hill called Cerro Colorado. On a series of three natural terraces human burials were found, some in fairly plain tombs, but others in deep "caverns", which give their name to this occupation, Cavernas. The tombs were often some 5 m (16 ft) deep. Beginning at the surface, the archaeologists excavated a pit a metre or two down to the layer of hardened calcium-carbonate (caliche) found throughout this region. At this point a narrow

The wind-swept Paracas Peninsula of the south coast of Peru is one of the most inhospitable places on earth. In summer the heat is unbearable, and it never rains; there is not a blade of grass to be seen. Worse still are the intense desert sandstorms that can blow for days at a time; indeed, the name Paracas is the local term for these terrible storms. But in 1925 archaeologists discovered that not only had people lived on the Paracas Peninsula, but that they had buried their dead in great splendour there as well.

excavation, the antechamber, less than one metre in diameter, was continued downward for another metre or two, and then widened out to form the "cavern", which could be several metres across. Inside the cavern a few or up to several dozen individuals were buried. These people were wrapped in several layers of textiles, some rather plain, others with woven and embroidered designs, and covered with a plain cotton cloth. Sometimes mummies were found in the antechamber. It is possible, given the extensive remains of disturbed mummies found at or near the surface, that the chambers were periodically cleared out and new mummies were interred in them.

Many of the human remains inside the mummy bundles were found to have skulls that were deformed — flattened and lengthened by being wrapped in childhood so that the bones would grow in a more aesthetically pleasing fashion. But even more notable were the large numbers of skulls that had apparently been subjected to surgery. Many of the skulls had holes cut in them, and pieces of the cranium removed. Such skull perforation is referred to as trephination or trepanation. Incisions were usually made using a stone knife in a sawing motion, although sometimes a continuous series of small holes was drilled around the circumference of the piece to be removed. Apparently, few of the patients died as a result of the surgery — there is evidence of

Deformados

ABOVE: Deformed skulls which were wrapped during childhood to persuade the bones to grow into a more aesthetically pleasing shape.

RIGHT: Human remains from Paracas.

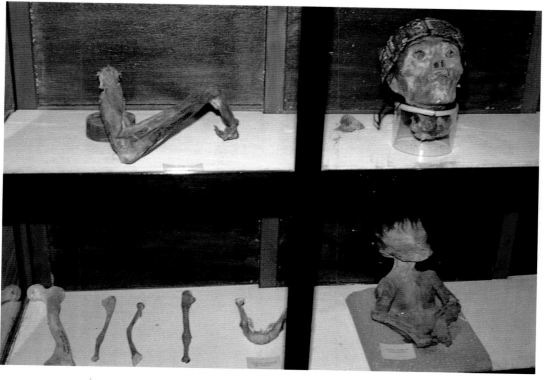

ABOVE: Mummies in crouched or sitting burial positions.

LEFT: A naturally dried mummy wearing clothing of astonishingly colourful design and advanced technical quality.

healing around the edges of the incisions, and in some cases the bone grew back completely. This could only have happened if the person were still alive.

The Cavernas people lived in small communities in areas to the north of Cerro Colorado. They apparently occupied subterranean houses, dug several metres deep into the dense sand. Given the terrible heat and wind on the peninsula, such living quarters were eminently practical; and later peoples found them useful structures for the burial of their dead. The archaeologists began excavation in one of these habitation areas, called Arena Blanca, and quickly came upon a dozen or so areas that were later used as cemeteries.

But perhaps the most spectacular finds came from the cemeteries at the necropolis of Wari Kayan, located between Cerro Col-

orado and Arena Blanca in another area of earlier Cavernas habitation. On 25 October 1927 Mejia and his assistants began a series of test excavations in an area that had apparently been used for habitation during the earlier Cavernas phase. Unlike Cavernas burials, these mummies were not placed in elaborately excavated tombs, alone or with other mummies, but were single burials. However, there were many of them, and the archaeologists quickly documented 429 individual burials.

The mummies that came out of the ground did not at first appear to be very prepossessing. Although numerous fragments of colourful textiles were seen on the surface, the intact mummy bundles themselves were wrapped in plain brown cotton cloth, sewn together with thick cotton thread. The bundles were generally triangular in form, more than a metre high and wide. But when the bundles were opened, some of the most astonishing and technologically advanced textiles were revealed.

Mummy 451 from Wari Kayan serves as a good example of these types of bundles. The body was placed, seated and flexed, on a deerskin mat inside a large basketry structure, almost like a large open bowl. Around the body were placed cotton textiles, found in deteriorated condition, mostly articles of clothing of various qualities. Around these were wrapped ten items of clothing of very good quality, including tunics, ponchos and mantles. Around those in turn were wrapped five ceremonial mantles of the highest quality. These were elaborately woven of several colours in block patterns, and the edges and blocks were filled with intricate embroidered figures of deities, humans, animals, and so on.

Work by Anne Paul has demonstrated that these large ceremonial mantles were probably made in workshops. The embroidery was supervised by skilled artisans who marked the designs and outlined the figures. Then other workers toiled to fill in the outlined areas with embroidery of different colours and stitches. Study of the different techniques of stitching has led Paul to suggest that several people worked on a single mantle in a workshop-like setting. The production of a single mantle probably took months. On some occasions unfinished mantles were included in mummy bundles. Mantles may have been prepared for specific individuals while they were living; and if the person died before the mantle was completed, it was included in the bundle anyway.

Returning to Mummy 451, after the mantles were wrapped around the shoulders of the bundle and draped over the other wrappings, a blue tunic, a turban and a sling were added. In this region the typical headdress was a turban, around which was wrapped a braided sling. The form of sling and the turban identified where an individual was from. Finally, the outer wrappings were added: a plain brown cotton cloth was sewn over the bundle. In all, the bundle formed a triangular profile 1.1 m (3 ft 7 in) high and 1.3 m (4 ft 3 in) wide, and it weighed 150 kg (330 lb).

The even more elaborate Mummy 310 included 56 garments. It was covered with 25 wrapping cloths and included 13 turbans, 18 mantles, five ponchos, two tunics and various other items; also ten pieces of gold.

There is little evidence that the bodies placed in the mummy bundles were artificially mummified in any way. There is some evidence of carbonization not only of the human remains, but also of the wrapping close to the body. The deterioration of the textiles closest to the cadavers suggests that no mummification procedures other than natural drying were used. ■

LEFT: An example of the amazingly well designed and executed textiles from Paracas.

OPPOSITE: A beautifully preserved mummy with a complete set of clothing, seen in front of a colourful mantle in geometric design.

THE TEMPLE OF QUETZALCOATL AT TEOTIHUACÁN

Sometime after AD 150 there seems to have been a shift in power that manifested itself in an architectural refocusing of the Street of the Dead. The Teotihuacanos blocked off much of the site by means of scattered walls. They then constructed a vast rectangular enclosure southeast of the pyramids. Measuring 400 m (just over 1300 ft) on each side, this architectural complex is known as the Ciudadela (the Citadel) and is believed to have functioned as an administrative centre for the city. Within its interior plaza are the remains of the famous Temple of Quetzalcoatl. Measuring 65 by 65 m (213 ft) at the base, this pyramid takes its name from the carved feathered serpents that adorn its façade.

The Mesoamerican Classic Period is marked by the florescence of many great cultures including that of Teotihuacán, an ancient city located northeast of Mexico City. Teotihuacán, or "the place of the gods," is bisected by a 6.5 km (4 mile), 40 m (130 ft) wide avenue which runs in a north-south direction. Along this street, known as the "Street of the Dead," are some of the greatest architectural monuments in the world. These include the Pyramids of the Sun and Moon, both built during the first century AD.

During the 1980s archaeologists conducting excavations at the Temple of Quetzalcoatl unearthed what was to be the first of many multiple burials associated with the construction of the monument. This type of mass "dedicatory" burial celebrated the completion of the building. Such burials are known from ancient Maya sites, but had only been hinted at in the case of Teotihuacán. In 1906, for instance, Leopoldo Batres found sacrificed children associated with the four corners on each of the tiers of the Pyramid of the Sun. In 1925 Pedro Dosal found a similar arrangement of individuals buried in the four corners of the Temple of Quetzalcoatl.

To date, the recent excavations of the mass burials at the Temple of Quetzalcoatl have yielded 113 complete skeletons and fragments of additional persons. Throughout these excavations archaeologists have noted the maintenance of symmetry in the positioning of the burials. For instance, burials found along the northern and southern sides of the pyramid seem to mirror each other not only in their physical placement but in the number of individuals found in the burials. Also similar are the types of grave goods interred with these individuals. Since this pattern of burial seems so marked, archaeologists are predicting that future excavations will bring the final count of bodies closer to 200.

The physical positioning of the individual bodies in the graves as well as their accompanying artefacts raise questions as to their identities. Eighteen were found in each of the mass graves located on the northern and southern sides of the pyramid. All were seated facing away from the centre of the pyramid as if "guarding" the contents of the great structure. Many of the individuals were found with their arms crossed behind them at pelvis level as if they had been bound at the time of burial. Several wore *tezcuilapilli*, discs worn on the back at hip level. These pyrite-encrusted mirrors are known to be part of the military costume worn by the later Toltec and Aztec warriors. If these are buried warriors at the Temple of Quetzalcoatl, then their warrior status may be underlined by the dozens of obsidian projectile points scattered throughout the burials. It is also possible that the points were to be used by the inhabitants after death to protect those buried in the interior of the pyramid from unseen forces.

In addition to projectile points, thousands of pieces of worked shell were found. These were parts of necklaces once worn by the individuals buried. Some of them are made up of shells which have been carved into the shape of teeth. In some instances they are attached to supports which mimic the form of human and canine jaws. In addition, necklaces of actual human upper jaws have been found; in total, the archaeologists discov-

An interior courtyard in the Palace of "Quetzal-Butterfly", probably HQ for one of Teotihuacán's warrior societies.

On the façade of the Temple of Quetzalcoatl the heads of feathered serpents alternate with mosaic headdresses.

View of the Pyramid of the Sun and, behind it, part of the Ciudadela at the ancient city of Teotihuacán. These massive constructions date to the first two centuries AD.

ered close to forty of them. This type of necklace is unique in Mesoamerica and its exact meaning remains a mystery.

In 1988 and 1989 the archaeologists moved their efforts from the edges of the pyramid toward its centre. They found more burials — one containing a group of eighteen individuals and another a group of eight. In both these instances the bodies wore accoutrements similar to those of the sacrificed warriors found on the perimeter of the pyramid. It is noteworthy that, rather than facing out, these individuals faced inward as if honouring a central person or persons buried in the pyramid's centre.

As they reached the centre of the pyramid, archaeologists found more mass burials. Although the graves had been disturbed by looters in ancient times, the remaining artefacts suggest that only the highest ranking Teotihuacanos were interred there. One complete skeleton was found with a pair of earspools, 21 large beads, a rectangular nose ornament, all of greenstone, as well as a large unusually shaped obsidian projectile point. A carved wooden baton was also discovered, its terminus in the form of a stylized serpent head similar to the heads carved on the front of the pyramid. This suggested to archaeologists that the individuals buried towards the centre held positions associated with a priestly office.

At the centre of the pyramid was a mass grave of some 20 undisturbed male skeletons. Some of the skeletons seemed to face an individual located at the eastern end of the burial, even though this individual was surprisingly non-distinct in terms of his accoutrements. Offerings were randomly distributed over the whole interment and included more than 400 greenstone items, 800 fine obsidian objects, 3400 shell pieces, slate discs, animal remains and items of wood and fibre. Two vessels were found with an image of the nature and water god Tlaloc.

Scholars have yet to resolve the mystery of these warriors. To date, two hypotheses as to the significance of the warriors in the Temple of Quetzalcoatl have been put forward. The archaeologists involved in the recent excavations believe that the warriors were the victims of a despotic rule which arose shortly after AD 150. Therefore, they may have been the unlucky members of a defeated earlier regime. If this were the case, then their buried presence would stand as an underlying threat to those citizens and outsiders who entered the Ciudadela to conduct their daily business. Alternatively, archaeoastronomer John Carlson has suggested that the numbers of individuals located in distinct groups of 8, 18 and 20 are significant and may suggest more of a sacred function for the individuals. He has pointed out that the traditional Mesoamerican 365-day year contains 18 months of 20 days. As for the number 8, he notes that it is associated with the eight years in the Venus almanac. Cycles of Venus have been shown to be important in the reckoning of Maya warfare, and Carlson suggests that the same may have held true for the Teotihuacanos. He believes that the remains found in the building may be those of enemy warriors and other prisoners captured in battle for sacrifice as part of a Venus warfare cult. Carlson notes that these two interpretations are not mutually exclusive. However, much work remains to determine the full meaning of the burials. ■

INGOMBE ILEDE

Ingombe Ilede is the Tonga name for "the place where the cow sleeps or lies down" and refers to a fallen baobab tree which resembled a cow. Initial investigations were undertaken in 1960 by J. H. Chaplin, then Inspector of Monuments for the Northern Rhodesian Commission for the Preservation of Natural and Historical Monuments and Relics, who was sent to investigate reports of a human burial discovered by workers digging trenches for water pipes. To his amazement, he found that " ... in the surrounding spoil heaps [from the construction work] there were many sherds and animal bones, while protruding from a small, deeper cut there were limbs with copper wire bangles on them."

Rescue excavations under less than ideal conditions by Chaplin and Mrs J. D. W. Anderson of Lusaka led to the recovery of eleven burials from what became known as the Central Tank Area. Most of these were richly decorated with jewellery, including tens of thousands of imported glass beads and bone beads; large numbers of bangles, mainly of copper, sometimes of iron, and in one case of gold; gold beads (found to have a purity of almost 18 carat), and Conus shells from the East African coast. Grave goods placed at the head and feet included copper crosses, bundles of copper wire, copper currency rods, a copper razor, iron hammers, tongs and drawing plates for the manufacture of copper wire, iron hoes and gongs.

The poor condition of some of the remains prevented determination of age and sex, but some were identifiable as adult or young adult males. Some had been wrapped in cotton or barkcloth shrouds, which were preserved as a result of contact with the copper bangles. The barkcloth was probably locally made,

The impressive stone-walled site of Great Zimbabwe was the capital of a large southern African Shona empire stretching from the Zambezi River to northern South Africa and eastern Botswana between about AD 1270 and 1450. In 1960-62 construction work for water tanks revealed two burial areas containing a series of elaborate graves of a fifteenth-century AD trading community called Ingombe Ilede, on the northern bank of the Zambezi River in southern Zambia.

but fragments of an exceptionally fine cotton cloth may have originated in India.

Further excavations in a second area of the site conducted by Brian Fagan yielded four more burials in 1961 and another 31 in 1962. These were mostly of infants and young adults, and generally not as richly decorated as those from the Central Tank Area. They contained grave goods such as copper bangles, glass and shell beads, and chicken as well as francolin bones.

The remains described indicate that the Ingombe Ilede economy was based on a mixture of agriculture, stock-keeping, fishing, hunting and collecting. The distinctive cross-shaped copper ingots found in some of the graves are identical to examples found at Zimbabwean sites south of the Zambezi River as well as at sites on the Zambian Copperbelt to the north, and suggest that Ingombe Ilede was part of a well organized trade system based on the Zambezi River.

Portuguese documents of the sixteenth century link Ingombe Ilede with the Mbara, a Zimbabwean metalworking people who originated in Central Africa north of the Zambezi River. Most

Some of the rich and varied grave goods found at the burial site of Ingombe Ilede - pottery, bangles and beads.

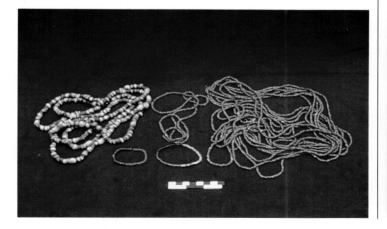

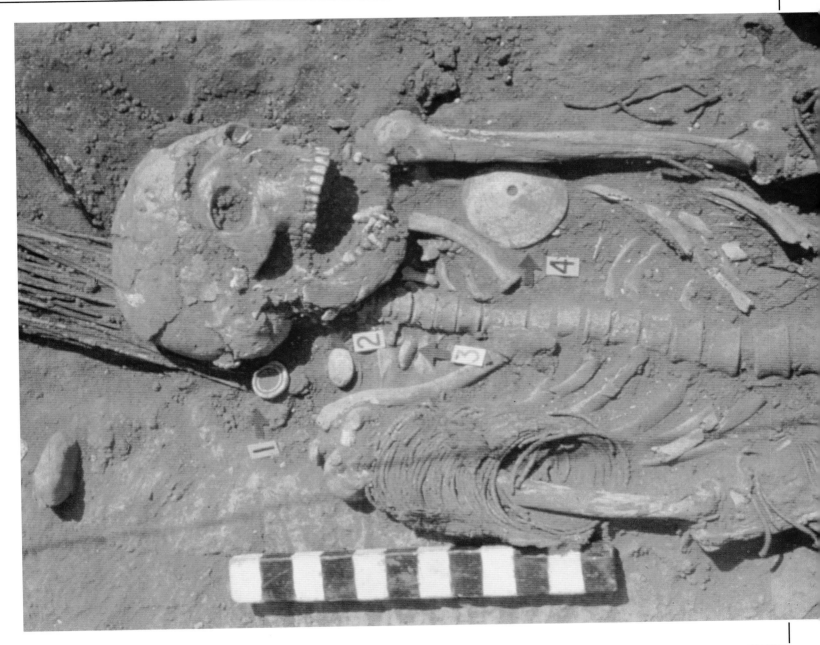

ABOVE: Ingombe Ilede burial with grave goods - copper currency rods at the head, copper bangles on the right arm, and Conus shells.

RIGHT: Cross-shaped copper ingots were cast in standardized sizes and probably used as a form of currency.

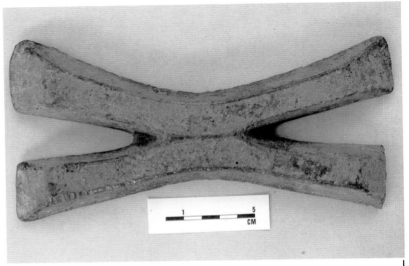

African linguists recognize a fundamental and long-standing difference between Western Bantu languages, which are spoken in Central Africa, and Eastern Bantu languages, which are spoken in East and southern Africa. The Ingombe Ilede people can be identified as Western Bantu speakers by their extended burials, a Western Bantu characteristic, and by their grave goods of gold ornaments, copper crosses, iron gongs and metalworking tools, which are Western Bantu symbols of authority and importance. Their burials suggest a socially stratified community, in which wealth from trade created social importance and political power. ■

VOICES OF THE SEVENTH CAVALRY

The events leading up to the Battle of the Little Big Horn are well-known. The 7th Cavalry, under the command of Lt Colonel George Armstrong Custer, the "boy-hero" of the Civil War, had been ordered by Brigadier General Alfred Terry to seek out the large force of Sioux and Cheyenne soldiers and their families, so that Terry could move them back onto the reservation. On finding the Indians encamped on the banks of the Little Big Horn River of Montana on 25 June 1876, Custer split his forces into three units under the command of himself (with 210 men), Major Marcus Reno (with approximately 140 men) and Captain Frederick Benteen (with approximately 115), and attacked the Indian camp. The camp, however, was far larger than he had anticipated — it is estimated that Custer faced up to 2000 mounted Indian warriors — and what had been intended as a classic pincer movement fell apart. All of Custer's command, as well as at least 40 of Reno's, were killed (we shall never know the extent of Indian casualties, although they were light, perhaps only

It is a truism of history that only the victors tell the tales of battle. Nowhere is this seen better than in the case of the Battle of the Little Big Horn, when George Armstrong Custer and his 7th Cavalry were decisively wiped out by a superior force of Sioux and Cheyenne. Because the Indians did not record all the battle's events, historians have never been able to figure out exactly what happened on that fateful day in 1876. But now, archaeology, aided by history and physical anthropology, has begun to fill in a few of the gaps.

100). These casualty figures are not large compared to the slaughter of the Civil War just a few years earlier, but the manner in which the command was wiped out, and the mystery surrounding the downfall of Custer, the "boy general", became the stuff of legend.

Although the survivors of Reno's command were able to reconstruct what happened to them, much is still unknown about the events surrounding Custer's own command. We still do not know if Custer died at the beginning of his charge into the village or whether he did indeed fight to the end.

In 1983 a grassfire gave archaeologists the opportunity to conduct an intensive survey of those portions of the battlefield still owned by the American government. The survey revealed excellent data on the distribution of artefacts, such as the guns and bullets used in the battle by both sides, and enabled the archaeologists Douglas Scott and Richard Fox to reconstruct in much more detail the actual movements of the two sides as the battle ebbed and flowed. Interestingly, the distribution and density of cartridges indicated that Custer's command did indeed mount a last-ditch defence, but whether Custer was one of the last cavalrymen to be killed is still unclear.

The burial detail, who arrived on 26 June after the Indians had left, realized that it was essential, because it was summer, to bury the dead as quickly as possible. Most were put into shallow graves, where they had fallen. Some simply had dirt or sagebrush thrown over them. Animal scavengers and human souvenir hunters quickly disturbed the bodies. In 1877 and 1879 reburial details came back to reinter the bodies in more permanent graves.

The archaeological crew directed by Scott located the remains of a number of the American soldiers who had died on the battlefield, and in 1992 Scott was given permission to re-excavate seven graves in the National Military Cemetery at the battlefield, to expand the size of his sample. Scientific analysis of skeletal remains can tell the archaeologists many things. Most obviously, it

RIGHT: General George Armstrong Custer, the swaggering boy-general of Western legend.

BELOW: An imaginative reconstruction of Custer's last stand at the Little Big Horn.

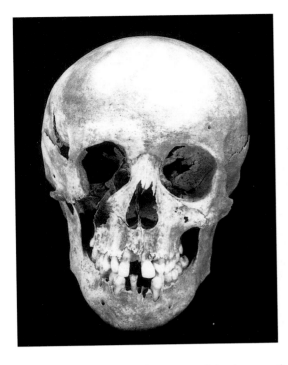

boasted well executed dentistry, having eight fillings in his mouth, four of them gold. His teeth were stained from smoking and chewing tobacco. There were no indications on his bones of the cause of death. By comparing the skeletal evidence with the roster of troopers of the same age and build, it has been possible tentatively to identify this trooper as Corporal George Lell. Contemporary reports have Lell being hit in the stomach during Reno's engagement and dying of wounds on 26 June 1876. Lell was born in Ohio and enlisted in 1873 in Cincinnati, the location of one of the country's first dental colleges. The dean of this college was Dr Jonathan Taft, well-known for his advocacy of gold fillings over tin. This would help explain the quality of Lell's dental work. The only problem with identifying the skeleton as Lell's is that his military records indicate he was 1.75 m (5 ft 9 in) in height, considerably taller than the skeletal estimate. However, it is possible that the measurements were erroneously taken at enlistment, a common enough error, it seems.

This individual skull was sufficiently well preserved for reconstruction on the basis of the facial features of the skeleton to give a remarkably accurate picture of what this man looked like when alive. The technique depends on meticulous measurements of modern cranial specimens to determine the location and thickness of particular facial muscles and soft tissue based on the shape and thickness of the bones themselves. Placing the particular muscles on the skull can be done with relative accuracy, the soft tissues with less. The skull is then built up with successive layers of modelling clay until an approximation of the face is achieved. Such features as hair and eye colouring and lip and nose shapes are then approximated, based on the expected racial type of the specimen. The final model is then compared with existing photographs of members of Custer's unit to see if a match can be made. ∎

can reconstruct the precise cause of death, sometimes in harrowing detail. For example, a skeleton was found at one of the skirmish lines. This individual was about 1.73 m (5 ft 8 in) in height and about 25 years old. He was a well-built man. He had been shot in the chest by a .44-calibre repeating rifle. After he had fallen to the ground, he had been shot in the head, probably with his own Colt revolver. His attackers had then smashed in his skull, shot arrows into him, and slashed his chest and back to indicate in the next life that he had been defeated in battle. Another cavalryman aged between 19 and 22, of similar height and weighing between 68 and 73 kg (150 and 160 lb), had had his skull fractured and his teeth knocked out. He had been shot in the chest twice, wounded in the wrist, and had then been slashed in the thighs with an axe. He had not died outright, but had lain in agony for a period of time. One trooper, buried in the National Cemetery in 1903 and re-excavated by Scott's team, showed clearly the bullet wound that had entered the right side of his head before exiting on the other side. The rectangular shape of the entry wound suggests that the bullet had lost its normal spin, instead tumbling into the skull, perhaps after it had ricocheted off another object. This poor man, 1.75 m (5 ft 9 in) in height, was only about 20 years old at death, and was identified tentatively as either Private Patrick Golden or Packer Frank Mann.

Scott, combining his archaeological and military expertise with that of dentists and forensic anthropologists like P. Willey, has even been able to gain remarkable insights into the dental health of the troopers, finding evidence on the skulls of such diseases as caries, abscesses, periodontitis, pre-mortem tooth loss and individual tooth attrition. One of these individuals was aged between 30 and 35 years old at the time of death, and was estimated to be in the vicinity of 1.65 m (5 ft 5 in) in height. His bones showed that he had suffered from malnutrition at some time in his life, he had osteoarthritis, and his hip-bones had been worn in a manner consistent with excessive horse-back riding. This trooper also

TOMBS

THE SHAFT GRAVES OF MYCENAE

There was no question about the identification of Mycenae, which was recorded by the Greek traveller Pausanias in the second century AD. A copy of Pausanias in hand, Schliemann chose to excavate within the citadel walls and in 1876, immediately inside the Lion Gate, he discovered the

Heinrich Schliemann had an unwavering belief in the veracity of the Trojan War as described by Homer, and sought to prove it through excavation. Following his initial success at Hissarlik in north-west Turkey, which he identified with Priam's Troy, Schliemann was eager to turn his attention to Greece, and pursue the heroes who had led the campaign against the Trojans. In particular he hoped to find the grave of Agamemnon, king of Mycenae, and leader of the Greek expedition to Troy.

a number of smaller, shallow graves, but these were largely destroyed by Schliemann's excavations. The shaft graves were marked by stone stelae, either plain or with carved decoration. The wealth of the burials, in particular the enormous quantity of gold, points to the fact that the grave circle was the

shaft graves within a circular enclosure wall. Schliemann excavated five graves and in 1878 a sixth grave was excavated by Stamatakis.

Schliemann's grave circle was used in the sixteenth century BC. It consisted of a group of six shaft graves (numbered I-VI), cut into the lower slope of the citadel, in an area which had been used for burials since the Middle Bronze Age. The shaft graves were enclosed within a low circular rubble wall. There were also

burial ground of the rulers of Mycenae.

A second grave circle was discovered accidentally during restoration of the so-called tomb of Clytemnestra, outside the citadel walls, in 1951. This was called Grave Circle B, to distinguish it from the one discovered by Schliemann, which was des-

Shaft grave circle A within the citadel of Mycenae contains six royal tombs, with lavish grave goods.

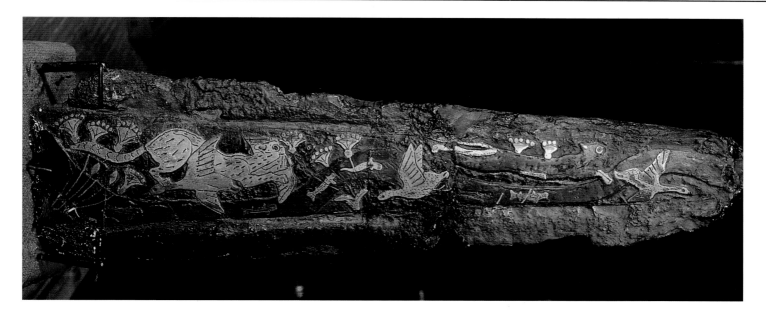

ABOVE: Among the most beautiful products made by Cretans for the mainland market, and found in the shaft graves of Mycenae, are gold-hilted daggers of bronze inlaid with gold and silver. This specimen depicts a cat hunting water birds.

LEFT: A gold mask from Mycenae, found in excavations undertaken after Schliemann's death.

The enclosure walls of both grave circles were probably built to encircle a space set aside specifically for the burial of important, royal personages, rather than to enclose already existing graves. The earliest graves in Circle B are small shallow pits or stone-lined cist graves, but the majority of graves from both circles are fairly substantial shaft graves, comprising large rectangular pits sunk into the earth and rock. The sides of the shaft were lined with a rubble wall, or a ledge was cut into the rock, to support wooden beams on which a roof of slate slabs or wattle rested.

The dead were placed on a layer of pebbles at the bottom of the shaft, usually in an extended position, and the grave goods were placed around the body. In Circle A the burials were usually laid out in an east-west direction, but the burials in Circle B had no consistent orientation. After the burial the shaft was roofed and the top part of the shaft, above the roof, was filled with soil raised in a mound, into which the stela was set. These graves were family tombs and contained more than one inhumation. Whenever a new burial took place the covering soil and roof would be removed, the earlier burial would be unceremoniously pushed to one side, together with the accompanying grave goods, and the new burial would be laid out on the floor. Often pottery from the first burial would be removed and placed on the relaid roof. An important part of the funerary ritual was a banquet by the side of the grave, and the debris of animal bones and shells would be thrown into the shaft. Drinking vessels, for libations offered to the dead or a toast drunk in their honour, were smashed against the sides of the shaft.

Nineteen bodies were found in the six graves of Circle A — seventeen adults and two children. Perhaps the most interesting of the burials is that of a male in grave V, which appears to have

ignated Grave Circle A. Grave Circle B was excavated by the Greek Archaeological Service under the direction of George Mylonas and John Papadimitriou between 1952 and 1954. Twenty-six graves were excavated, of which fourteen were shaft graves, similar to those found in Circle A. Only four of these graves were marked with stelae. The burials in Circle B appear to be slightly earlier than those in Circle A and on the whole are not as wealthily furnished, although the largest and richest burials in Circle B are comparable with the poorer burials in Circle A.

been mummified. The number of individuals buried in Circle B is difficult to establish because of the re-use of the graves. Anthropological studies of the skeletons from Circle B indicate that the men varied in height between 1.61 and 1.76 m (5 ft 3 in and 5 ft 9 in), and the women between 1.58 and 1.61 m (5 ft 2 in and 5 ft 3 in). Life expectancy was not long, only around 38 years, but these people enjoyed good health, were well nourished and had little dental disease. The men were massive and powerfully built, and were probably fearsome warriors. A forensic team has reconstructed the faces of a number of skulls from Circle B. These reconstructions reinforce the impression of a class of mighty warriors.

The most striking aspect of the funerary furniture of these graves is the sheer quantity of gold. There was an ever-increasing provision of wealthy grave goods, and the burials from Circle A were particularly lavishly equipped. There were some 13 kg (29 lb) of gold in the three wealthiest graves (II, IV and V), including 22 gold vases, in addition to which there were 30 silver vases and more than 70 vessels of bronze and copper.

The main classes of grave goods are personal adornments, weapons, tools, pottery, and vases of precious materials, such as metal, stone or faience. The dead were buried fully clothed, and the women were adorned with elaborate gold jewellery: necklaces, earrings, diadems with embossed decoration. Their garments were fastened by pins with rock crystal heads, and in Circle

The most famous of the Mycenaean masks, from shaft grave V. Dubbed the mask of Agamemnon, it predates that king's reign by centuries.

A the women's garments were adorned with numerous embossed gold discs. There were also gold signet rings and beads of amber and glass. The men in Circle A wore gold face masks. Although the burials in Circle B were less opulent, there was a male burial in grave Gamma with a face mask made of electrum (an alloy of gold and silver). Male burials were provided with an impressive array of weapons, spearheads, arrows, swords and daggers. The swords had elaborately decorated hilts in gold or ivory, and the dagger blades were decorated with fine inlay scenes of battle and hunting. Vases in precious materials were found with the later burials of Circle B and were commonly deposited with both male and female burials in Circle A. These include a variety of gold and silver cups, animal's head vases such as the famous bull's head *rhyton*, and from grave Omikron in Circle B a rock crystal duck vase. This extraordinary wealth was not a phenomenon restricted to the Mycenaean shaft graves, but is a trend common to the Greek mainland at the beginning of the Late Bronze Age.

The relationship between the two grave circles is problematic. Later treatment of Circle A suggests that the inhabitants of Mycenae revered the individuals buried there, whereas less respect was shown to the dead of Circle B — for while Circle A was undisturbed by later building activity in the fourteenth and thirteenth centuries BC, Circle B was severely encroached upon. The greater wealth deposited in Circle A suggests that the individuals buried there were the dominant ruling family at Mycenae, perhaps supplanting an earlier dynasty buried in Circle B. While the burials in both circles are several centuries too early to belong to Agamemnon and his followers, Schliemann certainly discovered the burial ground of the rulers of Mycenae. ■

Silver *rhyton* (drinking vessel) in the form of a bull's head, from shaft grave IV at Mycenae, sixteenth century BC.

DANISH BRONZE AGE LOG COFFIN BURIALS

In 1921 archaeologists at the National Museum of Denmark in Copenhagen were astounded at what appeared when they rolled back the carefully hemmed brown woollen rug that covered the contents of the oak coffin they had just opened. They saw the head of a young woman, between eighteen and twenty years of age, resting on her right cheek, a fine head of loose-hanging, shoulder-length hair hiding her face, hair that had once been tied by a hairband of twisted strands of fine black wool. A small bronze earring lay near where her left ear once was.

The archaeologists rolled back the rug further, revealing an outfit that scandalized the staid world of Danish archaeology: first, a

For about a hundred years, in the century around 1250 BC, the Danish landscape was dominated by the construction of huge burial mounds, cast up over the buried bodies of the Bronze Age élite. Of the 5000 or so tombs that span the region from Denmark to southern Sweden and Norway, and parts of north Germany, just a handful preserved some of the most remarkable burials from prehistoric Europe.

brown woollen short-sleeved tunic with a straight-cut neckline, then a knee-length skirt made of loose cords wrapped twice around slender hips, outrageously skimpy in the eyes of the Museum Director. In between, a large bronze belt disc, decorated with spirals and a raised spike, lay on her stomach. This was all that remained of a belt, into which would have been stuck the ornate bone comb that lay beneath the disc. The body of the girl lay, stretched out, with her arms by her side, bronze rings on each wrist, simple cloth wrappings on her feet. But the world was never to know her face. For after she was buried, over 3000 years before, beneath a mound at Egtved, Jutland, the preservative qualities of the

LEFT: Oak coffin from Guldhøj, Denmark. Such airtight coffins may contain bodies in an extraordinary state of preservation.

BELOW: Investigation of this oak coffin from Egtved caused consternation in the staid museum world.

RIGHT: The oak coffins from Borum Eshøj are now on display at the National Museum in Copenhagen.

tannic acid of the oak coffin had played their trick, preserving only the top horny layer of dead skin, nails, eyebrows and other hair, and beneath her hair only the brain of the Egtved girl remained for the archaeologists to admire. The yarrow flower placed by her left knee, above the rug and beneath a cow hide, showed she had been buried in the summer.

The secret of preservation lay in the great oak coffins in which the deceased were laid to rest. These coffins were made of tree trunks, which were carefully split lengthwise, hollowed out and, after the body of the deceased had been carefully arranged inside, put back together, creating a fine airtight seal. The coffins often rested on stone platforms on low mounds, with earthen mounds thrown up on top of the whole.

These burial mounds often contained the coffins of whole families, although most of the coffins rotted away

RIGHT: **This large bronze belt disc, decorated with spirals and a spike, covered the Egtved girl's stomach.**

BELOW: **The Egtved girl's woollen tunic, cord skirt and belt were all marvellously preserved.**

over time, leaving only a few imperishable grave goods such as bronze swords and ornaments. Next to the coffin of the Egtved girl was a space which may well have held her husband's coffin.

Beneath Borum Eshøj, one of the largest mounds, 111 m (364 ft) in diameter and 9 m (30 ft) high, three well-preserved oak coffins were discovered. In 1871 the first was opened. Over 2 m (nearly 7 ft) long, it contained the body of a woman, aged between 50 and 60, her long, once fair hair, now darkened by the tannic acid, held in place with a hairnet. She lay beneath a large woollen rug covered by an animal hide with hairs still attached. Clad in a short tunic with elbow-length sleeves and a full-length skirt supported by a long tasselled hide belt, the lady of Borum Eshøj was adorned with fine bronze ornaments: a fibula (safety-pin), dagger, belt-disc, and rings around her neck, arms and fingers. In the central, slightly longer coffin lay the outstretched body of a man of about the same age as the woman. He lay on the hide of a cow that was freshly flayed at the time he was buried, as could be deduced from the maggots preserved on it. Perhaps the cow was eaten during the funeral feast. This man was very well-kempt. He was wrapped in a woollen cape fastened by a wooden pin, and wore a cap and a woollen loin-cloth. His face was clean-shaven, his manicured nails and good teeth indicative of his high status. To one side lay a third coffin, buried later than the other two. Inside lay the body of a younger man, his wisdom teeth just erupting. By his side was a short dagger in a much longer scabbard with grooved decoration. Maybe his sword had been inherited by a younger kinsman.

Beneath the huge Muldbjerg mound lay a Bronze Age chieftain with his two wives. The chieftain's coffin was enclosed by massive oak planks, still with the original bark on them. As in so many other mounds, the body was covered by a woollen cape and rug, on top of which lay an untreated cow hide. He wore a short woollen coat upon which lay a sheathed bronze sword. On his head was a cap, covering his long hair, swept back and parted in the middle. As with his counterpart who lay beneath Borum

Eshøj, he was clean-shaven, and had carefully rounded fingernails.

The temptation of buried treasure lured grave robbers into some of these mounds even in antiquity, soon after the dead were buried. At Guldhøj, the well-preserved contents of a child's coffin were washed away by an ill-timed cloudburst shortly after the coffin was opened in 1891, leaving only three crab apples that had been buried with the child, and the black-haired goatskin in which the body had been wrapped. A second coffin contained rich grave goods, including an unusual folding stool, but only the hair and brain remained of the deceased. Keeping what they thought was the best till last, the archaeologists then turned to the third coffin, which seemed to be in the best condition. On opening this coffin, however, the investigators met with disappointment, as all they found was a hooked stick, the tool of thievery by which the rich contents had been extracted through a small hole in the end of the sarcophagus.

These "Mound People" were the upper class in a society that valued fine objects, some of which they took with them into the next world, and exercised great care over their personal appearance. Men were often carefully shaven, sometimes buried with their bronze razors. Both men and women carried decorated bone combs with them into the afterlife. Women wore their hair in elaborate nets held in place by hairbands. They knew the taste of alcoholic beverages. A birch-bark bucket in the corner of the Egtved girl's coffin, the last object placed inside, contained a brown deposit that on analysis turned out to be the remains of just such a drink, a mixture of beer and fruit wine brewed from wheat and cranberries, spiced with bog myrtle and sweetened with honey. The same young woman shared her coffin with the burnt remains of an eight- or nine-year-old girl, possibly a serving girl who followed her mistress into death.

The occupants of the oak coffins were at the top of a society

The ravages of time removed the face of the Egtved girl long ago, leaving her clothes to be modelled by a distant descendant.

whose economy was based on cattle breeding and farming. Their religion seems to have centred around beliefs concerning the sun and horses, beliefs given concrete expression in the model of a sun chariot drawn by a heavenly horse, which had been broken up and buried in the peaty fen at Trundholm as an offering to the gods. The horse motif can also be seen in the horse-head handles of the gold vessels ritually buried at Borgbjerg, a sacred hill which became a focus of sun worship. ∎

TOMBS IN THE PERSIAN GULF

Bahrain and the adjacent portion of Saudi Arabia are dotted with dense clusters of earthen mounds that turn out to be burials; some 170,000 of these tumuli occur on Bahrain alone.

Bahrain enjoys the benefits of an artesian system which delivers plentiful water to the northern end of this island nation, supporting the traditional towns and date plantations. The same aquiferous system breaks out at certain points on the nearby shore of Saudi Arabia, conferring similar gifts. In ancient times this natural endowment gave rise to Mesopotamian legends about the abyss (a word, and idea, borrowed from the Sumerian *abzu*, the watery deep), and Gilgamesh's epic search for eternal life. This Eden, named Dilmun, was also a real place, a centre of sea-going trade between Mesopotamia, southeast Arabia (Magan), and India during the Bronze Age.

Archaeology put a material face on Dilmun when a Danish group excavated at the capital city of the Bronze Age. They also opened some tumuli, and inside found items of the same culture, dated to around 2100-1700 BC, the height of the Mesopotamian trade. Subsequently others have excavated many more of these graves, giving a solid picture of their construction and content. The basic form of each tumulus is a central stone chamber, enclosed by a low ring-wall and covered by heaped-up earth and gravel. The mounds vary somewhat in size: the great majority measure 4.5 by 9 m (15 by 30 ft) in diameter and stand 1-2 m (3-6 ft) high, but the largest (called "royal tumuli") reach 30 m (100 ft) across and are 7.5 m (25 ft) tall. The smaller mounds generally contain a single chamber, set on or slightly into the original ground surface. The walls are rough courses of fieldstone, and several capstones cover the chamber. Sometimes a single elongated mound covers several chambers, a construction that grew by the addition of smaller, secondary chambers and ring-walls to the central structure. The larger tumuli may have stone-lined entrance shafts that give access to the central chamber; in the largest

Heaped-up earth and gravel, here half cut away, covers the central stone burial chamber of the Bronze Age tumuli of Bahrain.

Other burials, like these at Saar on Bahrain, form an underground honeycomb of tomb chambers.

tumuli the chamber may have two storeys. The chambers are normally rectangular, most often measuring about 1.20-2.40 m (4-8 ft) long, up to 1 m (3 ft) wide and around 1 m high. Very often, one or two alcoves lie at the northeast end of the chamber, creating an L- or T-shaped space, and additional pairs of alcoves sometimes appear midway along the chamber in the largest tumuli. The same architecture of chamber and ring-wall sometimes forms an extensive, interlocking honeycomb complex, placed below the ground surface without the mounded gravel superstructure, at the edge of a tumulus field proper.

The chambers normally contain one burial each, although occasionally a chamber may hold several people or, especially in secondary chambers, none. The dead were usually laid on their right side in a loosely flexed position, with the head in the alcoved end of the chamber (so that the head is facing north to northwest). Relatively few grave goods accompany the bodies, a poverty that persistent grave robbing has exacerbated. Pottery is the most common item of burial furniture, with one or two vessels serving the dead in most tumuli. Among the other less com-

monly found goods are shell or stone stamp seals, stone jars, baskets sealed with asphalt, ostrich eggshell cups, ivory objects, stone beads, items of copper jewellery, and copper weapons. A number of graves contain a joint of meat, usually sheep or goat, often in a charred condition, the final mortuary barbecue. The skeletons represent people of all age groups and both sexes, and show a life expectancy of nearly 40 years. The high incidence of tooth decay, and intentional extraction of rotten or abscessed teeth, suggests a diet high in dates, a crop for which Bahrain is famous.

Further east in the Persian Gulf, in the modern United Arab Emirates and Oman, the ancient Magan was also engaged in the Bronze Age trade. Indeed, the copper of Magan was one of the most important items of this trade, and archaeological research has discovered places where copper ore was smelted to make the ingots for trade. The people of Magan practised distinctive burial rituals that are very different from those of Dilmun, and that seem to reflect a basically different social organization. The tombs of Magan, southeast Arabia, are superficially similar to those of Dilmun, formed as above-ground tumuli of stone. But this resemblance disappears inside the tombs, where very different architectural concepts and burial practices reign. The earliest tombs of Magan, dated to around 3000-2500 BC, present a single, relatively small chamber 1-2 m (3-6 ft) across within the very

thick, solid stone walls of a domed, round tumulus. The tumulus walls were built as several concentric envelopes around the central chamber, and the entire structure ranged up to 9 m (30 ft) across and 3.5 m (12 ft) high. The burials themselves are heavily disturbed and the skeletons poorly preserved, though in several cases enough bones remain to establish that several people shared a single chamber. The grave goods are also sparse, being limited to some pots, a few copper rivets, pins, and stone and faience beads.

A new type of tumulus emerged around 2500 BC. These far more elaborate tombs were faced with dressed stone blocks, equipped with a formal entrance through the side, and set on a platform. In several cases, depictions in low relief of people, camels, ibex and other animals decorate the exterior. Inside the graves, walls divided the tumulus into at least two, and up to ten, separate chambers. In some cases stone slabs running across the interior walling created two distinct floors, the lower of which might extend underground. These circular structures, some 3-12 m (10-40 ft) across, probably had a flat roof, formed by slabs braced up by the interior walls. Each of these tombs was used over multiple generations, with new interments continually being introduced through the doorway. When the crush of bodies threatened to take up the floor space, the older ones were swept up against the back walls, creating more room for the recent arrivals. In one known instance the remains of approximately 250 individuals are accumulated in the rooms of a single tumulus, the more recently buried being laid out in serried ranks. And as each burial included its complement of burial goods, these tombs can be extremely rich in pottery, both imported and local, as well as

ABOVE: The Bahrain graves form tumulus fields so dense that one mound almost treads on another's skirts.

OPPOSITE: The reusable tombs of Oman and the UAE had portals (through which new interments could be introduced) that sometimes bore animal and human figures carved in relief.

stone vessels, jewellery and weapons. A study of genetically determined characteristics of teeth shows that the dead of several families used the same grave; these families were probably related to each other as a clan that jointly owned a particular tumulus.

After around 2000 BC, various other burial forms emerged to replace these elaborate tumuli in southeast Arabia. The most common new type was an elongated oval dug into the ground, and variations on that theme. Despite being very different in architecture, and much less sophisticated, in comparison to the earlier tumuli, these second-millennium BC tombs continued to house multiple burials — as before, a single structure might hold the remains of 100 or more bodies - and their accompanying goods. Towns never developed during the Bronze Age in this region, and communities of farmers and pastoralists were widely scattered across a harsh landscape. The persistence of collective burials in southeast Arabia reflects the persistence of clans as a social organization appropriate to these conditions. In contrast, towns did develop in Bahrain, in connection with the Mesopotamian trade. This more commercial and urban milieu encouraged the emergence of individual instead of group identity, and the creation of separate tombs for each of the dead. ■

KLASIES RIVER MOUTH
CAVE 5

At Klasies River Mouth Cave 5, infants and young pre-adults, who would have had low social rank, had unexpectedly elaborate graves, contrary to the expectation that there would be a correlation between the social rank of a living person and the "wealth" of the goods placed in the grave. It is thought that this could be a consequence of the existence of a reciprocal gift exchange system, like the one called *hxaro* among recent southern African hunter-gatherers. *Hxaro* resulted in children having ornamentation which they had been given available for placement in their graves, while the material "wealth" of adults and the elderly was generally not available for this purpose.

Rock shelters and caves in the southern coastal belt and adjacent mountains of South Africa record a distinctive rich Later Stone Age culture called the Wilton between about 7500 to after 2000 years ago. These shelters were also the repositories of considerable numbers of burials of the period, some of which had variable amounts of grave goods and, occasionally, painted burial stones, a practice apparently unique to this region of southern Africa at the time.

A cemetery in a coastal cave

A spectacular series of caves and rock shelters at Klasies River Mouth, so named for their location near the mouth of the Klasies River on the southern South African coast, is extraordinarily rich in archaeological remains from the past 120,000 years. The main cave complex has produced some of the earliest known remains of modern-looking or "near-modern" humans dating from 100,000 or possibly 120,000 years ago. Klasies River Mouth Cave 5 (KRM 5), a tunnel-like cavity some 90 m (295ft) long with its entrance almost entirely blocked by a huge sand dune, lies about 2 km (1 1/4 miles) east of the main complex, some 18 m (60 ft) above sea level. It has also produced human remains, though these tell a social rather than a biological evolutionary tale.

A shell midden on top of the sand dune near the front of KRM 5, containing the cultural and dietary debris of Later Stone Age people, was excavated by Johan Binneman of the Albany Museum in Grahamstown in 1984. Six burials were identified, of which five were excavated, while the sixth remains unexcavated but visible in the excavation cutting wall. Radiocarbon dates of the

Cliff face showing the entrance to Klasies River Mouth Cave 5.

excavation layers indicate that the burials date between about 4250 and 2000 years ago.

The KRM Cave 5 burials

The five excavated burials had all been placed in shallow hollows filled in with shell midden material. Apart from one skeleton of an infant, which was placed on its right side, the skeletons were lying in a flexed ("curled up") position on their left sides, and all five were placed lying in a northeasterly direction.

KRM 5/1 was probably a young female, some 16-18 years old at death, whose face had been badly damaged by cut and scratch marks as well as splintering, indicating an injury that might have caused her death. The hollow in which she was placed was lined with a thin layer of plant material, covered by a layer of red ochre. There was a thick layer of red ochre below her hips, and she was covered with a layer of sand mixed with red ochre.

Red ochre-stained ostrich eggshell beads were found around her neck, chest and hips: 269 around the neck and shoulders, and 735 around the hips. The placing of the beads around the neck and shoulders suggests that they were originally either embroidered onto a piece of leather, or sewn together as a decorative pendant, which was hung around the neck by a string of ostrich eggshell beads. The beads around the hips were laid down in strings and may have been attached to two serrated *Turbo sarmaticus* (commonly known as the ollycrock or alikreukel, from the

Klasies River Mouth 5/1: burial of a female of 16-18 years decorated with strings of ostrich eggshell beads and shell pendants.

Dutch for "periwinkle") shells. There were also two serrated oyster shell pendants and 272 ochre–stained *Nassarius* (estuarine mollusc) shells around the shoulders. Items found in the grave fill included three *Turbo* shell 'buttons', ten *Tricolia* (pheasant shell mollusc) shell beads, and a piece of polished bone.

KRM 5/2 was a young male, between 18 and 20 years old at death. His skull was not present and might have been removed when the burial hollow for KRM5/6 (which was not excavated) was dug. There were no grave goods or ochre directly associated with this skeleton (the oldest individual found), but the grave fill contained ostrich eggshell beads, *Nassarius*, *Bullia* (plough snail mollusc) and *Tricolia* shell beads as well as *Turbo* pendants and "buttons" and a bone point.

KRM 5/3 was an infant with a rich collection of grave goods. Strings of *Bullia digitalis*, *Tricolia* species and *Nassarius kraussianus* shell beads were draped around the upper part of the skeleton, while strings of ostrich eggshell beads were found around the left leg and hip. A cormorant beak may also have been ornamental. There were *Turbo sarmaticus* "buttons" and *Fissurella aperta* (key–hole limpet) shells around the ochre-stained skull. A split cobble stained with ochre and charcoal was laid on top of the skeleton.

KRM 5/4, also an infant burial, was richly adorned with four oyster pendants on the chest, strings totalling 1108 *Nassarius* shell beads, and ostrich eggshell and *Tricolia* beads. KRM 5/5, yet another infant, had no shell grave goods, but the red ochre-stained skull still had lumps of ochre attached to it and the bones were covered by a thick layer of yellow ochre.

In a second excavated area further back in the cave, Binneman found a small quartzite slab with a small red antelope painted on it, associated with a radiocarbon date of nearly four thousand years ago. Previous excavations at KRM 5 by Ronald Singer and John Wymer in the late 1960s also yielded a painted stone. This had a red oval-shaped grid pattern on both sides and was found just above a layer radiocarbon-dated to just over 4000 years ago. It is possible that these painted stones might be associated with as yet unlocated burials. Painted stones from other sites in the region are sometimes, but not necessarily, linked with burials.

A hunter-gatherer burial place

Among Stone Age hunter-gatherers like those who buried their dead at KRM 5, children and young people have low rank because they are not yet involved in many duty or status relationships. Rank and social importance increase with age as the

Klasies River Mouth 5/3: infant burial richly decorated with shell beads. Also visible in the centre of the picture is a cormorant's beak. The skull is stained with ochre.

individual becomes involved in increasing numbers of social relationships. Why, then, were the graves of infants and sub-adults at KRM 5 so elaborate?

Simon Hall, now at the University of the Witwatersrand, and Binneman have suggested that the richness of these graves might be a consequence of the existence of a reciprocal gift exchange network like the *hxaro* institution which has been described among the !Kung and other Bushmen of Botswana. This involves giving gifts to exchange partners to create an obligation and thereby ensure access to food and other resources in other areas when they are scarce in one's own locality. The *hxaro* networks are maintained by the discrete delayed exchange of gifts like ostrich eggshell beads, arrows and blankets. More than two-thirds of the possessions of the !Kung are obtained through *hxaro* exchange.

Symbolic *hxaro* exchanges are made for infants during the first six months of their lives, and thereafter children are given many gifts without the requirement of reciprocity, to emphasize the value of the child. Children and young people therefore have quantities of possessions available for grave goods as they have not yet formalized the reciprocal side of their *hxaro* relationships. When an adult dies, some of the possessions are buried with the deceased, but most are passed on to *hxaro* partners by the children or relatives so that the reciprocal network will remain secure. Very old individuals who die will have given away their possessions during their *hxaro* years in order to build up a support network for their declining years. The richness of the graves of the young people at KRM 5 may also symbolize their denied productive potential; they became in death what they did not achieve in life. ∎

HOCHDORF

One of the most remarkable finds of the late 1970s in Central Europe was the lavish burial of a Celtic chief at Hochdorf, in the German state of Baden-Württemberg.

The burial mound at Hochdorf was especially important because it was unrobbed (most other tombs of this period had been plundered in antiquity or modern times) and as a result the finds were extraordinarily rich. It was fully excavated in 1978 and 1979. The Hochdorf tomb dates to the late Hallstatt period, between 550 and 500 BC, and is one of a number of such burials from this period in Central Europe that have been termed "princely tombs". This was a period of important change in Central Europe, during which powerful leaders emerged as a result of commerce and manufacturing. It was also the time during which Celtic art and decorative styles developed.

Germany and eastern France. They were then buried next to their seats of power in lavish tombs. For example, the spectacular tomb at Vix is located at the foot of the *oppidum* of Mont Lassois. Similarly, along the upper Danube in southern Germany, the hillfort called the Heuneburg was surrounded by nine burial mounds including the Hohmichele, which is preserved up to 13 m (43 ft) high. In southwestern Germany near Stuttgart, a Celtic mountain stronghold at the Hohenasperg was also surrounded by a ring of such "princely tombs", but almost all

During this period it was common for these Celtic leaders to establish their residences in hillforts, or *oppida*, which are found throughout southern

of them had been robbed in ancient times. In 1977, however, an amateur archaeologist, Renate Liebfried, notified the State Antiquities Office of Baden-Württemberg of the existence of a burial mound about 10 km (6 miles) west of the Hohenasperg at a town called Hochdorf.

Although the Hochdorf tumulus has been estimated to have been 6 m (20 ft) high in its original state, by the mid-1970s it had become so eroded that it was hardly visible above the surface of the ploughed field in which it was located. Intensive archaeological investigation in this area since the nineteenth century had failed to identify it as a prehistoric burial mound. It was only in February 1977 that it was possible to recognize the Hochdorf mound as an Iron Age tumulus with a stone ring, of a size similar to that of the other "princely tombs" in the region. By this time erosion and ploughing had placed the mound in even greater danger of destruction, and it was decided to excavate it completely in an intensive research campaign.

The excavations led by Jorg Biel began on 5 July 1978 and lasted until 30 November. The following year, they began on 7 June and again lasted until November. The total cost of the field-work was about DM 440,000, or nearly $300,000 by exchange rates at that time, a very expensive undertaking. Excavations were extremely difficult, owing to the wealth of the burial goods and their concentration in the tomb. In some places whole blocks of soil were taken out intact and excavated delicately in the laboratory to separate the finds from the surrounding matrix of soil. Conservation work on the artefacts was also very painstaking, and lasted until 1985.

The excavation of the tumulus, 60 m (200 ft) in diameter, revealed a central burial shaft, 11 by 11 m (36 by 36 ft) and about 2.5 m (8 ft) deep. Inside this shaft were two wooden structures, one within the other, and each covered with a timber roof. The outer one was constructed of oak timbers and formed a box 7.5 m (25 ft) square and about 1.5 m (5 ft) deep. Inside this was another oak box, 4.7 m (15 ft 4 in) square and 1 m (3 ft 3 in) deep. Within the inner box was the burial and all its associated offer-

Above: Reconstruction drawing showing the location of the body of the Hochdorf "prince" on a recliner, textiles on the floor, cauldron and wagon. Note the drinking horns hanging from the wall.

Left: The Hochdorf "prince"'s skeleton as excavated, lying on a bronze recliner and with golden neck-ring, bracelets and belt.

ings. The space between the boxes was filled with stones, which were also heaped over the inner chamber, about 50 tons in all. Unfortunately, this weight caused the roof of the burial chamber to collapse shortly after the burial, before the corpse had even decomposed. In all, the tumulus is estimated to have comprised 7000 cubic metres of soil.

At the north side of the mound low stone walls had formed a gate into the central burial chamber before it was secured with the stones. These were then covered over by the mound. When the mound was built up, manufacturing by-products and residues from the working of gold, bronze and iron were included in its fill, indicating that there were workshops close by the tomb which apparently produced many of the grave goods. Traces of

comb, an iron razor, five amber beads and three iron fish-hooks. Numerous gold ornaments decorated the clothes and even the shoes of the deceased, including fibulae, cuffs, and bands of hammered gold. The walls of the burial chamber were hung with fabric curtains, while the wooden floor was covered with a timber rug. Hung on the wall of the chamber were nine drinking horns.

The man was lying on a bronze recliner which has no known parallel in Celtic Europe. It was upholstered in furs and textiles and was supported by eight bronze female figures with upstretched arms. Scenes of wagons and dancers are embossed on the large bronze surfaces of the back and sides of the couch. At the foot of the recliner was a large bronze kettle, believed to have been manufactured in a Greek colony in southern Italy, which was decorated with three lions. Residue in the kettle was from mead, which played a large role in Celtic ritual. Also inside the kettle was a small gold bowl.

huts which may have served as these workshops were found at the perimeter of the mound area.

The burial chamber of the Hochdorf tumulus had an extraordinary level of preservation, not only of metals but also of wood, leather and textiles. The individual interred in the mound was a man about 1.83 m (6 ft) tall and between 30 and 40 years old. On his head he wore a conical birch-bark hat. Around his neck was a gold hoop and on his chest a small bag with a wooden

On the other side of the burial chamber was a four-wheeled wagon, made of iron-sheathed wood, with harnesses for two

horses. Wagons are common elements in Celtic "princely tombs", but this iron sheathing is unique. Including its tongue, the wagon is 4.5 m (15 ft) long, extending nearly the entire width of the chamber, its massive ten-spoke wheels supporting a rather lightweight platform. Its construction indicates that it was only really suitable for ceremonial use. Piled on the wagon were still more grave goods.

Who was the man in the Hochdorf burial mound? During this period Greek imports from the Mediterranean were reaching Central Europe and were being exchanged for goods and materials such as furs, honey, grain and amber. This trade passed up the Rhône valley from the Greek trading colony at Massilia (now the

RIGHT: Gold bands decorated shoes made of a perishable material, probably leather.

BELOW: The bronze recliner, as it appears after conservation, on which the skeleton in the Hochdorf mound was found.

modern city of Marseilles) and then overland to the Danube and Rhine drainages to the east and the Seine to the north. In this area it connected with the emerging commercial networks of Central Europe, which could be called "the first European Economic Union". It appears that the control of this trade permitted some Celtic chieftains to become extraordinarily wealthy. We can speculate about the power structure during this period: were there "dynasties" or did the chieftains fulfil a different, possibly religious, function?

The Hochdorf tumulus and the other princely graves of Germany and France provide a rare glimpse of Celtic aristocratic life and death. Strongholds like Mont Lassois, Heuneburg and Hohenasperg give us evidence of the large central settlements where the "princes", their families and their retainers lived. Smaller Hallstatt settlements shed light on how the common people lived, although such sites have been neglected in favour of the spectacular tombs and strongholds. Tutankhamen's tomb provided an important glimpse of the élite society of dynastic Egypt, and the Hochdorf tomb is in many respects a find of similar importance for Celtic archaeology. A full understanding of the society of this period, however, will require the analysis of much more evidence from ordinary sites. ■

PHILIP OF MACEDON

Aigai was known from Plutarch's life of Pyrrhus, king of Epirus, to be the burial place of the Macedonian royal family. Plutarch recorded that after the invasion of Macedonia in 274/3 BC the Gaulish mercenaries "set themselves to digging up the tombs of the kings who had been buried there; the treasure they plundered, the bones they insolently cast to the four winds."

One of the most dominant features of the small town of Vergina in Macedonia is the prominent "Great Tumulus", measuring some 110 m (360 ft) in diameter and 12 (39 ft) m high. Vergina itself has been recognized as Aigai, the first capital of Macedonia.

If the identification of Vergina with Aigai was correct, this would imply that there were royal tombs in the vicinity. Excavations on the Great Tumulus were finally commenced in 1952, although the main work was conducted in 1962 and 1963; all failed to find the main tomb. However, further work was carried out at the site in the late summer of 1977 by the Greek archaeologist Manolis Andronicos. As the trench was cut into the mound traces were found of a ceremonial area where offerings had been made to the dead person buried there.

The first tomb discovered in the mound had already been looted. However, the wall paintings were particularly well preserved, with scenes of the seizure of Persephone by the god of the underworld, Pluto. Soon afterwards another larger tomb was discovered a little to the northwest. As the façade was cleared, remains of a painted frieze were found showing a hunting scene; one rider recalled the image of Alexander the Great from the so-called "Alexander mosaic" found at Pompeii. Andronicos presumed that this tomb too had been robbed, but on clearing the façade realized that the great marble doors were still closed, implying that the contents of the grave remained intact. Digging above the vault, the excavators identified the remains of the funeral pyre, and in the debris three gold acorns, small pieces of charred ivory, iron horse trappings, two iron swords and a spearhead were found. The roof of the tomb was itself covered with a thick layer of stucco. The archaeological team removed the keystone to the vault — a technique learned from Macedonian tomb-robbers — and Andronicos used a ladder to enter the tomb. Although the walls were undecorated, unlike Tomb I, Andronicos realized, to his delight, that the tomb contents were intact.

Around him were groups of grave goods: a bronze shield-cover and greaves (leg armour), as well as an iron helmet, all leaning against the wall alongside bronze vessels. One of the objects was a large bronze vessel with finely pierced sides; inside was found a clay lamp, and the bronze vessel had acted as a lantern. Near the shield-cover numerous gold and ivory fragments were found, clearly from an ornate shield, possibly depicting the mythological fight between the Greeks and the Amazons. On the other side of the

A small ivory head (3.2 cm or 1¼ in) was found in the main chamber of Tomb II at Vergina. The bearded middle-aged man has been identified as Philip II through the similarity to coin portraits.

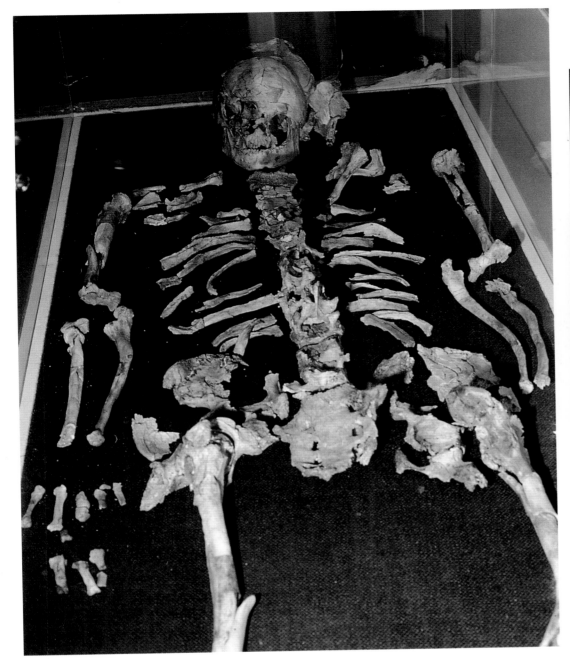

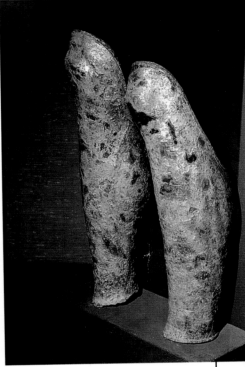

Above: Pair of gilded bronze greaves found in the antechamber of Tomb II at Vergina. The left greave is much shorter than the right, suggesting that the left leg was weaker. Remains of leather padding were found inside the greaves.

Left: The cremated remains of the person buried in the gold *larnax*. The body seems to have been buried like a Homeric hero.

chamber was a stack of silver vessels including cups and jugs. On the floor Andronicos could detect what appeared to be the remains of decayed wooden furniture. Elsewhere in the chamber an iron cuirass decorated with six gold lion heads was found.

Excitement increased when small ivory portrait heads were discovered. These appear to have formed part of the relief decoration of a wooden couch which had been placed in the main chamber. Andronicos considered them to be representations of members of the Macedonian royal family — known from the coins they issued. His identifications included Alexander the Great and his father Philip.

Within the main chamber, at the centre of the back wall, was a marble sarcophagus. On opening the lid a solid gold chest (or *larnax*), weighing 11 kg (nearly 25 lb), was discovered, bearing the distinctive Macedonian star burst. When the chest itself was

opened the excavators discovered the cremated remains wrapped up in a purple cloth, along with a gold wreath of oak leaves and acorns. The wreath itself seems to be the same one from which the gold acorns found on the pyre above the vault had come.

The burial procedures recall that of the heroes from Homer's *Iliad*, in particular the collection of the cremated remains of Hector which were placed in a gold urn and wrapped in soft, purple robes:

"Then they laid what they had gathered up in a golden casket
and wrapped this about with soft robes of purple, and presently
put it away in the hollow of the grave, and over it
piled huge stones laid close together. Lightly and quickly
they piled up the grave-barrow ..."

(Homer, *Iliad* 24.794–801; translated by Richmond Lattimore)

Clearly, whoever was buried in this chamber wished to be considered on the same level as one of the Homeric heroes.

There was still an antechamber which lay between the main chamber and the façade. As Andronicos suspected that it too might contain debris on the floor, it was decided to make an opening in the wall rather than to move the internal marble door. When the chamber was entered, a further sarcophagus was found containing another gold *larnax*; inside were the remains of a cremated woman wrapped in a gold and purple cloth, and with these remains was a gold diadem. The age of this woman has been determined as being between 23 and 27. On the floor of the chamber was debris from furniture and possibly textiles. In the

doorway to the main chamber was a gold case for a bow and arrows, decorated in relief with battle scenes. Next to it were a pair of greaves, clearly made for somebody who had a slightly shorter left leg.

Andronicos was then faced with a dilemma about the identity of the corpse. He felt that the remains were likely to be those of Philip II, father of Alexander the Great, who was murdered in 336. Certainly the material could be dated stylistically to the

This gold *larnax* contained the cremated remains of a man aged between 35 and 55. In the centre of the lid is the starburst, symbol of the Macedonian royal family.

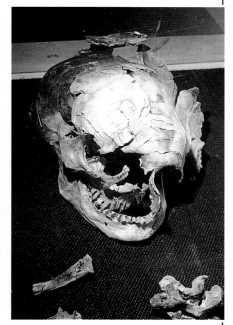

Other suggested identifications have included Alexander's half-brother and Philip's elder son, Arrhidaios, who was assassinated in 317. He was buried, with Eurydice his queen, at Aigai "as was the royal custom". Certainly the large number of pieces of silver plate as well as the two gold chests point to a wealthy, if not royal, burial.

mid- to late fourth century, and there was the support of the ivory portraits. An inscription *Machata* on a silver strainer has been linked with the Machatas who, as Andronicos recognized, was the brother-in-law of Philip II through his wife Phila.

Subsequent research involved the use of forensic science in reconstructing the face of "Philip". The man was probably aged between 35 and 55, and would have stood about 1.67 to 1.72 m (5 ft 6 in to 5 ft 8 in) tall. The scientific study showed that the cremated individual had suffered a major wound to the right side of the face, almost certainly blinding him. Such a description corresponds with the identification of Philip who is known to have been wounded by an arrow during a city siege in one of his many campaigns.

The Great Tumulus was also found to contain a third burial chamber. This again took the form of an antechamber and main chamber. The cremated remains had been placed inside a large silver *hydria* (water-jar), decorated with a gold wreath of oak leaves; this person was apparently a boy aged between twelve and fourteen.

The identification of the dead man buried in the main chamber of Tomb II is still disputed, although the link with Philip has found common acceptance. The presence of the Macedonian royal symbol on so many of the grave goods as well as the lavishness of the material placed within the tomb make it likely that this was indeed a member of the Macedonian royal family buried in the ancestral resting place. ■

ROYAL BURIALS OF EARLY IMPERIAL CHINA

The Qin Terracotta Army is perhaps the best known discovery in Chinese archaeology, but there are many other spectacular tombs from the following Han dynasty. At Mancheng, south of Beijing, the adjoining graves of a provincial king, Liu Sheng, and one of his consorts were hollowed out of the rock of a hillside after his death in 113 BC. The tombs have a similar structure consisting of an entrance passage and four inner chambers, both graves covering about 3000 m³ (100,000 ft³). The identity of the tombs' occupants is known from inscriptions on the bronzes and lacquerware found with the burials. According to the *Shiji* ("Historical Records"), King Liu Sheng "was fond of drink and women and had over 120 children." The bodies of both Liu Sheng and his consort in Tomb 2 were dressed in ex-

China was first unified under the Qin dynasty of 221-207 BC. The tomb of Qin Shi Huangdi, the First Emperor of the Qin, is a massive mound of rammed earth located near Xi'an in Shaanxi Province. To its east Chinese archaeologists have uncovered three large pits containing the famous Terracotta Army. These life-sized clay figures, more than 7000 of which have been found so far, were the guards for the dead emperor. The amazing realism of these figures has provided a wealth of information on armour, hairstyles and physical types in ancient China.

quisite burial suits of small rectangles of jade sewn together with gold thread. Each suit contains around 2500 jade plaques. Burial in this extravagant manner was a carefully guarded privilege, usually only afforded to the kings of the empire. Ancient Chinese religious beliefs held that jade would preserve the physical body. From the several examples of these suits that have been discovered so far, however, we know that this preservative power was not effective in practice.

The other grave goods at Mancheng were equally noteworthy. Comprising a total of some 4200 items, they were found in all of the tomb chambers except for the entrance passages. Tomb 1 contained the remains of six chariots with 16 horses, 11 dogs and a deer. Tomb 2 had four chariots and 13 horses. Other finds included bronze and ceramic vessels, lacquerware, textiles, and gold and silver needles possibly used for acupuncture.

In 1972 a group of three tombs dating from slightly earlier than Mancheng was found south of the Yangzi River at Mawangdui on the outskirts of the city of Changsha. In January of that year, construction work on an underground military hospital was stopped when a mysterious cold gas suddenly began seeping from a layer of white clay. It was soon determined that this gas was coming from the inside of a well-sealed ancient tomb, and salvage excavations were begun. What was uncovered over the following two years was one of the most important burial sites in ancient China.

The three shaft tombs at Mawangdui were covered by a large earth mound 500 m (1640 ft) in circumference. Tomb 1 was the first to be excavated. The burial chamber contained a series of wooden coffins sealed with white clay and charcoal. The innermost coffin was covered with a T-shaped painting on silk; the body of a woman was found inside, wrapped in twenty layers of embroidered silk and brocade. The corpse was remarkably well preserved with the skin still soft and the hair and eyelashes intact. The age of the woman was estimated at about 50.

Tomb 3 was excavated next, and found to contain the skeleton of a male who had died at about 30 years of age. As well as silks, lacquerware and weapons, Tomb 3 produced over 30 books copied onto silk. An inscription on a wooden slip found in the tomb enabled archaeologists to date the burial to 168 BC. More detailed information on the occupants of the Mawangdui graves

Terracotta warrior designed to protect the as-yet unexcavated tomb of the First Emperor of Qin at Xi'an.

came from Tomb 2 in the shape of jade and bronze seals bearing the characters for "Li Cang" and "Marquis of Dai". According to the *Shiji*, Li Cang died in 186 BC. The woman in Tomb 1 is therefore probably his wife. Since the second Marquis died in 165 BC, the occupant of Tomb 3 may be a second son of the first Marquis.

The grave goods at Mawangdui include an amazing variety of items including clothes, musical instruments, weapons, silk paintings and books, pottery, cereals and fruits, and lacquerware. The exceptional preservation at the site means that the items in each of these categories are all of great significance for the study of ancient China. Perhaps the most important treasures in the tombs, however, were the books copied on silk. Many of these were lost documents, their existence known only from brief citations in other texts. The books comprise major works dealing with matters such as astronomy, medicine, politics and ritual. With these texts in hand we can begin to understand something of the philosophical basis of the elaborate burials at Mawangdui.

Elsewhere in Han period China, brick tombs were common amongst the aristocracy and provincial élites. The interiors of some of these were decorated with stone and ceramic reliefs or painted murals. Beyond the Chinese Empire, local rulers as far as Japan and Southeast Asia were brought into the Han sphere of influence. The royal cemetery of the Kings of Dian in modern Yunnan province in southwest China has provided abundant evidence of the lifestyles and customs of this non-Chinese state. Particularly famous are the bronze human and animal figures on bronze drums from the cemetery at Shizhaishan. From the different hairstyles and clothing on these figures, it has been possible to use historical and ethnographic information to link them with the ethnic minorities of the Yunnan region, providing further insights into the "lost bodies" of ancient China. ■

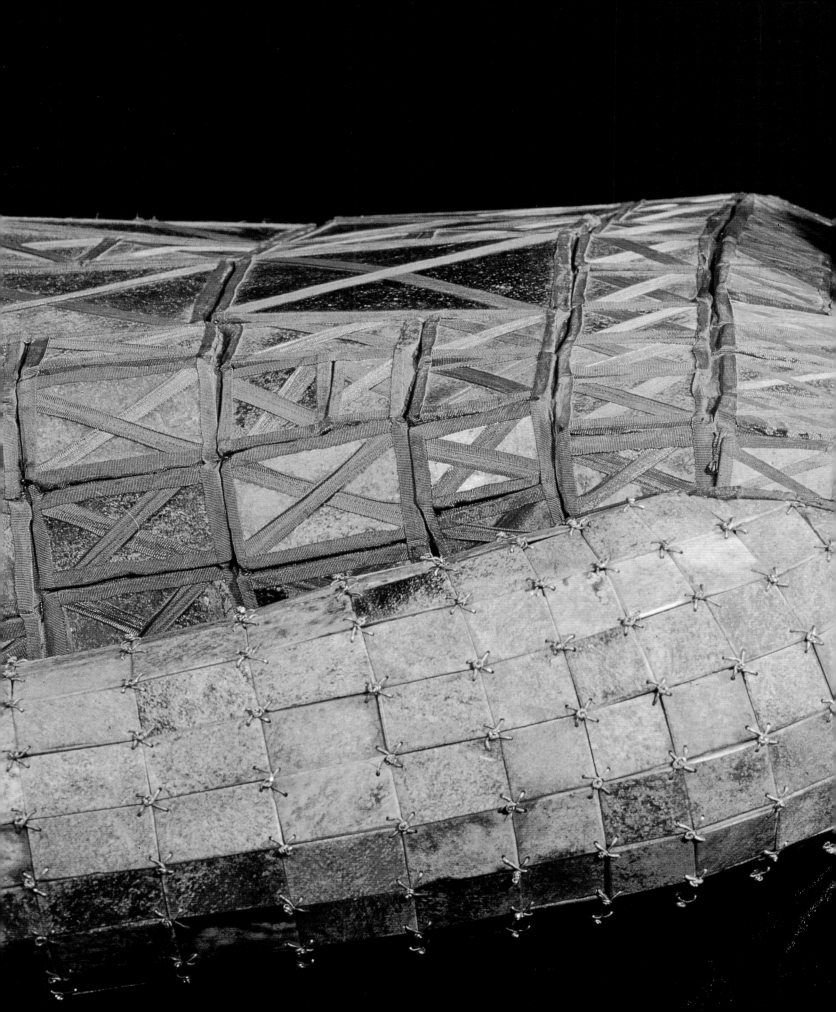

THE LORDS OF SIPÁN

Between the first and seventh centuries AD the Moche civilization stretched along the north coast of Peru. One of the driest deserts in the world, this region was tamed by ancient inhabitants who built irrigation projects to water the fertile desert. The Moche inherited a land rich in agricultural potential, and rich in the bounty of the sea as well. They also controlled an area rich in metals and mineral resources. Moche society supported many skilled artisans who specialized in working gold and silver, bronze production, bead-making, weaving, and many other artistic pursuits. And the best of their labours became offerings and grave goods in the royal tombs.

A few days after the grave-robbers made their discovery, they began to argue among themselves over how the treasure was to be

On the night of 16 February 1987 a group of grave-looters digging clandestinely in an adobe mound in northern Peru broke into the richest undisturbed tomb ever found in the New World. It was the royal tomb of a Moche ruler, who had lived more than 1500 years before.

divided up, and one disgruntled looter informed the police, who raided several of the homes of the looters and confiscated many of the pieces. They then called in the Peruvian archaeologist Walter Alva, director of the Bruning Museum in nearby Lambayeque. When he arrived at the police station he expected to be shown some broken pieces of pottery, which he had often been called in to identify before. When the policeman opened a plain brown paper bag and took out a large golden bead in the form of a human face, Alva was stunned. The police then proceeded to lay out on a table several dozen pieces. Alva could not believe his eyes: here before him were greater riches than anyone had known existed in the Moche culture.

Alva immediately decided that the location of the looted tomb must be sealed off, and that archaeologists must carefully map the pyramid-mound to provide the exact context of the tomb. This required an armed guard, posted 24 hours a day. The news of the discovery had spread like wildfire, and dozens of potential looters had shown up with their shovels, hoping to find pieces of treasure for themselves. They were less than pleased to find their access to the site cut off. In the meantime the looters began to sell the treasures they had hidden from the police to rich collectors in Peru and elsewhere, thus preventing archaeologists from accurately reconstructing the contents of the tomb.

But Alva persevered, and began by cleaning out the rest of the tomb opened by the looters. He found several artefacts, including a copper sceptre, which they had left behind in their haste to extract the gold and silver objects. While cleaning out this first tomb, the archaeologists noticed something: nearby was

Excavations at Sipán, showing graves at different levels.

ABOVE: Treasure is uncovered during the excavation at Sipán, including gold and silver beads.

RIGHT: Some of the heavily eroded adobe burial mounds at Sipán.

an area in which the adobe blocks that formed the mound had been removed, and the area filled in with soil. They began to excavate down into this disturbed area, and to their great surprise located an intact burial chamber. First they came upon the remains of a man who was buried with his feet cut off. Was he the guardian of something of value below? Had his feet been cut off to prevent him from leaving his post?

Further excavation demonstrated that this was indeed the case. They had found the guardian to another royal tomb. In the space hollowed out inside the pyramid-mound the archaeologists found a wooden coffin, in which the body of a Moche ruler was buried amid a plethora of artefacts. They called him the Lord of Sipán, named after the small village nearby. Arranged around his coffin were five others, containing two men (one of them buried with a dog) and three women. There were offerings of ceramics in niches created by removing adobe blocks around the burials.

The rich burial of the Lord of Sipán, showing treasures including pectorals.

A body *in situ* with Moche pots.

Nothing, however, could be compared with the contents of the coffin itself. The coffin was a wooden box held together with copper straps. On top of the other materials in the coffin were two banners: cloths covered with small pieces of sheet metal — gilded copper — and depicting human figures. Beneath the banners were a series of elaborate objects including pectorals made of thousands of shell beads, head ornaments, and a tunic covered with squares of sheet gold. Immediately over the body were found pieces of jewellery the ruler had been wearing, or which had been placed on the body. The most spectacular of these was a necklace of twenty hollow beads in the form of exquisitely wrought peanuts. They formed a double strand with two rows of five silver beads on the left and two rows of five gold beads on the right. This arrangement of beads in groups of ten, but bilaterally symmetrical with gold on one side and silver on the other, is a reflection of concepts of duality that pervaded life in the Andes. Among the Inka, who would not exist for another thousand years after the Lord of Sipán was buried, gold represented the sun and all things male, and was associated with the right. Likewise, silver was associated with the moon and all things female, and the left.

The body of the Lord was poorly preserved, but physical anthropologists were able to determine that he was a man of about 40 years of age. Beneath the body were found even more artefacts: a golden headdress, metal "back-flaps" (pieces of sheet metal with bells that were worn below the waist on the backs of Moche warriors), more shell pectorals, and a variety of other artefacts.

But this was not all. Further excavation in the mound revealed yet another royal tomb, this one referred to as Tomb 2, or that of the Old Lord of Sipán. Like the first tomb, this one included a royal personage in a wooden coffin, surrounded by other men and women who had been buried with him. The coffin was filled with treasures rivalling those in the first tomb. But there were some interesting differences. The Old Lord was wearing a necklace of ten gold beads, each of which had a solid back, and a spider web front. Perched on each web was a golden spider with a human face on its back.

The Moche culture, at least until recent discoveries, has been known primarily for its monumental architecture and its ceramic art. In each valley within its realm the Moche built enormous mud brick pyramids. The largest one, called the Pyramid of the Sun, is found in the valley that gives the culture its name, and it is estimated that more than 125 million mud bricks went into its construction. At the time it was built, it was probably the largest man-made structure in the New World. Moche is perhaps best known for its ceramics, which were sometimes painted with elaborate scenes of religious and political rituals. Other vessels were modelled in the shape of animals or people, and depicted many aspects of Moche life. "Portrait pots" were jars modelled in the form of a human head; facial features were so carefully executed and are so distinctive that they were probably portraits of actual Moche people, perhaps their rulers.

The discovery of the tombs of the Lords of Sipán has made it apparent that Moche culture was much more complex than archaeologists had previously realized, and that Moche rulers were much more powerful than archaeologists had ever suspected. ■

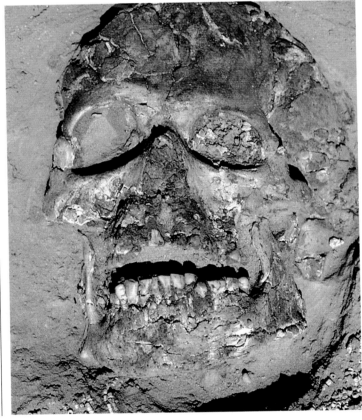

The face of the Lord of Sipán, a man of about 40 years of age. Note the tiny beads around his neck.

MONTE ALBÁN, TOMB 7

Monte Albán in Oaxaca, Mexico is one of the most spectacularly placed ancient cities of Mesoamerica. Situated on top of a mountain, the city looms 300 m (1000 ft) above the floor of the Valley of Oaxaca and is strategically located at the junction of three great river valleys, the Etla, Tlacolula and Zimatlán. Beyond the wealth of material found interred with its occupants, Monte Albán's Tomb 7 has interested archaeologists because of its bi-cultural nature: it presents components of both Zapotec and Mixtec cultures, both of which had laid claim to the city during different periods. The site of Monte Albán was inhabited as early as the Preclassic Period (c. 500 BC) and had become the Zapotec capital by 200 BC. Although the site was deserted by this group after AD 750, it remained an important pilgrimage site for the later cultures who moved into the area, especially the Mixtec.

In January 1932 the Mexican archaeologist Alfonso Caso came upon what is one of the most celebrated finds in Mexico while excavating in the northern sector of the site: Monte Albán's Tomb 7. Besides the tomb's nine occupants, Caso found ornaments made of cast and hammered gold and silver as well as objects of jade, rock crystal and carved bone. With over 500 Mixtec grave goods of high quality, it was considered at the time to be one of the richest tombs in the world.

While the actual construction of Tomb 7 can be credited to the earlier inhabitants of the city, the Zapotecs, Caso determined that the Mixtecs reused it for their own purposes some time after the twelfth century. The bi-cultural nature of the tomb was indicated to the archaeologist by a number of factors. First, remnants of Classic Period (c. AD 600) writing found on the walls and construction techniques were clearly Zapotecan and compared favourably with other well known examples of Za-

RIGHT: View of the North Acropolis at Monte Albán, Oaxaca, Mexico. Tomb 7 is located just beyond the mound on the right.

BELOW: The famous gold pectoral from Tomb 7 at Monte Albán was cast by the "lost wax" process.

potec burials from around the site. Second, Zapotec ceramics, offerings directed towards an earlier burial, were found scattered about the floor of the antechamber located in the extreme eastern area of the tomb. In the absence of Zapotec artefacts from other chambers, Caso reasoned that the Mixtecs must have removed the older remains before reusing the tomb.

Caso's men originally entered the tomb via an opening they had made in the roof. However, once the layout of the tomb had been established, the archaeologists dug a trench towards the front of the crypt which enabled them to enter through the original door. In ancient times the Zapotecs had reached the tomb via a portal located in its eastern antechamber. This was followed by a larger room with a ceiling constructed of flat stone slabs. A narrow passage covered by a single stone lintel formed a passage connecting this first chamber to an even larger rectangular room, which differed from the first not only in size but also in its construction. Stretching some 6 m (20 ft) in length, it was roofed by a series of paired beams forming an inverted V. Although this was less stable than a simple post and lintel construction, the Zapotec architects made a deliberate choice to mimic the shape of the same type of pitched roof that would have covered their homes.

Hundreds of years later the Mixtecs cleared the tomb of its older Zapotec inhabitants and placed nine bodies, along with grave goods, in both the eastern and western chambers. Rather than entering through the original door, they made an opening through the ceiling of one of the rooms. They then placed their bodies within. From the pattern of bone distribution and remnants of fibres, it was clear to Caso that the bodies were originally "bundled". In this form of burial a body, in foetal position, is encased in swathes of fabric or placed in a large woven bag. Once bundled, the bodies in Tomb 7 were placed in a seated position along an inclined ramp which sloped towards the original entrance to the tomb. As time went on, the woven fabric perished and the bones of the skeletons collapsed upon themselves.

Of all the artefacts associated with the Mixtec bodies, it is the carved bones found in the tomb that have led to most speculation as to the identity of the inhabitants. The bones are from jaguars and eagles and are tapered at either end. Images carved into the bones are in high relief, and in some examples the background has been inlaid with turquoise, so that the imagery is more easily readable. The bones have been classified into three types: 1) those that depict persons, names, places, and scenes resembling those found in the Mixtec codices (manuscript volumes); 2) those containing calendrical references; and 3) those with alternating and repetitive iconographic motifs.

Caso cited the bones as evidence supporting his contention that the occupants of Tomb 7 were Mixtec. He based this on the calendrical data recorded on the bones as well as on the presence of many of the place names mentioned in the texts. These place names are similar to the Mixtec sites named in both the Codex Selden and Codex Bodley, two famous Mixtec screen-fold codices.

It was not until 1994 that two scholars, Sharisse D. McCafferty and Geoffrey G. McCafferty, made further inquiries as to the identity of one particular occupant of the tomb. "Skeleton A" is the most complete skeleton of the group. This body was placed in the tomb in a seated position at the end of the western chamber, its gaze directed toward the other occupants. This position of honour implies that the body had a greater social importance than that of its companions. At the time of its discovery, it was identified as that of an adult male of about 55 years of age who suffered from Paget's disease — an ailment that results in a visible thickening of the skull. However, the pelvis found with this body was smaller than is usual for a male, leading to later speculation that the remains might be those of a female.

Since the osteological evidence for this body was less than conclusive, the McCaffertys decided to look for clues to the identity of the individual by focusing on objects found in the context of the tomb. The 34 oddly shaped bones drew their attention immediately, since they recognized the shape as being characteristic of weaving battens. They noted also that the highest concentration of these bones was found immediately behind Skeleton A. Since the functional counterparts of these supposed battens are much larger, the McCaffertys reckoned that the small bones were symbolic references to weaving implements. Adding credence to the identification of the bones as symbolic battens were the clay spindle whorls also found in the context of the tomb. Ear-

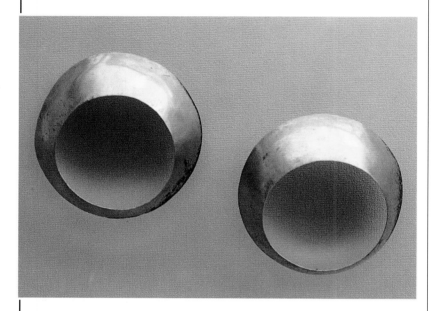

LEFT: The elegant ear plaques (top) and gold collar (below) accompanied the élite occupant of Tomb 7.

RIGHT: Complex B at Monte Albán, of Zapotec construction, was reused by the Mixtecs in later centuries.

lier, Caso had suggested that their presence might suggest that one of the tomb's inhabitants had been a woman.

Much has been written about the symbolic importance of weaving battens in Mesoamerica. Documents from the Conquest Period indicate that the Aztecs used battens not only for weaving but also as gifts given to baby girls as prescriptive symbols of their gender identity. At the same time, battens are carried by female deities in many Aztec and Mixtec codices and in this context are wielded as weapons alongside shields. For this reason the battens not only seem to be associated with weaving and women's roles, but cross traditional gender associations that lie in the male realm of warfare and sacrifice. However, it is well known that high-ranking Aztec males often took on the guise of female deities, wearing their garments and assuming the spiritual powers of those same deities. Could the individual in Tomb 7 at Monte Albán be a male impersonating a female Mixtec goddess? If so, then which deity and how were its attributes significant vis à vis the social function of the impersonator? The McCaffertys' research has opened up an entire line of questions about ancient Mixtec beliefs and gender. As more Mixtec tombs are re-examined in the light of these questions, it seems likely that more clues will be uncovered regarding the identity of Skeleton A. ■

THE TOMB OF PACAL
AT PALENQUE

The success of the ancient Maya kings of Palenque can be attributed to a number of factors. For instance, the city's geographic location at the junction between the lowland and highland regions greatly facilitated trade with other Maya sites. Further, the five rivers flowing in and around the city guaranteed a constant source of water for the city's inhabitants and their crops. It could be argued, however,

The discovery of Pacal's tomb at Palenque in 1952 not only revealed the wealth of Maya kings but showed that the temples found in the Maya area were more than mere testaments to the glory of the ancient kings; they could also have a mortuary function.

that it was the charismatic kings' own abilities in directing their peoples' energies towards advantageous pursuits that assured their distinct position in history. Hieroglyphic texts carved into the walls of the limestone buildings recall important events in the lives of the kings such as war, accessions and births. The dynasts' greatness is also proclaimed by the architectural campaigns that resulted in palaces and temples located throughout the site.

BELOW: A life-sized jade mask with shell and obsidian eyes was placed over the face of the dead ruler.

Of all the buildings at Palenque, by far the most famous is the Temple of the Inscriptions. This was the final resting place of the great ruler Pacal. The nine-tiered pyramid derives its modern name from the continuous text running along the back wall of the temple on top of the structure. Although it appears austerely white in its present state, examinations of the monument made within the last twenty years have shown that this building was originally painted red.

The Temple of the Inscriptions was first examined by the Mexican archaeologist Alberto Ruz Lhuillier in the late 1940s. While examining the limestone slabs that make up the floor of the temple on top of the pyramid, he noted that one of them had a double row of holes with stoppers. When this slab was removed, the top of a stairway was revealed. Access down the stairway was initially impossible owing to the stone and rubble used by the ancient Maya to fill the passage. Ruz and his men would spend the next two years carefully removing the rubble from the corbelled vaulted passageway. As they progressed, the excavators noted that the passageway changed directions at a landing located midway down the pyramid. Altering their course, they came to an abrupt end at the level of the plaza. Further passage was blocked by a huge triangular slab. Here the archaeologists found a cist containing ceramic, jade, shell and pearl offerings. Additionally, they uncovered the bones of a half dozen youths in the same area who had apparently been sacrificed, perhaps in honour of the pyramid's main inhabitant.

On 15 June 1952 the slab was removed and Ruz's men discovered the final resting place of Pacal. The vaulted crypt is located almost directly below the central axis of the pyramid, 27 m (90 ft) below the floor of the temple and roughly 1.5 m (5 ft) below the level of the plaza. It is 9 m (30 ft) in length, 4 m (13 ft) wide and 7 m (23 ft) high. Occupying most of the floorspace is a huge monolithic limestone sarcophagus on supports. Measuring

OPPOSITE: The Temple of the Inscriptions at Palenque was the final resting place of the great seventh-century Maya ruler Pacal.

some 4 m (13 ft) in length, the sarcophagus is carved on all sides with reliefs. Nine over-lifesized stucco figures are attached to the surrounding walls of the crypt and seem to stand guard over the deceased ruler.

Inside the sarcophagus, excavators found an uncharacteristically tall male skeleton laid out in state. The ruler held a jade bead in each of his hands and had an additional bead in his mouth. Two jade figurines were also placed alongside him. His body had been adorned with a heavy jade diadem, earplugs and rings. A belt with masks surrounded his waist and, below that, the ruler wore a jade and tubular-beaded hip-cloth characteristic of Palencano kings. Most striking was the lifesize jade mosaic mask with eyes made of shell and obsidian which had been carefully placed over his face. The abundance of jade artefacts found inside the sarcophagus is not surprising. For the Maya, jade was considered to be a precious stone which represented condensed moisture, including breath. It therefore seems likely that the jade that accompanied the great ruler guaranteed continuation of life after death.

Ruz also found an assortment of grave goods outside the sarcophagus. For instance, beneath it there were clay vessels and plates which archaeologists reasoned were intended to be used by the ruler in his afterlife. In the same area, two lifesize stucco heads were also found. These had been torn from full-length statues located elsewhere on the site. The resemblance between these heads and the mosaic mask worn by the individual was striking and has led scholars to believe that all these representations constitute actual portraits of the ruler. On the surface of the sarcophagus, stone celts had been carefully laid out. Since celts are important emblems of Maya authority it is likely that these allude to the deceased king's power and prowess in battle.

Ruz's discovery in 1952 went beyond the simple revelation of the wealth of Maya kings. Through this work he was able to show, once and for all, that the temples found in the Maya area were more than mere testaments to the glory of the ancient kings. He proved that they could also have a mortuary function. Even so, the riddle of the actual identity of the tomb's inhabitant remained unsolved until a higher level of glyphic decipherment had been achieved by epigraphers in the 1970s. The texts lining the walls of the Temple of the Inscriptions stated that the building

ABOVE: One of the stucco heads found beneath Pacal's sarcophagus. The ruler's sloping forehead, the result of deliberate childhood cranial deformation, was considered to be a mark of élite status and beauty.

RIGHT: On the sarcophagus lid, the ruler Pacal is depicted falling into the gaping skeletal maw of the underworld. The cosmic importance of the event is indicated by the vertical bands of hieroglyphs flanking the ruler. The symbols represent planets, the moon and the sun.

In this reconstruction the sarcophagus lid has been rolled back to expose Pacal's extended body.

had been dedicated in AD 692. Other texts revealed that Pacal was born on 26 March AD 603, and had acceded to the throne at the age of twelve in AD 615. According to the texts the king's death occurred when he was 80 years of age on 31 August AD 683. This information is at variance with the osteological evidence which places the age of the individual in the mid-40s. Since it is also stated that construction of the monument began in AD 675, clearly Pacal himself must have been involved in the planning and construction of his own mortuary monument. However, he died before the temple was completed. It was left to Pacal's son, Chan Bahlum II, to finish the pyramid's façade and the temple on top. Each of the 69 steps which front the pyramid can be associated with a year of rule in the great king's life.

Just as the texts revealed more about Pacal's life, so the iconography of the sarcophagus provided insights into Classic Period Maya beliefs. The imagery carved into the surfaces of Pacal's sarcophagus constitutes a private expression of piety and worthiness directed towards unseen forces by the ageing king. Originally painted red — the colour of blood and life — the monument visually proclaims Pacal's ascendancy into death and his ancestry. Along its sides, portraits of the king's ancestors are depicted emerging from the earth, as if physically and ideologically to validate the complex image carved on the upper surface of the sarcophagus. A segmented border containing celestial symbols surrounds a bisymmetrical composition. Pacal, located centrally, falls into the gaping skeletal maws of the underworld. A mirror sign, fixed into his forehead, indicates that he is depicted at the moment of his rebirth as a divinity. Jutting out from the mirror is a smoking celt, an emblem of God K, a deity known to be associated with lineage and lineage blood.

The ruler's placement in a bowl before a stylized tree is a refer-

ence to his piety. Bowls such as these were associated with the blood sacrifices often offered before trees and before monolithic monuments called "stelae". The tree on the sarcophagus lid represents the "world tree" that stands at the centre of the Maya cosmos and serves as an *axis mundi*. Its branches stretch into the sky while its roots penetrate earth. It is not surprising that Pacal chose to depict himself and his death as a sacrificial offering placed before this tree, for it is believed that such trees provided access to both realms. This imagery, along with the jade accoutrements associated with the ruler's body, would assure Pacal's successful entry into the Maya afterlife. ■

IGBO-UKWU

Discoveries at Igbo-Ukwu, about 40 km southeast of Onitsha, on the fringe of the forest in southeastern Nigeria, began in 1938 when Isaiah Anozie was undertaking the mundane task of digging a cistern and to his astonishment unearthed a number of bronze artefacts. They were bought by the administrative officer in the area and later presented to the Nigerian Museum, where they were recognized as having a style and decoration quite unlike previously known West African bronzes from places like Benin and Ife, and deserving investigation.

Many complex societies emerged in West Africa during the second millennium AD, but little is known of the processes of the late first millennium AD that led to their development. Discoveries of a stunning collection of bronze and copper artefacts, as well as the 1959-60 excavation of the burial chamber of a high-ranking person by Thurstan Shaw at Igbo-Ukwu in southeastern Nigeria, indicate that, by the ninth century AD, wealth was in the hands of a few people who had religious authority and probably also political power.

In 1958, Thurstan Shaw was invited to excavate at Igbo-Ukwu and dug at the compounds of Isaiah Anozie (designated Igbo Isaiah) and Richard Anozie (Igbo Richard) in 1959-60 and at that of Jonah Anozie (Igbo Jonah) four years later. Shaw recalls that:

"Igbo-Ukwu was far and away the most nerve-wracking excavation I have undertaken. This was partly because I very soon realized that I was onto something unique and important .... in the night after the first bronze was discovered [an attempt was made] to steal it from under my bed ... Sometimes one had to make a choice between what was archaeologically desirable and what was physically practicable. One of the hardest things in these circumstances is professional loneliness; you have no one with whom to discuss and share the decisions that have to be taken and the interpretations that have to be made."

During demolition of a goat house and wall in order to clear an area for excavation at Igbo Isaiah, in addition to the 1938 collection, a remarkable cache of richly decorated bronzes was found only 0.5 m below ground. Apart from items like bronze bowls, bosses, bells, chains, ornaments, anklets, wristlets, staff heads, scabbards and an altar stand, there were several pots decorated in a highly ornamental style, as well as large numbers of glass and carnelian beads. The most remarkable item was a 320 mm

(12½ in) high vessel of a leaded bronze (an alloy of copper and tin, with lead, almost certainly locally made) waterpot set on its own stand and enclosed in ropework. It was made by the "lost wax" process, as were most West African bronzes, by substituting molten bronze in the place of a clay-covered wax or latex model, and the way the method was used suggests local invention. It seems that these items comprised a collection which was housed in a repository or small structure — there is evidence of a roof that collapsed — which was abandoned for an unknown reason.

A burial chamber

Extraordinary though the Igbo Isaiah repository collection was, cistern digging led to the discovery of the even more astonishing find of a burial chamber, the floor of which lay 3.5 m (11 ft 6 in) below the surface, at Igbo Richard.

Between 1–2.5 m (3–8 ft) below the ground, beads, two copper wristlets (one associated with extremely decayed bone), and enamel from the teeth of at least five people were discovered. The next half metre produced no finds, but deeper probing exposed first a stylized bronze leopard skull with a copper supporting rod sinking vertically into the ground, then a confused mass of copper, bronze, bone, ivory and iron items, as well as over 100,000 glass and carnelian beads. There were three ivory tusks, but they were too decayed to know whether they had been carved or used as horns. In the middle of this collection was a

Bronze shell from Igbo-Ukwu.

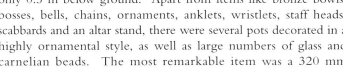

Reconstruction of a ninth-century dignitary's burial chamber at Igbo-Ukwu.

LEFT, ABOVE AND BELOW: Fine examples of intricate Igbo-Ukwu bronzework, including two pennants, one in the form of a ram's head decorated with two grasshoppers, the other of a human head with facial scarification.

circle of spirally twisted copper bosses and a similar one of bosses set in wood 200 mm (8 in) below it, apparently the remains of a stool. A partially preserved skull completely surrounded by beads, and the badly preserved limb bones of a single male individual, lay nearby.

This was clearly the burial chamber of an important person. His tomb had been lined with wooden planks, joined by iron clasps and nails, and the floor was covered with matting. It seems the corpse was placed on the stool in a corner of the chamber. The arms were rested on copper brackets, and a fan holder and fly-whisk were set in his hands. His ceremonial attire included quantities of beads, a beaded head-dress and copper crown, a copper chest plate and wristlets of blue beads set in copper wire. A wooden roof had been erected over the chamber, and the remains of at least five individuals, presumably servants or slaves, were placed above this.

Four radiocarbon dates, including one on wood from the stool in the burial chamber, indicate a ninth century AD age. This was initially thought to be too early for the sophisticated bronze technology and imported glass beads, some of which ultimately came from India, implying far-flung trading connections, but is now considered applicable in the light of growing evidence for pre-Arab trading networks in West Africa.

A titled man

Shaw suggests that the dignitary in the burial chamber was a titled man rather like an Ozo in recent Igbo communities. This title is the highest of a series of graded titles that are earned rather than being hereditary. Traditionally, the burial of an Ozo was a public affair in which the grave goods proclaimed his status in life. The repository of bronze vessels at Igbo Isaiah and the regalia in the burial chamber are considered comparable to the materials kept by an Ozo in a shrine for use in rituals to secure the favour of ancestral spirits and for other duties required by his title, such as settling disputes.

The seeds of the centralization of religious and probably also political and administrative authority, which culminated in the rise of states in West Africa in the 2nd millennium AD, are probably also reflected in the extraordinary Igbo-Ukwu bronzework. This was the work of highly accomplished local craft specialists who, contrary to previous ideas of importation, used local methods and are considered to have developed their own techniques to create what William Fagg has called the "strange rococo, almost Fabergé-like virtuosity" of their craft. The Igbo-Ukwu bronzes in fact contribute the earliest sub-Saharan African evidence for the use of copper alloys in art. The very use of bronze at this time was unusual in comparison with elsewhere in the world, where brass was the most commonly used alloy. Copper alloys are known to have been linked with the insignia of kingship that developed in the Nigerian forest during the 2nd millennium AD. Igbo-Ukwu thus appears to document the beginnings of an indigenous process of increasing social stratification that led to the development of West African states in the 2nd millennium AD. ∎

EARLY PACIFIC ISLANDERS

The cultures of the remote and isolated islands of the Pacific Ocean are very diverse. This diversity is reflected in physical characteristics, language, material culture and social organization. Melanesia, Micronesia and Polynesia are the three main divisions of the region. Although many Pacific societies are small-scale and kinship-based, there are more complex forms of social organization, especially in Polynesia.

The discovery and settlement of the Pacific islands began more than 30,000 years ago in what is now Melanesia and involved impressive feats of voyaging and navigation. Just under 4000 years ago groups of people thought to be the ancestors of the Polynesians rapidly colonized the southwest Pacific as far as Tonga and Samoa. By 1000 years ago Polynesians had settled Easter Island, the Hawaiian Islands and New Zealand.

The peoples of the Pacific treat their dead in a variety of different ways. Large stone or earth tombs are found in several parts of the Pacific. The spectacular ruins of the ceremonial centre of Nan Madol, on Ponape in the Caroline Islands, include the chiefly burial enclosure of Nan Douwas. The structures at Nan Madol are artificial platforms of coral rubble faced with basalt. The outer wall of Nan Douwas is up to 8.5 m (28 ft) high, and has a raised gallery for exposing corpses before burial. Within the enclosure are three massive tombs and an inner enclosure, which contains another massive tomb. The tombs were ransacked in the late nineteenth century by a visiting Englishman who removed an impressive range of grave goods. These included necklaces, bracelets and pendants of shell and other shell artefacts such as fish hooks and adzes.

Tonga also has burial mounds, and these seem to vary according to the status of the person buried. Commoners were buried in simple earth mounds, while chiefs were buried in coral slab chambers in circular earth mounds. Members of the ruling dynasty were buried in large rectangular tombs with stone-faced terraces known as *langi*. Two earth burial mounds have been excavated. Each contained about 100 inhumations, some wrapped in bark cloth, and was presumably the burial place of a single descent group or clan.

For the Maori of New Zealand, like most Polynesians, the ceremonies of death and burial are extremely important. Treatment of the dead was commonly elaborate. A wide range of burial methods is recorded ethnographically and archaeologically. In historic times ceremonies commonly had two parts. First came a mourning ceremony followed by a temporary burial or exposure of the corpse. Then later the bones would be recovered, cleaned and displayed, and finally interred in a secret place.

Wairau Bar is typical of early New Zealand settlement sites in that the burial ground is very close to the living areas. The site was mainly excavated in the 1940s and early 1950s by Jim Eyles and Roger Duff. Evidence of shell middens, ovens, pits and remains of structures was found as well as burials. The oldest burials date to about AD 1150, and the site seems to have been in use for perhaps three hundred years. Some of the burials are extraordinarily rich and elaborate. Most people were buried face down, although a few were buried in a flexed position with knees drawn up. One person was interred in a wooden coffin. There were also some secondary burials where the bodies had either been exposed or previously buried somewhere else and later exhumed. Grave goods accompanied many of the people interred at Wairau Bar. These included necklaces of bone, whale ivory, shark teeth and shell. Pierced moa eggs were placed in some graves; they may have been water containers or perhaps offerings of food. Some individuals were also buried with joints of moa (flightless birds, now extinct). Argillite adzes were also found; some had clearly never been used and were probably valuable ceremonial items - one man was buried with no fewer than fourteen adzes.

Studies of the skeletal remains by the physical anthropologist Philip Houghton have provided a very detailed picture of the Wairau Bar community. The burial ground included both men and women. The soil conditions meant that the bones were quite poorly preserved. The generally more fragile bones of children and infants have not survived at Wairau Bar, except in a couple of

A reconstruction of the cave burial at Lake Hauroko in New Zealand, around 300 years old.

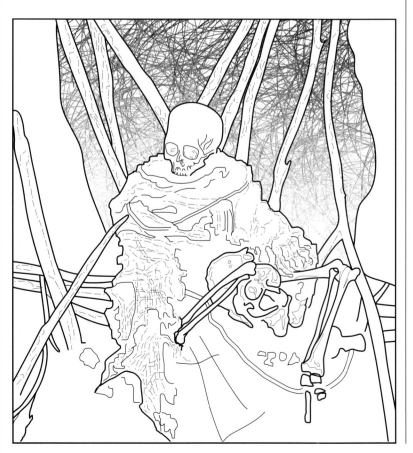

Roy Mata

One of the most startling archaeological discoveries ever made in the Pacific is the collective burial of Roy Mata in the New Hebrides. We owe the knowledge of his name and existence to detailed oral traditions on the island of Efate, which recount the arrival in the New Hebrides of a group of high-ranking men who introduced a new form of matrilineal social organization. Roy Mata was one of them and, when he died, he was buried on the small island of Retoka off the coast of Efate, together with several of his followers who had committed suicide and others who were killed as sacrifices.

In 1967 excavations by the French archaeologist José Garanger provided remarkable documentation for this tradition. He was shown a group of standing stones on Retoka island. He went on to excavate a remarkable series of burials of Roy Mata and his retinue. Roy Mata's grave was marked by two large stone slabs and some marine shells. In the pit beneath, he himself lay on his back, with a man and woman to his left and a single male to his right. A young girl lay across their feet. Between Roy Mata's legs was a secondary burial of a woman, perhaps a wife who had died before him. Surrounding this burial were no fewer than 35 other individuals; most were men and

women buried in pairs, with the woman frequently clasping the man. It seems that the men may have been drugged before burial, while the women were often alive and conscious. The bodies were richly adorned with necklaces and bracelets made of shell and bone. One woman wore 34 shell bracelets; some wore armbands, skirts or loincloths decorated with hundreds of tiny shell beads. Burials of pigs and scattered, possibly cannibalized human bones indicate some of the ritual that must have accompanied this burial.

Radiocarbon dating puts Roy Mata's burial at about AD 1265. This fits well with the oral tradi-

tion that puts the arrival of Roy Mata and his companions sometime before a devastating volcanic eruption in the region, dated to around AD 1400.

Other similar ritual sacrificial burials are known, although they are not usually on this scale. Garanger also excavated three smaller burials in the New Hebrides, on the island of Tongoa, with attendant sacrifices and also dating to around AD 1400.

RIGHT, BELOW AND OVERLEAF: Many burials from the Roy Mata site are richly adorned. Roy Mata is identifiable by the secondary burial between his splayed legs.

cases as traces in the soil. The average age at death was about 28, and nobody was older than the early 40s. The community seems to have been well fed, and there is no evidence of violent death. Most people still had all their teeth, which were in good condition with relatively little wear, suggesting a diet of relatively soft foods. Human remains from later periods, by contrast, usually have very worn teeth, indicating changes in diet, and greater dependence on harsh and gritty foods such as fern root.

A wide range of burial practices were in use throughout the prehistoric period in New Zealand. As time went on, however, there was a trend for burials to be away from settlements, and caves were increasingly used for final disposal of the remains. Often these were secondary burials, but some examples of partly desiccated complete bodies are known. One unusual example comes from a small cave on Mary Island in Lake Hauroko in the South Island. A young woman, in her late twenties, was seated on a bier of stakes, with her knees drawn up to her chest. She had been placed in the entrance to the cave looking out over the lake. She wore a remarkably well preserved cloak of woven flax, which had a dog-skin collar and strips of feathered bird skin inserted into the fabric while it was being made. The woman was buried about 300 years ago. ■

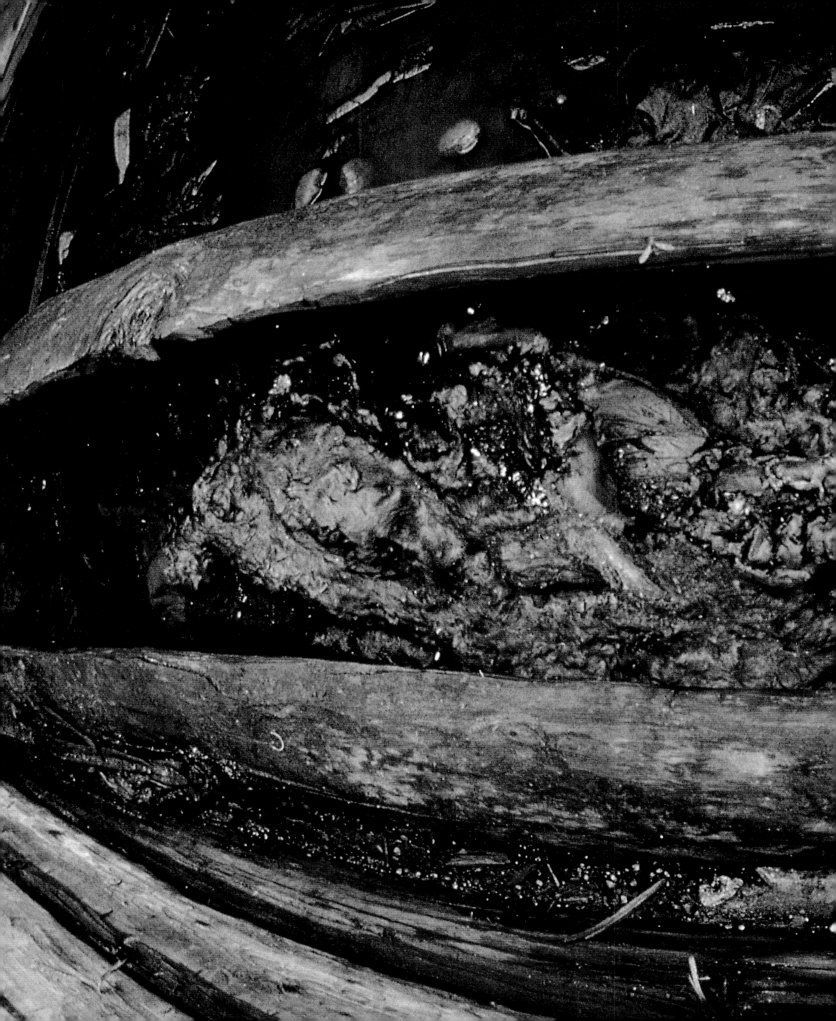

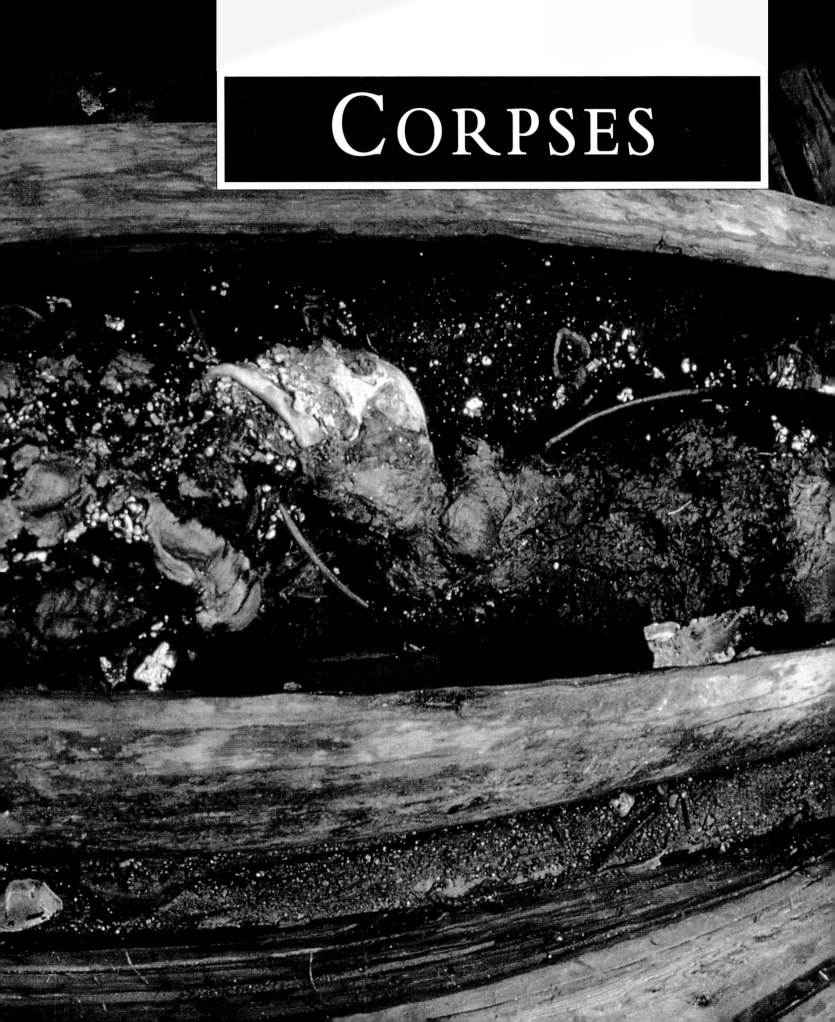

CORPSES

DISCOVERING THE ORIGINS OF NEW WORLD HUMANS

Determining the time and place of the first migrations into the American continent has been controversial ever since scientists began to look seriously at the problem at the turn of the century. Whilst most scholars agree that humans came into the New World from northeast Asia over the Bering Strait area (perhaps by boat, but more likely by foot), there is much less agreement on when this took place, with estimates ranging anywhere between 40,000 to 12,000 years ago.

The anthropologist Robert Williams has studied this problem from a genetic perspective, analyzing blood samples of approximately 5000 American Indians. He found that one particular blood protein fell into three distinct sub-groups and that their genetic "distance" (similarities and dissimilarities) allowed him to postulate three distinct migrations into the New World. The first occurred before 15,000 years ago and was ancestral to all later Central and South American Indians, and to most North American populations; the second, between 14,000 and 12,000 years ago, was ancestral to Athabascan populations, who live in both

Recent advances in genetics have given archaeologists a whole new set of tools for unravelling the complicated history of human migrations throughout the world. One area in which these new techniques have great potential is in understanding the peopling of the New World. Unfortunately, archaeologists have all too few opportunities to study the genetic make-up of past peoples.

Alaska and the American Southwest; the third, about 10,000 to 9000 years ago, was ancestral to modern Inuit and Aleut populations of Alaska and the Far North of Canada.

As techniques have become even more sophisticated, scientists have been able to take advantage of lucky finds of well preserved human remains. A particularly exciting set of finds has been made recently in Florida, and although much of their potential remains untapped, they give archaeologists a tantalizing glimpse of what research in the twenty-first century might look like.

Windover Pond is a peat bog located near the town of Titusville in Florida. In the early 1980s workmen trying to drain the bog made a remarkable discovery, for the peat had preserved the remains of over 160 individuals, covering the full age range from new-born babies to people in their 70s, who had apparently been deliberately placed in the bog as part of a burial rite. These bodies were found with a variety of textiles, clothes, bags and mats, together with well-preserved bone and wooden tools.

The Windover material, which has been in storage for ten years, is now being examined with new scientific tools. Scientists are now in the process of soaking ancient preserved clothing in cold water to remove all the salt. Then they intend to freeze-dry the material and finally cover it with parylene, which will protect the delicate fabric without damaging it. James Adovasio (an archaeologist famous for his researches into the first peopling of the New World) and his colleagues have already discovered that these ancient textiles were woven very tightly, as tightly as modern machine-made garments, in fact. The care with which these garments were woven suggests that this ancient hunting-and-gathering lifestyle was stable, with plenty of time to devote to the creation of finely made fabrics.

The fact that some of these people lived into their 70s also suggests a fairly comfortable existence. Moreover, archaeologists have also found the re-

Excavations at Windover, Florida were made directly into the peat deposits, drained so as to reach materials 2 m below the pond bottom.

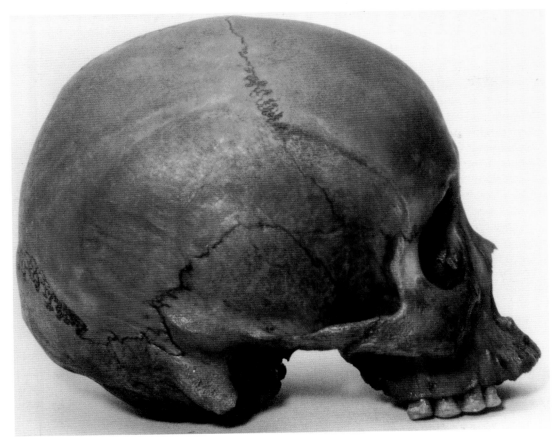
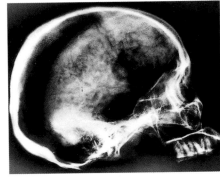
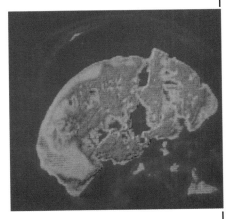

This skull of a young Native American man, almost 8000 years old, found at Windover, has yielded preserved DNA. A lateral X-ray showed material which resembled the brain inside the skull. It proved to be peat surrounding a residual brain. When the skull was placed in a scanner, the brain was found to be largely undamaged.

mains of disabled teenagers who must have required extra attention to keep them alive.

Ninety-one of these bodies have remains of their brains intact. In 1984 Glen Doran, an archaeologist at Florida State University, recovered the remains of a human brain from a skull approximately 7500 years old. The skull, based on tooth wear, belonged to a 27-year-old male.

The potential of these brains for scientific research is being realized at another Florida bog site, Little Salt Spring, located near Charlotte Harbor in the southwest part of the State. The site comprises a freshwater sinkhole about 60 m (200 ft) deep. It was particularly attractive to prehistoric humans during periods when surface water was scarce.

The earliest evidence for use of this locale dates back to approximately 12,000 years ago. On a ledge were found the remains of a giant land tortoise, which had been killed with a sharply pointed wooden stake. The tortoise had then been overturned and the flesh cooked inside its shell. Later Paleoindians, about 9500 years ago, had lived around the edges of the sinkhole, leaving behind the remains of their hearths, bone refuse and pine stakes still found upright in the sediment. The sediments preserved the remains of a wooden non-returning boomerang. As water levels continued to rise during the early Holocene period,

the locale became less attractive to local inhabitants, and occupation temporarily ceased about 9000 years ago.

However, around 8500 years ago water levels began to drop, and 1500 years later Archaic Period peoples were using the locale in great numbers. The archaeological remains of their occupation of Little Salt Spring cover 20,000 sq. m (215,000 sq. ft), and the combination of the hard water and peat created an airless environment perfect for preserving organic materials. Chemical analyses showed that the high level of dissolved solids in the water lends itself to rapid mineralization of organic materials. The water is almost oxygen-free beyond the first few feet, and its temperature is remarkably constant. This also would slow down bacterial growth and thus enhance organic preservation.

During the period 6800 to 5200 years ago, Archaic peoples buried an estimated 1000 individuals in the soft banks of the sinkhole. The cemetery covers approximately 6000 sq. m (65,000 sq. ft). Their bodies were buried extended, on beds of wax myrtle, or with leaf-covered branches placed between their arms and bodies. Besides numerous stone projectile points and other normal archaeological remains, archaeologists, led by Carl Clausen, the State Marine Archaeologist for Florida, found the remains of a wooden tablet, on which was inscribed the profile of a long-necked (or long-billed) bird.

The preservation at Little Salt Spring was in some instances remarkable. For instance, the Swedish scientist Svante Pääbo recovered DNA from fragments of the brain recovered from a 6000-year-old skull found in 1988. His analysis suggests that the Indian was unrelated to the three previously identified aboriginal waves of migration thought to have entered the New World. ■

THE ICEMAN

The world's oldest fully preserved human body was found on 19 September 1991 by German hikers near the Similaun glacier, in the Ötztaler Alps of South Tyrol. The Iceman constitutes the first prehistoric human we have ever found with his everyday clothing and equipment, and presumably going about his normal business; other similarly intact bodies from prehistory have been either carefully buried or sacrificed. He brings us literally face to face with the remote past.

At an altitude of 3,200 metres (10,600 feet) the hikers spotted a human body, its skin yellowish-brown and desiccated. It was four days before the body, and its accompanying objects of leather, grass, flint and wood, were removed by Austrian authorities and taken to Innsbruck University. There were already suspicions that the corpse might be old, but nobody had any idea just how ancient.

The body was handed to the Anatomy department of Innsbruck University for treatment, after which it was placed in a freezer at −6°C (10°F) and 98% humidity. Subsequent investigation determined that the corpse — called Similaun Man, Ötzi or simply the "Iceman" — had lain 92.6 m (302 ft) inside Italy, but most initial research has been carried out in Austria and Germany. However, apart from some body scans and radiocarbon dating, very little has yet been done with the corpse. Considerable work has been carried out on the objects that accompanied him. According to the investigators, he was probably overcome by exhaustion on the mountain — perhaps caught in a fog or a blizzard. After death in a gully, he was covered by enough snow to protect his body from predators but was nevertheless dried out by a warm autumn wind, before becoming encased in ice. Since the body lay in a depression, it was protected by the movement of the glacier above it for 5300 years, until a storm from the Sahara laid a layer of dust on the ice that absorbed sunlight and finally thawed it out.

However, this version of events seems somewhat unsatisfactory: it is hard to understand how the body could be both covered with snow and dried out by wind; and how a glacier could pass over the gully, and entomb the body in ice without disturbing it. In fact, the body was rotated in the opposite direction to the glacier's flow, and it had 20 to 24 metres (65 to 80 feet) of ice above it. The weight alone should have crushed the corpse, even if it remained unaffected by the glacier's flow. A far better explanation for the body's condition is that it was preserved in the same way as the many frozen carcasses of mammoths and other Ice Age animals in Siberia and Alaska. They were preserved by the build-up of ice in the sediments that enveloped the bodies: the ice layers desiccated the soil and dehydrated the carcasses. Unlike freeze-drying, where the original form remains intact, this process shrivels the body. It has been likened to placing a tightly wrapped stew in a freezer — at first it expands and swells its container, but after some months the moisture separates out and forms ice-crystals inside the container. Finally, the stew shrinks and desiccates, surrounded by a network of ice-crystals. If the situation is seen from this perspective, it is probable that the Iceman was preserved in similar conditions to the mammoths (which also often lost their hair in the process), and may not have been in a glacier at all. This process would explain why X-rays of the skull show a severely shrunken brain, a sign of extreme dehydration.

The body is that of a dark-skinned male in his mid- to late 40s, with a cranial capacity of 1500-1560 cc (91½-95 in³). He was only about 1.57 m (5 ft 2 in) tall, and his stature and morphology fit well within the measurement ranges of Late Neolithic populations of Italy and Switzerland. The corpse currently weighs only about 54 kg (120 lb). Preliminary analysis of his DNA confirms his links to Northern Europe — his mitochondrial sequence (a type of DNA passed on by females and inherited solely through one's mother) belongs to the most common group in modern Europeans.

His teeth are very worn, especially the front incisors, suggesting that he ate coarse ground grain, or that he regularly used them as

The late Rainer Henn from Innsbruck's Institute of Forensic Medicine, who collected the Iceman from a mountain in the South Tyrol.

ABOVE: The Iceman's fingernail, showing the location of the three lines indicating episodes of ill-health on its dorsal side.

RIGHT: The Iceman's back, showing its tattoos.

a tool; there are no wisdom teeth, which is typical for the period; and he has a marked gap between his upper front teeth. His facial hair was shaved. When found, he was bald, but hundreds of curly brownish-black human hairs, about 9 cm (3½ in) long, in the vicinity of the body and on the clothing fragments indicate that he had recently had a haircut. His right earlobe has a pit-like and sharp-edged rectangular depression, indicating that he probably once had an ornamental stone fitted there.

A jackhammer used in a crude attempt to dislodge him from the ice severely damaged the left pelvic area. A body scan has shown that the brain, muscle tissues, lungs, heart, liver and digestive organs are in excellent condition, though the lungs are blackened by fire, probably from open fires, and he has hardening of the arteries and blood vessels. His intestines contained the same type of harmless threadworms as are found in those of modern people. His left arm is fractured above the elbow: this almost certainly occurred during his recovery, when he was forced into a coffin. There are traces of chronic frostbite in one little toe. He has eight rib fractures, which were healed or healing when he died.

There are groups of tattoos, mostly short parallel vertical blue lines, half an inch long, on both sides of his lower spine, on his left calf and right ankle, and a blue cross on his inner right knee. These marks may be therapeutic, aimed at relieving old wounds and the osteo-arthritis which X-rays have revealed in his neck, lower back and right hip.

The body's nails had dropped off, but one fingernail was recovered. Its analysis revealed not only that this man undertook manual labour, but also that he underwent periods of reduced nail growth corresponding to episodes of serious illness — four, three and two months before he died. The fact that he was prone to periodic crippling disease may help explain how he fell prey to adverse weather and froze to death. Further indications of sickness come from traces of a fungus, similar to the modern *Aspergillus fumigatus*, which have been found in his lungs: this fungus often attacks those ill with other diseases, and, it is thought, would have left him gasping for breath.

Archaeologists are particularly interested in the items found with him, which constitute a unique "time-capsule" of the stuff of everyday life, much of it being made of organic materials that were preserved by the cold and ice. An astonishing variety of woods, and a range of very sophisticated techniques of work with leather and grasses, can be seen in the collection of 70 objects which add a new dimension to our knowledge of this particular period.

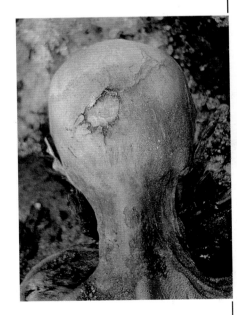

The axe, 60 cm (24 in) in length, has a head of copper; it was bound to the yew handle with leather thongs. As the blade is only 9.5 cm (3¾ in) long and 4 cm (1½ in) wide, it would not have been a very efficient woodcutting tool, though nicks on the blade match marks on the bow.

The bow, of yew wood, is almost 180 cm (6 ft) long. One side is flat, the other rounded. Its odour at room

ABOVE: Back of the Iceman's head.

OVERLEAF: The Iceman on the mountain, emerging from his icy matrix.

temperature suggests it was smeared with blood or fat to keep it pliable. A quiver of deerskin contained 14 arrows, only two of which were ready for use. Their 75-cm (30-in) shafts, made of two pieces, are of dogwood and viburnum wood, and had points of stone or bone fixed to them by pitch. The two finished arrows had double-sided points of flint, and triple feathering whose placement meant the missiles would spin in flight and indicated an advanced ballistic design. The quiver also contained an untreated sinew (possibly for use as a bowstring), a ball of fibrous cord, bone or antler spines tied together with grass, and various objects of flint and bone, together with pitch — it may have constituted some kind of repair kit.

The dagger or knife has a sharp flint blade, only c. 4 cm (1½ in) long, set into an 8-cm (3-in) ash-wood handle. Polish on the blade indicates that it was used to cut grass. A woven grass sheath was also found. What was originally assumed to be a stone-pointed fire-striker was found to be a thick "pencil" of linden wood with a central spine of bone, probably used for retouching and sharpening flint objects. A U-shaped stick of hazel and two cross-boards of larch are thought to be the frame of a backpack which may have contained some animal bones and residues of the skin of chamois and other small animals, found nearby: blood residues from chamois, ibex and deer have been found on some of the implements.

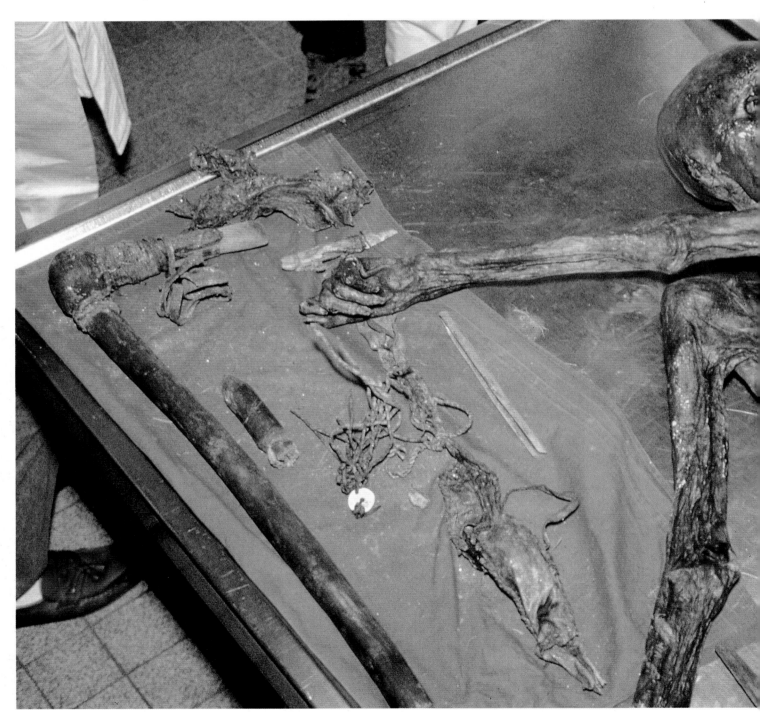

Other finds include a braided grass mat and a coarsely woven net of grass fibres (possibly a carry-bag); a birch bark container with a raw blackthorn (sloe) berry in it, indicating that the Iceman died in the late summer or autumn; a leather pouch; a flat marble disc threaded onto a "necklace" decorated with 20 leather straps; and two lumps of an agaric tree-fungus strung on a knotted leather cord: this kind of fungus grows only on birch trees, and has antibiotic properties, although it is also possible that the lumps were used as tinder, like the pyrites and charcoal also found in the collection. The quantities of moss found with the body were probably used as toilet paper.

What is assumed to be the man's clothing was found in dozens

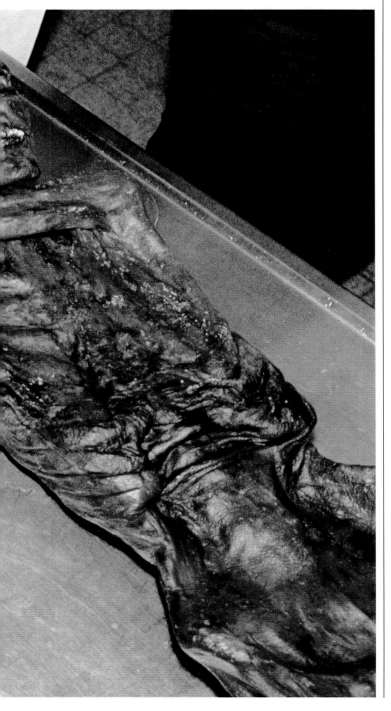

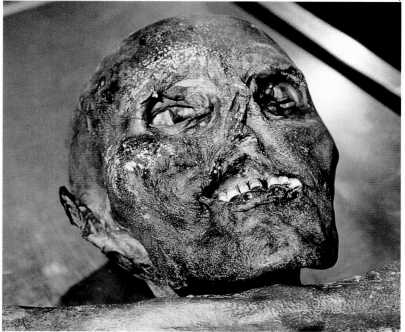

ABOVE: The Iceman's face.

LEFT: The Iceman with his axe and other possessions. Marks on his left temple, as well as the folding of his left ear, suggest that he originally lay on his left side with his head resting on a rough, hard support.

of fragments, and many are still missing — perhaps removed by early visitors to the site. When found, the body wore only its leather leggings and the equivalent of size 5 or 6 leather shoes, well worn — all packed with insulating straw. The shoes had many lace-holes, and showed signs of constant repair. A rain-cloak of woven grass, similar to those worn by shepherds of the region until recent times, is thought to be present, as well as a fur cap with a leather strap. Opinions are still divided as to whether this man wore leather trousers or a kind of fur and leather skirt. The latest attempt to piece together the many patches of deer, chamois and ibex skin has led to the claim that he wore a jacket of tanned hide, with alternating vertical stripes of black and golden fur; the patches are stitched together with very fine thongs, but the garment has also been badly repaired in many places with a grass thread — perhaps by the Iceman himself.

Fifteen radiocarbon dates have been obtained from the body, the artefacts and the grass in the boots: they are all in rough agreement, falling within a range of 3365-2940 BC.

Initial suggestions, based on the altitude of the find, that this man might have been a shepherd have been rejected since he has no shepherding equipment, and the altitude is in fact very high for grazing, even in the milder climate of the period. The traces of animal hair and blood on some tools have thus led to the idea that he was a hunter, albeit attached to a farming village in the valleys. Recently, however, analysis of the outer layers of his hair has shown them to be heavily contaminated with copper and arsenic (a pollutant associated with copper-smelting), so he may have been a coppersmith: extracting the metal from ores like malachite or azurite would have produced much contamination. ∎

PAZYRYK AND THE UKOK PRINCESS

Today a number of lavish burials are known scattered throughout the Altai region. The most famous are the ones in the Ust Ulagan Valley, excavated between 1929 and 1949 (commonly known as "Pazyryk" graves after the local word for burial mound which was applied to this locality), and several excavated on the Ukok Plateau between 1990 and 1995.

The Altai Mountains on the border of Russia with China and Mongolia are a remote and beautiful corner of the globe. These treeless grasslands, several thousand feet above sea level, are nearly deserted today. Between two and three thousand years ago, however, they were the home of horse-riding nomadic pastoralists who lived hard lives and who buried the members of their aristocracy in sumptuous tombs. Through an accident of preservation, the contents of these tombs were literally "frozen in time" and thus give us a glimpse of life in this region during the last millennium BC.

formation about the Iron Age societies of this remote region, and about the peoples with whom they had contact, notably the Chinese and Persians.

The Ust Ulagan tombs were excavated by the Russian archaeologist Sergei I. Rudenko. They consisted of a group of five large and nine small burial mounds, along with other stone structures such as stone circles

They date to the Iron Age, about 400 BC, and contained not only superbly preserved bodies of people and horses but also lavish textile and leather objects. Such finds provide a wealth of in- and alignments of vertical stones. Rudenko discovered them in 1924 and investigated the first large mound in 1929, then turned to the remaining four large mounds between 1947 and 1949.

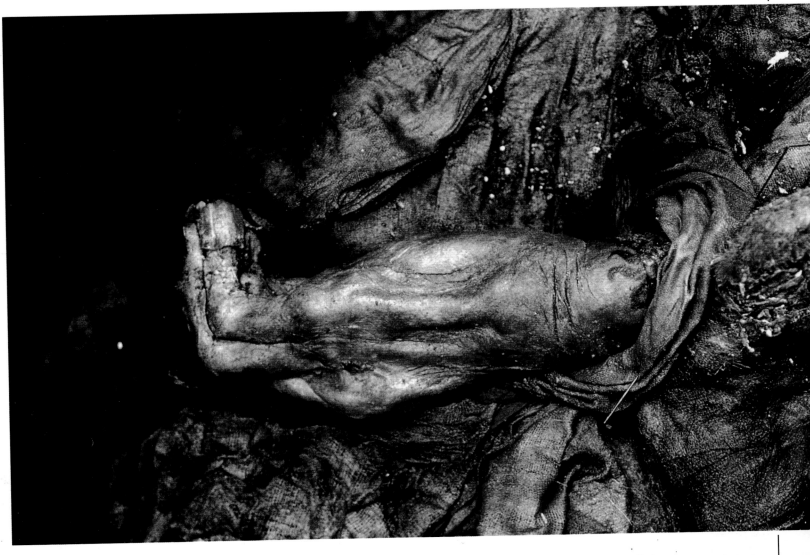

LEFT: Researchers examine the preserved corpse of the Ukok "Princess" in her log coffin after she has been freed from the block of ice.

ABOVE: The forearm of the Ukok "Princess" has a tattoo with a stylized representation of an antlered deer.

OVERLEAF: The body of the "Frozen Princess" in the expedition hut.

The tombs appear on the surface as low earthen mounds covered with stones. The large ones excavated by Rudenko are between 36 and 46 m (118 and 150 ft) in diameter, while the smaller mounds are 13 to 15 m (43 to 49 ft) across. Each large mound conceals a central tomb shaft between 4 and 5 m (13 and rather over 16 ft) deep. Only the soil from the tomb shaft was used for the construction of the mound, which accounts for the low height of the barrows. These shafts were certainly dug during the warm season, for otherwise the ground would have been frozen hard. Within the shafts were timber chambers, consisting of two nested log boxes, in which the primary burial and grave goods could be found. Over these were layers of more logs and stones which filled the shaft up to the base of the mound. The smaller mounds have smaller and lower timber chambers, which

in some cases were too small to accommodate all the grave goods inside.

Shortly after the Ust Ulagan tombs were built during the Altai summer, the warm air that remained in the chambers after their construction rose. The water vapour in this air condensed on the stones in the grave fill and in the mound. This condensation trickled back down into the grave. More moisture from the mountain mists also seeped through the mound and the shaft's fill into the chamber. All this wetness saturated the corpses and the accompanying grave goods and then froze solid during the icy Siberian winter that followed. The mound above then insulated the frozen tomb and kept it from thawing, and thus the Ust Ulagan burials remained refrigerated in ice for over two thousand years. The only disturbance came from ancient grave-robbers, who dug into each of the mounds and robbed them of many of the objects they contained. What they left behind was so extraordinary that we can only speculate about the original richness of these tombs.

Barrow 2 was the least disturbed by the robbers (probably because it was very solidly frozen) and contained the most spectacular finds. The burial chamber was lined with felt wall-hangings. Within it the embalmed bodies of a man and a woman had been

placed in a coffin made from a hollowed-out larch trunk, on which were cut-out leather silhouettes of deer. On the man's body were remarkable tattoos covering the arms and part of a leg. These tattoos depicted imaginary and real animals, including griffins, rams, birds, snakes and deer. The coffin also contained a woollen rug which had been wrapped around the bodies, along with items of clothing made from linen. Elsewhere in the burial chamber were more textiles and clothing, leather objects, wooden furniture, gold and silver ornaments, and mirrors.

The other barrows were looted more severely, which caused decomposition of many of the objects, but what remained indicates a similar level of richness. In Barrow 5, as in Barrow 2, a man and a woman were interred in a hollow-log coffin, and the corpse of the woman wore a wooden headdress. The walls were hung with felt which had appliqués of lion-like figures and birds. The unusual aspect of Barrow 5 was that the coffin had been wedged under a group of timbers which protruded through the wall of the burial chamber, clearly in a deliberate effort to make sure the lid of the coffin stayed closed in perpetuity.

The head of the Ukok "Princess", as reconstructed by the anthropologist Tatyana Baluyeva.

During their looting of the Ust Ulagan barrows, the robbers generally ignored the numerous horse burials, between seven and fourteen per tomb, which were off to one side from the main burial chambers. For this we can be grateful, since some of the more remarkable finds are associated with the horses. The horses' bodies were preserved in some cases, most notably in Barrow 5, along with extraordinary furnishings: bridles, saddles and cloth horse-coats. Among the horses was a large four-wheeled wagon with a felt canopy ornamented with appliquéd figures of swans.

The Ust Ulagan burials, while spectacular, had nonetheless been severely damaged by the looting and by the relatively crude excavation methods employed by the archaeologists. For many years no archaeologists returned to the Altai to seek new burials, possibly unlooted ones. In the summer of 1990, however, the Russian archaeologist Natalya Polosmak renewed the search for Iron Age tombs at Ukok, high in the Altai steppes on the Chinese border. That year she found the burial, unfortunately looted, of a 40-year-old man and a 16-year-old girl with weaponry and ten horses. Three summers later, in July 1993, Polosmak discovered another frozen tomb at Ukok, that of the now-famous "Frozen Princess". The barrow was excavated carefully to reveal an unlooted frozen tomb with the tattooed body of a woman, about 25 years of age, in a log coffin, with textiles and leather items, and wooden salvers bearing cuts of mutton and horsemeat. She wore an elaborate, tall wooden headdress. Just outside the burial chamber were six horses, each killed with a

blow to the head, with patches of their chestnut-brown manes and their felt saddle-covers preserved in extraordinary detail.

Another 2500-year old frozen tomb, this time of a man, was found on the Ukok Plateau in the summer of 1995. The new mummy, a man nicknamed "The Warrior" or "The Horseman", was found in the same area as the "Princess" at an altitude of 2200 m (7220 ft). Like the "Princess" he had been buried in a wooden coffin in a log-lined chamber dug into the permafrost which preserved the remains under more than 2 metres (7 feet) of ice. Aged about 25 to 30, he seems to have been killed in battle with an enemy or an animal, judging by the wound in his stomach. His face and hands did not survive well, but the rest of his skin and musculature and his two long braids are in good condition, as is the spectacular large tattoo of a deer on his right shoulder. He was wearing a cap of thick wool, high leather boots, and a coat of marmot- and sheepskin in exceptionally good, "almost new" condition. Buried alongside his horse, he was accompanied by a bow and arrows, an axe and a knife. The horse wore a harness richly decorated with figures of griffins and animals carved in wood and covered with gold-foil.

Like the "Princess" before him, the man was transported to Moscow's Biological Structures Research Institute — where

The "Princess" in Moscow, being treated in a tank of chemicals, such as formaldehyde and alcohol, to kill microbes.

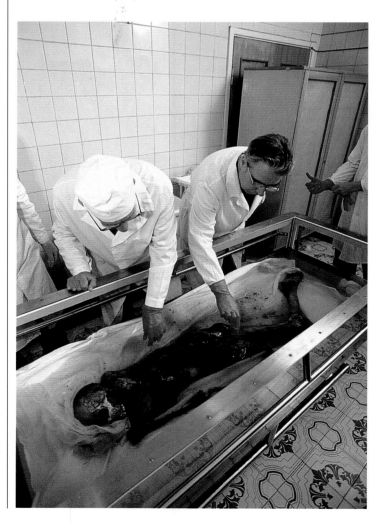

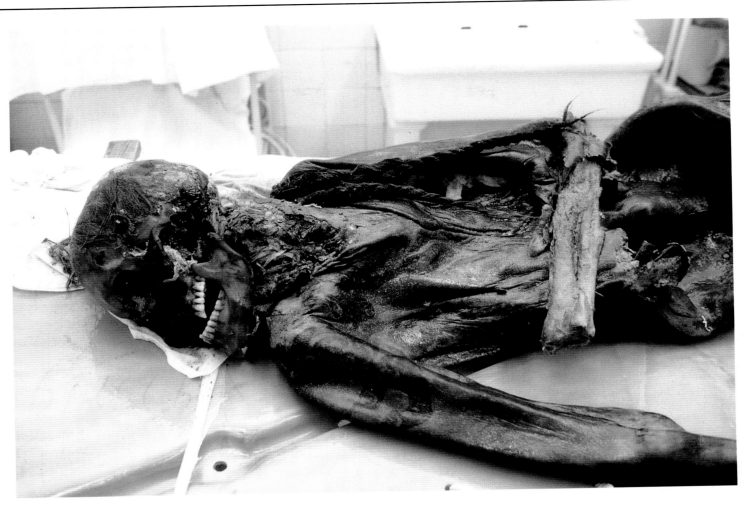

ABOVE AND RIGHT: The body of the "Warrior" or "Horseman". Note the elaborate tattoo of a deer on his right shoulder. His braided red hair is remarkably well preserved.

Lenin and other Communist leaders were turned into mummies. Thanks to the speed of this transfer (in contrast to the long delays that beset the Princess), the treatment was relatively straightforward, involving the immersion of the body in a secret chemical cocktail in a thick glass tank. Both bodies had had their internal organs removed, and had been embalmed by a method that scientists do not yet fully understand. The modern Russian embalmers hope the two mummies will attract worldwide attention ... and new clients for their services.

The people who interred their dead in tombs like the ones at Ust Ulagan and Ukok were nomadic horse-riding, sheep-herding folk, having many traits in common with Central Asian nomads today. They also had much in common with the Scythians, who lived far to the west in the steppes north of the Black Sea and who also buried their élite in rich tombs and featured animals prominently in their art. More importantly, the finds in the frozen tombs, particularly the textiles, show that these people had contact with Persia and China at this time, based on similarities in patterns and the use of materials such as silk. The use of modern scientific techniques such as DNA analysis in the study of the Ukok tombs will be able to tell us much more about their lives.

The artefacts from Pazyryk can now be seen in the Hermitage Museum in St Petersburg, while some of the finds from Ukok are on display in Moscow. In 1995 the government of the Autonomous Altai Republic, upset that the spectacular finds were being taken off to institutes in Russia for conservation and display, passed a law prohibiting further excavation of these tombs. ■

LOST CAUCASOIDS OF THE TARIM BASIN

This evidence consists of scores of desiccated human bodies dating from about 4000 to 2000 years ago. What has excited archaeologists most about these mummies is that almost all have clear Caucasoid facial features including long noses, deep-set eyes and blond or brown hair. A few Caucasoid mummies had already been discovered early this century, but most of the finds have been made since the late 1970s by Chinese and Uyghur archaeologists. Over 100 mummies are now known from at least a dozen sites around the edges of the Tarim Basin, in addition to thousands of skeletons with reportedly Caucasoid features.

The mummies are extremely well preserved, many with intact hair, internal organs and clothing. One man from Zaghunluq,

The Tarim Basin lies at the very heart of the Eurasian continent. Before the West European maritime empires altered the structure of world trade in the sixteenth century, the Basin was the focus of a wide variety of ethnic and economic exchanges. Because of its remoteness and harsh desert climate, the history of the region remains poorly understood. In recent years, however, an unusual and dramatic type of archaeological evidence has begun to revive interest in what is now China's westernmost Xinjiang Province.

near Qarqan, and thought to date to about 1000 BC, still has a sun-ray design painted on his left temple, a symbol that has been linked with Mithras, the solar deity of the ancient Iranians. Another man from Subeshi at Toyuq, and dating from some five centuries later, bears the scars of a primitive surgical procedure, an incision on his neck

sewn up with horsehair sutures. A woman from this same site wore a 60 cm (2 ft) high black, brimmed conical hat identical to the witch's headgear of European folklore. The "Beauty of Loulan" is the name given to a female mummy dated to about 1800 BC. Found near the Chinese nuclear weapons testing ground at Lop Nur, this woman has become a symbol of resurgent Uyghur nationalism in Xinjiang.

One of the most striking features of the Tarim mummies is their clothing which includes boots, trousers, stockings, coats and hats made of leather, felt and wool. This clothing shows strong links with that of Indo-European peoples who lived far to the west. Analysis of a 3200-year-old fragment of twill weave wool with a blue, white and brown plaid design from Qizilchoqa, near Hami, has shown it to be both stylistically and technically almost identical to textiles known from Western Europe in the same period. A convincing explanation for this similarity has yet to be found.

The bodies from Zaghunluq and Loulan had had a yellow substance rubbed onto them before burial. This as yet unidentified material appears to have had a preservative effect on the skin. Most of the Tarim mummies, however, were not subjected to any sort of deliberate mummification process. Their bodies were naturally preserved in the extremely dry and saline soil of the region. Since the average January temperature in the Tarim Basin is -7° C (20° F), it is probable that corpses buried in the winter would have been particularly slow to decompose.

One important task that the international project currently studying the mummies has set itself is to look at the genetic characteristics of the corpses. New techniques mean that very small samples of ancient DNA can be amplified and analyzed with relative ease. Preliminary results from samples taken from the Tarim mummies support links with the European populations they resemble facially. Other work is being conducted on the genetic make-up of the modern inhabitants of the Tarim Basin in an attempt to see to what extent the genes of the Caucasoid mummies

3000-year-old desiccated corpse with Caucasoid facial features found in the Tarim Basin, Central Asia.

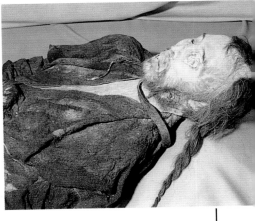

From the 1890s a series of ancient manuscripts was discovered in the desert oases of the Tarim Basin. Though written in the Brahmi script of north India, these texts were in a previously unknown language. This language was soon found to belong to the Indo-European family and was given the name "Tocharian" after a Central Asian people known from classical authors as the "Tócharoi" or "Tochari". Within the Indo-European family, Tocharian is closer to the western Celtic, Italic, Germanic and Greek languages than to the Slavic or Indo-Iranian branches. It was once thought that the Tocharians had migrated to Central Asia from Western Europe, but it is now more common to see Tocharian as an ancient and independent branch of Indo-European. Debate still continues, however, over the origins and identity of the Tocharians.

Can the Caucasoid mummies of the Tarim Basin be linked with the Tocharians? This is a possibility now being seriously considered by scholars of the region, but any such equation is by no means problem-free. The major difficulty is one of chronology: the Tocharian texts date roughly from between AD 500 and 700, more than 2000 years after the earliest mummies. At best, therefore, the mummies may have spoken an ancestral form of Tocharian. A satisfactory answer to the Tocharian problem will necessitate a better understanding of the origins of the Indo-European language family as a whole, and here lies perhaps the most exciting potential contribution of the Tarim mummies. ■

may have been preserved by the local Uyghurs and Chinese.

The discovery of the Tarim mummies has excited a great deal of recent interest all round the world with many newspaper articles expressing surprise that "Europeans" should be found in ancient "China". To some extent this surprise derives from the widespread contemporary assumption that the ethnic and political make-up of the world was the same in Antiquity as it is today. One of the great strengths of archaeology is that it can often question such ill-founded assumptions, but it is extremely rare for us to have the range and quality of evidence relating to prehistoric ethnicity that has come from the Tarim Basin. The popular appeal of the Tarim mummies no doubt lies in the shared human fascination in seeing such phenomenally preserved bodies from so long ago. But for the archaeologist the mummies are equally interesting for the light they may be able to throw on what was hitherto a somewhat obscure problem in Indo-European linguistics — the so-called Tocharian problem.

HERCULANEUM AND POMPEII

One of the most famous individuals to be caught up by the eruption of Vesuvius was the Elder Pliny, best known for his work the *Natural History*, but who was at the time commander of the Roman fleet at Misenum at the mouth of the Bay. His nephew, the Younger Pliny, wrote a description of the events in a letter to Cornelius Tacitus. His uncle had gone to assist with the evacuation and ended up at the house of his friend Pomponius:

The eruption of the volcano Vesuvius on 24 August AD 79 destroyed two prospering towns on the edge of the Bay of Naples, in southern Italy. Pompeii was to be covered with a deep layer of volcanic ash, whereas Herculaneum was overwhelmed by hot mud. Those people and animals caught by the disaster seem to have perished, many with their possessions intact.

"By this time the courtyard giving access to his room was full of ashes mixed with pumice-stones, so that its level had risen, and if he had stayed in the room any longer he would never have got out. He was wakened, came out, and joined Pomponius ... and they debated whether to stay indoors or take their chance in the open, for the buildings were now shaking with violent shocks ... Outside ... there was the danger of falling pumice-stones, even though these were light and porous ... As a protection against falling objects they put pillows on their heads tied down with cloths ... My uncle decided to go down to the shore and investigate the possibility of any escape by sea ... Then the flames and smell of sulphur which gave warning of the approaching fire drove the others to take flight and roused him to stand up. He stood leaning on two slaves and then suddenly collapsed, I imagine because the dense fumes choked his breathing by blocking his windpipe which was constitutionally weak and narrow and often inflamed."

(Translated by Betty Radice)

Although Pliny's body was discovered, many do not seem to have escaped the twin dangers of collapsing buildings and the sulphur fumes. Stories soon started to circulate about the sudden destruction. Just over a century after the eruption the Roman senator Cassius Dio recorded the story that the assemblies of both Herculaneum and Pompeii had been in session at the moment that the destruction fell.

During excavations in the last couple of centuries, victims of the eruption have been discovered. It was Giuseppe Fiorelli who, as director of excavations at Pompeii from 1860 to 1875, devised a way of obtaining a cast of the bodies as they were found. At Pompeii when the bodies decomposed, a space filled with the skeletal remains was left in the compacted ash. Fiorelli realized that if the voids were filled with plaster, then an impression of the body would be found — a method which can be compared to the creation of bronze statues by the "lost wax" technique. The detail is such that individual features of

LEFT: View of Herculaneum.

OPPOSITE: The House of the Trellis at Herculaneum, where hot mud carbonized the wooden trellis-work of the upper storey.

clothing and build can be recognized. Indeed, the technique was extended to other organic materials such as furniture, wooden doors and even food.

One of the bodies found in the excavations of the so-called "Skeleton Alley" was of a girl prone on the ground. She had pulled her tunic up over her face, almost certainly to try and breathe in the face of the fumes; but it was to no avail, and she suffocated. Alongside her was a young girl wearing expensive sandals, and a large man, perhaps their servant. At the house of Vesonius Primus in the northwestern part of Pompeii the excavators came across the contorted remains of a watchdog, still wearing his bronze-studded collar; in the panic of evacuation nobody had thought to unchain him. The remains of animals other than guard dogs are rarely found during the excavations at Pompei. Almost certainly any horses or mules were used during the mass escape: evidence for this includes the wagon of amphoras being delivered to the House of Menander, where the draught animals had been unharnessed.

It has been estimated that as many as 2000 may have died at Pompeii, perhaps as much as one tenth of the population. One reason for the large number of casualties was that the gates and narrow streets restricted the movement of people. A group found by the Porta Ercolano seems to have consisted of a mother and baby, with two young girls still clinging to her dress. Another group of Pompeians was found by the Porta di Nuceria. One of them, apparently a beggar, was found with a sack in which he had placed offerings; on his feet were high-quality sandals which may have been supplied through the generosity of the community. Some of the inhabitants would have stayed indoors waiting for the crowds to diminish, and others seem to have been trapped. This appears to have been the case with a man found in the House of

RIGHT: Plaster casts at Pompeii reveal the dress and physical features of the dead.

BELOW: Aerial view of Herculaneum showing a main street on the left, and at the top the remains of the palaestra and baths.

the Vestals who apparently survived the initial disaster. He and his guard dog seem to have been unable to escape, the man dying of starvation; his remains then appear to have been gnawed by the dog until it too died.

At the House of Menander in the southern part of the town more remains were found. The steward of the house, Eros by name, was found stretched out on his bed; clearly he had not wished to desert his post. He was surrounded by his belongings including his purse containing some ninety coins. Elsewhere in the house a group of bodies was found huddled at the foot of the stairs. As these people seem to have been carrying a lantern at the time of their death, it is possible that they were trying to salvage belongings from the villa when they were overcome by the fumes and suffocated.

At one of the suburban houses, the villa of Diomedes, a large group of bodies was found in the cellar. Some of the adult women still wore gold bracelets and were presumably members of the family who owned the house. The others may well have been household slaves or others associated with the family. The

This guard dog at Pompeii died still chained to the wall.

group seem to have been looking for an escape route as another figure, often identified as the head of the household, was found with a silvered key lying near a door. Another body lay beside his. Clearly they had been trying to take some of the most valuable items with them.

At the Temple of Isis the priests were sitting down to a meal of eggs and fish at the time of the eruption. The meal was abandoned and they systematically collected up the sacred objects belonging to the goddess, placing them in a sack. In the Triangular Forum some members of the group were crushed by the collapse of one of the porticoes, and some of the gold plate was lost. The remainder sheltered in a house where they were trapped by the ash; the last found a hatchet and managed to break his way through a series of partitions, only to be foiled by the ash which had built up in the street and stopped his escape.

Some of the residents did manage to leave the city. Most of the gladiators seem to have got away from their barracks; all except two unfortunates who were found still manacled in their cells where they must have died an agonizing death.

At Herculaneum the hot mud carbonized any organic remains, and it has not been possible to recover remains of the inhabitants in quite the same way; indeed at one time it was believed that most people had escaped. However, recent excavations by the coastline have shown that many people were drawn to the shore where they were probably hoping to find some escape; some 150 bodies have been found in this area of the excavations. The skeleton of a 25-year-old woman was found to have been seven months pregnant; traces of her blond hair were still attached to the skull. Groups of people were found packed at the back of the ten boat sheds which were tucked into the town wall; one chamber contained seven adults, four children and a baby. Nearby was the upturned hull of a boat — perhaps carried there by the force of the mud from a nearby shipyard — and the skeleton of a short man, 45 years old. Elsewhere in the town the charred remains of a baby were found still lying in the wooden cradle where it had been abandoned. As the study of the skeletal remains continues, it should be possible to gain valuable information about a wide cross-section of the population of Herculaneum. ∎

At Pompeii people found themselves trapped and unable to escape.

INKA MOUNTAIN SACRIFICES

Dubbed the "Ampato Maiden", she was discovered in a stone-lined pit near the top of the mountain called Ampato by the American anthropologist and mountaineer Johan Reinhard. Nearly perfectly preserved in every detail, she was the closest thing to a living Inka that scientists could hope to meet. But she was not the first such mountain-top sacrifice discovered, nor is it likely she will be the last. Archaeologists now realize that the Inka made human sacrifices to deities on many sacred, snow-capped peaks in the Andes of South America.

In 1954, about forty years before Reinhard's discovery, the frozen remains of an Inka boy were found near the summit of Cerro el Plomo in Chile. He was wearing a tunic made of llama wool, and his face had been painted red with yellow stripes. Buried with him, in the stone-lined crypt, were a silver figurine of a human, dressed in elaborate clothing and wearing a feather headdress, and a small gold figurine of a llama. Sacrificed to the mountain deity some 500 years earlier, he was so well preserved that he looked as if he

In the autumn of 1995, headlines splashed around the world: the frozen remains of an Inka maiden had been found near the summit of a mountain in the high Andes of southern Peru. She had been left as an offering to the mountain gods some 500 years ago.

had just lain down for a nap.

Ten years later, in 1964, the mountaineer Erich Grogh located another frozen burial near the summit of El Toro in northwest Argentina. The remains were those of a young man, perhaps twenty years old, who was wearing only a sort of breech-cloth. Like the boy in Chile, he had been placed in a stone-lined pit and left to freeze to death. Perhaps his lack of clothing was deliberate, intended to hasten the freezing process. It seems most likely that he was drugged, and little aware of his surroundings at the end.

The Inka were mountain people. Their capital at Cuzco was located at 3350 m (11,000 ft) above sea level in the Andes, in what is today Peru. The Inka conquered a vast empire, which

ABOVE: Members of the 1964 expedition to Argentina's Cerro del Toro, with the mummy they found there at 6300 m (20,650 ft).

RIGHT: The mummy bundle found in 1985 on Aconcagua, Argentina, at 5300 m (17,400 ft).

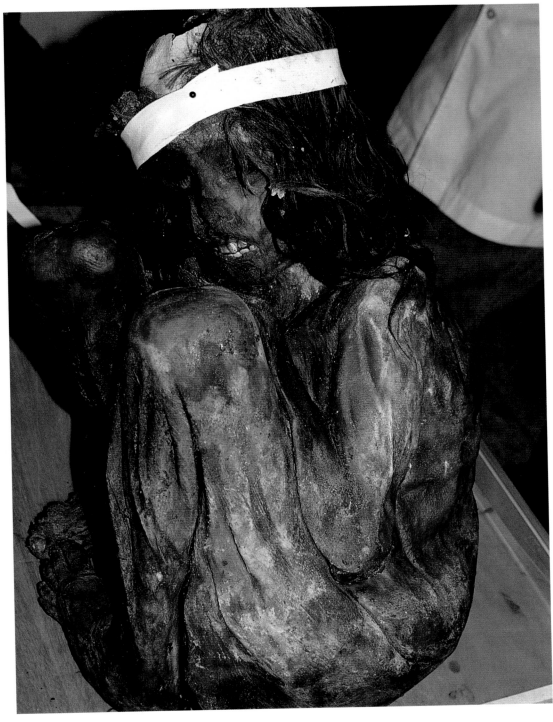

lations, the Inka also worshipped natural features: springs, interesting rock formations, and, perhaps most importantly, mountains. Snow-capped peaks especially had particular meaning for the Inka, and the most revered of them were called "apu". Such mountains were said to be inhabited by mountain deities, and offerings were required on special occasions, or whenever necessary to appease the anger of the mountain gods. On the summits of many mountains the Inka built small shrines or ceremonial centres.

It is no surprise that the Inka made offerings to these important sacred places. But what is remarkable is that many of these offerings were placed at elevations well in excess of 6000 m (20,000 ft) above sea-level, in areas of permanent snow cover, at elevations that would challenge the most skilled of modern mountaineers. How did they develop the technology and mountaineering abilities to scale such peaks? In part, the Inka may have been aided by more than ten thousand years of adaptation to the mountain environment by their ancestors. Not only do native Andean people have exceptionally large lung capacities in order to cope with decreased oxygen at high altitude, but they also have more efficient circulatory systems, keeping their hands and feet warm at all times.

they called Tawantinsuyu (Land of the Four Quarters), stretching through modern Ecuador, Peru, Bolivia, Chile and northwest Argentina. This impressive empire lasted only about a century, however, from roughly 1450 until 1532 when the Inka were conquered by the Spanish. The Inka were efficient rulers who incorporated conquered provinces into a single empire-wide political and economic structure.

In their conquests the Inka made special note of sacred places in their new territories, and instructed their new subjects in aspects of Inka religion. In addition to their rich pantheon of gods, including the sun, the moon, and various planets, stars and constel-

Human sacrifices were not common among the Inka. Normally sacrifices were made of such things as *kumpi*, a fine cloth woven from vicuña wool, or crushed *Spondylus* shells from the warm waters off Ecuador. Animals were sometimes sacrificed, especially pure white llamas. Only rarely were humans — usually children — sacrificed at particular shrines or during special events. But the sacred mountain deities were different. They required human offerings: the sacrifices of adolescent or young adult Inka, both male and female.

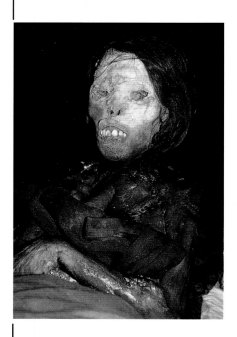

In the last few years, the anthropologist Reinhard has made a number of discoveries of Inka mountain-top sacrifices. Near the summit of Pichu Pichu in southern Peru he found the frozen body of a young Inka woman, eighteen years old. Like the young man in Argentina she wore no clothing, but, unlike him, appeared to have been killed by a blow to the head before being left in her stone-lined tomb. Other Inka sacrificial victims were strangled or smothered before being left as offerings to the mountain deities.

It is important to note that these bodies, although usually referred to as mummies, were not actually mummified or embalmed by the Inka. Rather, they became solidly frozen, and partially dehydrated from the cold, dry mountain air at these extremely high altitudes. Preservation of the remains after discovery requires that they be

ABOVE AND RIGHT: Scans reveal that this Ampato maiden died from a sharp blow to the skull, probably while kneeling.

BELOW: With the sacrificial burial of this 8-year-old girl on Ampato was pair of tiny sandals made of plant fibres and Alpaca straps.

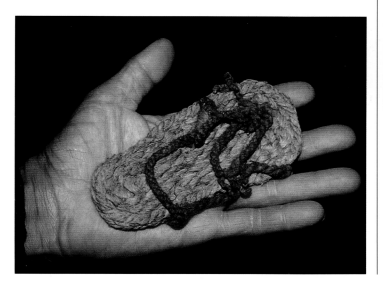

maintained at freezing temperatures and low humidity. The frozen remains of these Inka are so well preserved that it has been possible to determine the blood types of the victims. Indeed, the boy from Chile was found to carry a virus that causes warts — the first evidence that scientists had that viruses existed in the New World prior to the Spanish Conquest.

The Inka preoccupation with mountains can also be seen in the location of their most famous site, Machu Picchu, the private

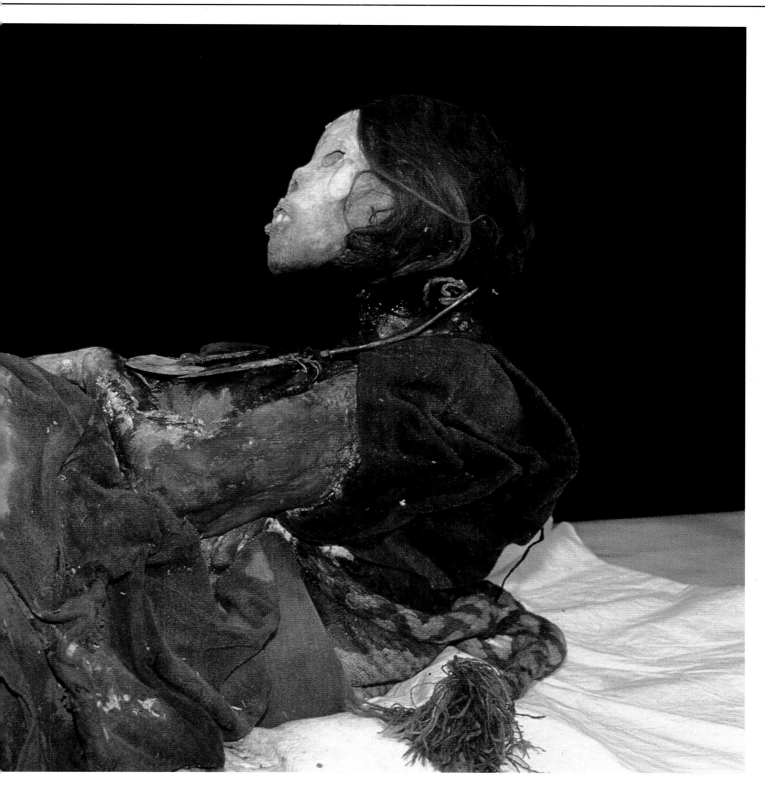

royal estate of the first great Inka emperor, Pachacuti. Machu Picchu's location is vividly depicted in nearly every photograph taken of it. The site lies on a ridge between two mountains, the larger Machu Picchu behind, and the uniquely pointed Huayna Picchu in front of the site. Less obvious is the site's location with respect to three sacred snow-capped peaks in the surrounding Andes. To the south of Machu Picchu is Salcantay, and the site is actually located on a distant spur of that mountain. To the east and west of the site lie Veronica and Pumasillo respectively. The sun rises and sets directly over these mountains on the days of important religious festivals.

The Inka were first and foremost a people of the mountains. They lived and grew crops — maize and potatoes — at high altitudes in the Andes. They worshipped hills and mountains, and especially snow-capped peaks. These *apus* demanded the greatest sacrifices from the Inka — offerings of young women and men. ∎

BOG BODIES OF BRITAIN AND DENMARK

On 13 May 1983 a round, peat-covered object was discovered by workers cutting peat on the edge of Lindow Moss, an ancient peat bog overlooking Wilmslow in Cheshire, in northwestern England. The workers, Andy Mould and Stephen Dooley, were on the lookout for objects that might block the peat-extracting machinery. This soft and pliable find looked like a burst football, and they jokingly called it a Dinosaur's Egg. They discovered their mistake when, after washing the object, a severed head with tissue and hair still attached emerged from its peat wrapping.

The discovery prompted a local man to confess to the murder of his wife, who had mysteriously vanished 23 years previously.

The discovery of numerous bodies preserved by the tannic acid in the bogs of northern Europe has caused sensation after sensation. They attest to the brutal ritual demands of Iron Age beliefs, described in the accounts of Classical authors such as Tacitus who wrote of human sacrifice among Celtic and German tribes.

He was convicted, but the skull was subsequently dated by radiocarbon to about 1740 years before, proving that this was no recent murder victim returning to wreak revenge, but rather one of a long series of Iron Age bodies given up after nearly 2000 years by the bog whose remarkable qualities had preserved them. A year later, on 1 August 1984, the discoverer of Lindow Woman pulled what he took to be a stick from another piece of peat-cutting machinery and threw it at his colleague. This "stick" turned out to have a

The remarkable preservative powers of the bogs have kept the long hair of this girl from the Swabian bog in place, tied in the so-called "Swabian knot", for over 2000 years.

Grauballe Man, found in 1952, had had his throat cut from ear to ear.

human foot at one end, and was the leg of the person who became known as Lindow Man.

Nearly 200 individual bog bodies have been reported from the British Isles over the years, but Lindow Man is the best known and the best preserved. More than 30 years ago Peter Glob reported over 150 such finds, including men, women and children, from the bogs of Denmark in his classic study *The Bog People*, in which he discussed two of the most famous examples, Tollund Man and Grauballe Man.

Bog bodies are priceless treasures for archaeologists who are more accustomed to extracting what meagre information they can from the dry bones of the long deceased. Thanks to the preservative powers of the bog waters, many details can be obtained about the health, lives and deaths of these Iron Age bodies. We know that Lindow Man was well-built, in his twenties, 1.68 m (5 ft 6 in) tall, and weighed about 60 kg (132 lb). Before his death he was generally in good health, except for suffering from worms and a touch of rheumatism, although he would scarcely have been aware of either of these conditions.

Like many of his Danish counterparts, Lindow Man met a violent, gruesome death. When the face of the Tollund Man first emerged from the peat in 1950, those present at the scene were deceived by his tranquil expression. When the peat around his neck was removed, the noose around his neck was testimony to his brutal demise. Lindow Man had been struck from behind on the head with an axe, struck in the back with such force that one of his ribs was broken, and then, unconscious but still alive, he was garrotted with a cord tied around his neck. The dead man then had his throat slit, before his body was dropped face down into a pool in the bog. Other bog bodies show similar ends. One of the earliest recorded discoveries, made in 1773, the body of a man from Ravensholt, on the island of Fyn in Denmark, had his hands tied behind his back before having his throat cut. His body was then dropped in the bog, covered by branches as if to weigh him down. The body of a woman, originally mistakenly identified as Gunhild, the scheming wife of Erik Bloodaxe, had been pinned in the bog with stakes before being covered with branches.

Although some of the bodies were clothed, notably the women

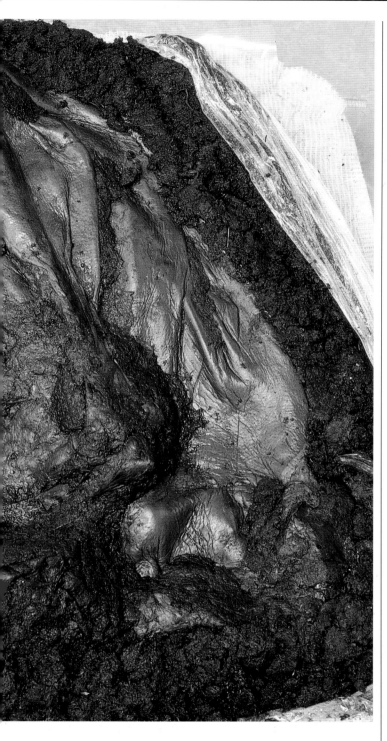

pany them, although some bogs, such as Borre Fen in Denmark, have given up several bodies. However, one of those from Borre, a woman, was found with a baby and a pottery vessel.

Many of the bog bodies have smooth uncalloused hands and carefully rounded fingernails, suggesting that they were people of high class who were not involved in manual work. The finger-prints from the carefully manicured hands of Grauballe Man, whose head popped out of the peat of Nebelgard Fen in central Jutland in April 1952, were so clear that they were immediately identified as a whorl pattern on the right thumb and an ulnar loop pattern on the right-hand index finger, patterns that are still common in the modern Danish male population. This would have been sufficient to identify him, had he had a criminal record.

Such is the nature of bog preservation that the skin, hair, flesh and internal organs survive, while the once hard bones are reduced to a spongy mass. Because of this, archae-ologists can reconstruct the last meals of these victims of the peat from their gut con-tents. Shortly before he was killed, Lindow Man had eaten a meal of wholemeal bread, probably unleavened and cooked on a griddle over an open fire, made of finely ground wheat and barley. He had drunk some of the water from near the bog, and traces of sphagnum moss were found in his gut. From the digested state of his stomach contents we know that Tollund Man ate his last meal between 12 and 24 hours before he died. This was a vegetarian gruel, consist-ing of barley, linseed, "gold-of-pleasure" (*Camelina sativa*), knotweed and a whole variety of arable weeds.

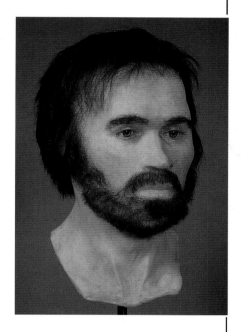

Modern forensic techniques have enabled archaeologists to recreate the face of Lindow Man, his gaze brutally extinguished 2000 years ago.

The absence of any traces of summer or autumn fruits or leafy greens in the stomach of either Tollund Man or Grauballe Man, as well as other bog bodies, suggests that these men died in either winter or early spring. It is possible that they were sacrificed in rituals relating to the mid-winter celebrations disapprovingly noted by Roman authors as culminating in gory ceremonies. The Iron Age was a time when the gods were appeased by mak-ing sacrifices in the watery fens, not only of people but also of gold and other treasure. A fine example is the magnificent silver cauldron from the Gundestrup bog in Denmark. This splendid piece, decorated inside and out with scenes of deities and sacri-fice, had been imported into Denmark sometime after 200 BC. Before being deposited in the bog as a votive offering to some god whose name is now long forgotten, the cauldron had been cut up into small pieces. The scenes on the Gundestrup cauldron are vividly brought to life by the remarkable bog bodies. ■

from Borre Fen, many of the deceased were thrown into the bog naked or near-naked. Lindow Man wore only a fox-fur armlet around his upper arm. Tollund Man wore only a pointed skin cap, and a smooth hide belt at his waist. It is likely that they had been stripped before being killed and dumped, for even if clothes they had been wearing had disintegrated in the bog, their skins would have borne the impressions of the textiles. On the other hand, the woman from Huldre Fen in Denmark wore two lamb-skin capes and a check shirt, and a head-scarf fastened by a bird bone pin on her head. Most of the bog bodies seem to have been deposited in the mire alone, with no material objects to accom-

THE FRANKLIN EXPEDITION

On 19 May 1845, under the command of the veteran explorer Sir John Franklin, two ships, the *Erebus* and *Terror*, with a crew of 129 officers and men, set sail from England, determined to forge a passage. However, Franklin failed like others before him, and it was not until a Canadian anthropologist, Owen Beattie, excavated the graves of three of Franklin's crew and autopsied the bodies that the world finally knew the full and grisly fate of Franklin's Expedition.

After Sebastian Cabot failed in his attempt in 1508 to find a short cut to the Pacific Ocean by sailing through the maze of islands north of the Canadian mainland, European explorers long sought the Northwest Passage. By the nineteenth century, grasping this elusive prize had become a source of national pride as much as commercial need, and so in 1845 the British government financed the most costly, best organized and best equipped attempt to date.

From a note left by the crew and found by Captain Francis M'Clintock, who had been sent out in 1857 to find the remains of Franklin and his crew, the essentials of Franklin's route are known. It appears that, after leaving England in 1845, the two ships got as far north as Bathurst Island. However, pack-ice forced them to retrace their route, and by September 1846 they had decided to winter by Beechy Island, off the coast of the much larger Devon Island and only about 1700 km (900 nautical miles) from the North Pole.

During this terrible winter three of the crew died and their bodies were buried in well marked graves. Able-Bodied Seaman John Torrington, 20 years old, died on 1 January 1846; John Hartnell, 25 years old, died three days later. Finally, on 3 April, Royal Marine William Braine, aged 33, died.

As the summer broke up the ice, Franklin decided to sail south, but as in the previous year, September of 1846 saw them ice-bound again, this time off the coast of King William Island. For twenty long months the crew battled the elements. On 26 April

1848, with Franklin and 23 crew already dead, the survivors made the momentous decision to abandon the ships and head south on foot. Their hope was to reach the mainland and then to row up the Back River to the nearest fur trade post. They pulled boats loaded not only with the essentials for survival, such as food and guns, but such non-essentials as a writing desk. These survivors never made it, and the Franklin Expedition passed into the annals of maritime legend.

Numerous expeditions were sent out by the British government, and the remains of some of the men were found. However, the investigators never really got to the bottom of the mystery: why had this well stocked and well organized expedition come to such a disastrous end? It was left to archaeology, over one hundred years later, to provide the answers.

Owen Beattie is a physical anthropologist at the University of Alberta in Canada. He had long been interested in the Franklin Expedition, and in 1981 was able to collect a number of bones from Franklin's crew who had died on King William Island. Beattie found evidence on some of the bones of scurvy, a physically debilitating disease common among sailors, and which was caused by a lack of vitamin C (the expression "limey" for an Englishman actually comes from the fact that the Royal Navy fed citrus fruits to their sailors to try to combat this disease). More importantly, Beattie found that one of the bones showed evidence of cannibalism, thus confirming reports from contemporary Inuit that the crew had been reduced to eating each other.

In 1984, Beattie, engrossed by the Franklin mystery, took a small group of scientists to Beechy Island to excavate and autopsy the remains of the three men who had died there in 1846. Because of the extremely cold and icy conditions, there was a good chance that the bodies would still be fairly well-preserved and thus offer Beattie a clue to the causes of death. Under Canadian law Beattie had to treat all the human remains with great reverence, even to the point of individually mapping each of the many small stones covering the graves so that, after reburial, the graves could be rebuilt exactly as they had been found. Beattie also made great efforts to track down the descendants of these men. Brian Spencely, a Canadian, is a great-great nephew of John Hartnell, and he served as the team's photographer. Donald Bray, still living in England and another descendant of John Hartnell, provided Beattie with letters written by Hartnell's mother to her two sons (John's brother Thomas had also sailed and died on the expedition).

During the summer of 1984 Beattie excavated the body of John Torrington. His coffin was made of mahogany, and on its lid a heart-shaped piece of metal cut from a tin can had been affixed. On this was inscribed Torrington's name, age and date. The body was incredibly well preserved. By melting the ice in which the body was encased, Beattie was able to see that the body had

This drawing of the Franklin Expedition's three graves shows the bleak desolation of Beechy Island.

RIGHT: John Hartnell, as he reappeared after 140 years of solitude.

OVERLEAF: The body of John Torrington, still held by the cotton strips his shipmates used to prepare his body for burial.

been laid to rest in sailor's uniform, a handkerchief had been tied around the chin to keep the mouth closed, and the face had been covered by a piece of blue cloth. The scientific team removed pieces of bone, hair and tissue for later analysis, and then the body was reinterred.

In 1986 Beattie returned to Beechy Island with a larger medical and scientific team in order to excavate the remains of John Hartnell and William Braine. Both of these bodies too were extremely well preserved. Hartnell still had his cap on, and his body was wrapped in a shroud. Beattie and his crew found that Hartnell's body had been autopsied immediately after death, presumably by the expedition's doctor. Braine, the oldest of the three, must have been extremely emaciated, weighing an estimated 40 kg (90 lb) at death. Besides taking tissue samples of the bodies, scientists with Beattie X-rayed the bodies in the field. As with Torrington, the bodies were meticulously treated and reinterred exactly as they had been found.

The autopsy reports showed that all three men had died of tuberculosis, a common enough disease, and possibly pneumonia. However, most interestingly, all the bone and hair samples showed massively inflated levels of lead, far higher than normal. Beattie had found similarly high levels in the other skeletal samples he had recovered in the early 1980s. Excessive lead in the body would physically weaken men and, in the harsh Arctic environment, this would have been catastrophic. Moreover, excessive lead also causes a breakdown in the ability to think clearly and logically. If the officers were similarly affected — and there is no reason to think otherwise — then their ability to make clear decisions, so crucial in the fight for survival, must have been severely impeded.

The lead could have come from only one source — the tin cans in which all the food was stored. At that time, the walls of tin cans were joined together and their tops attached with a solder made from a mixture of lead and tin. Lead would have been constantly leaking into the food and contaminating it. So, although lead poisoning itself did not kill the men, its long-term effects on their physical and mental capacities clearly played a part in determining the fate of the Franklin Expedition.

Beside the three graves were the remains of the expedition's camp, dominated by a huge rubbish dump of tin cans (a total of 8,000 were carried on the two ships). The dump stands as mute testimony to perhaps the ultimate cause of why the Franklin Expedition ended in disaster. ■

MUMMIES IN
THE FAR NORTH

Qilakitsoq is a remote spot on the west coast of Greenland, about 450 km (280 miles) north of the Arctic Circle. The name means "the sky is low", an undoubted reference to the fogs that cling to this rocky land. This spot was occupied by people whom archaeologists assign to the Thule culture, which originated in Alaska and then spread westward about a thousand years ago. These people hunted sea-mammals with sophisticated weapons and boats, as well as land mammals like the caribou. They also made beautiful objects from ivory and antler. The Thule Culture people were termed Skraelings by the Vikings who encountered them, and are the ancestors of the modern-day Inuit, who still inhabit the Arctic. Qilakitsoq was a winter encampment, comprising a number of stone and turf structures. From this site hunters could capture seal, walrus, beluga, narwhals, polar bear, reindeer and birds.

In 1972 two brothers, Hans and Jokum Grønvold, were out ptarmigan-hunting close to this deserted settlement when they came across a crevice about 200 m (650 ft) from the closest structure. In the crevice was an oddly shaped pattern of stones, and on removing these stones the Grønvolds found the mummified remains of six women and two children laid to rest in two separate graves. Although they reported their finds immediately to the authorities, it was only in 1977 that Jens Rosing, the new director of the Greenland Museum, realized their significance and had them transported to Copenhagen for further analysis by the pathologist J. P. Hart Hansen and the archaeologists Jørgen Meldgaard and Jørgen Nordqvist.

The mummified bodies had been stacked on top of each other, five in one grave and three in the other. They were all dressed in warm clothing made of sealskin, presumably to keep them com-

Mummification occurs naturally under conditions of extreme cold or dryness. Two examples of this from the Far North have given scientists a rare opportunity to examine the lifestyles and health of humans inhabiting the most northerly reaches of our planet.

fortable for their final journey to the Inuit Land of the Dead. Their clothes were functional certainly, but also beautifully made. Additionally, each set of bodies had been sandwiched between sealskin covers. These covers were radiocarbon-dated to between approximately AD 1425 and 1525. These people belonged to the Thule Culture.

The bodies ranged in age from a six-month-old baby to three females all aged about 50 years old. No adult males were present. The baby's body was in the best condition; because of its small size it would lose its body heat most quickly and thus be preserved the best. Indeed, so good was its preservation that its discoverers at first thought they had found a small doll.

Anatomical examination of the pelvis showed that a four-year-old boy probably suffered from Down's Syndrome. One of the 50-year-old women had suffered malnutrition, a broken collar-bone and missing front teeth. More importantly for her, she had suffered from a cancer which had spread from her nasal passages into her left eye and which must have caused her great pain. One mummy had very high levels of soot in the lungs, presumably from the use of blubber lamps. The bones showed no evidence of tuberculosis or infectious diseases like smallpox. Hair samples had very low levels of mercury and lead, indicative of an extremely unpolluted environment.

Other mummies had good amounts of subcutaneous fat, indicating that they were well-nourished. The faecal material in the lower intestines of one body contained bits of hair from reindeer, seal and arctic hare, as well as bird-feathers, lice and various plant remains.

One final prize for the archaeologists was the presence of facial tattoos on five of the women. These tattoos had been made by needle and thread dipped in a mixture of soot, ash and plant juices. They showed different artistic styles, perhaps indicating that the women had come from different communities.

Utqiagvik is an archaeological site located in Barrow, Alaska, and is contemporary with Qilakitsoq. This site consists of the remains of 60 historic and prehistoric houses. It was a winter settlement, occupied by families who during the summer would have dispersed to hunt and fish throughout the region. During one

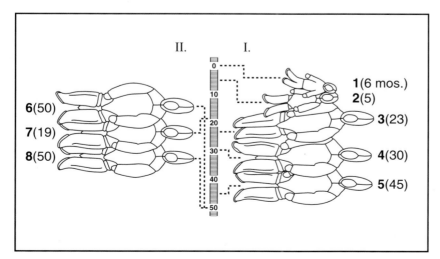

II.   I.

6(50)
7(19)
8(50)

0
10
20
30
40
50

1(6 mos.)
2(5)
3(23)
4(30)
5(45)

LEFT: The two groups of bodies at Qilakitsoq and their ages.

RIGHT: A child mummified at Qilakitsoq still speaks to us down the centuries.

winter storm one of the houses had been flattened by an *ivu*, the local Inupiat term for a coastal ice-surge, which brought tons of ice down on top of it.

In 1982 illegal collectors were digging on the site of Utqiagvik when they came across the remains of human bodies. Fortunately, also working at the site was the archaeologist Albert Dekin, who had been hired by the local community to carry out archaeological studies before development destroyed the site. Dekin recognized the importance of these finds and instigated scientific investigations before the collectors could do much more harm.

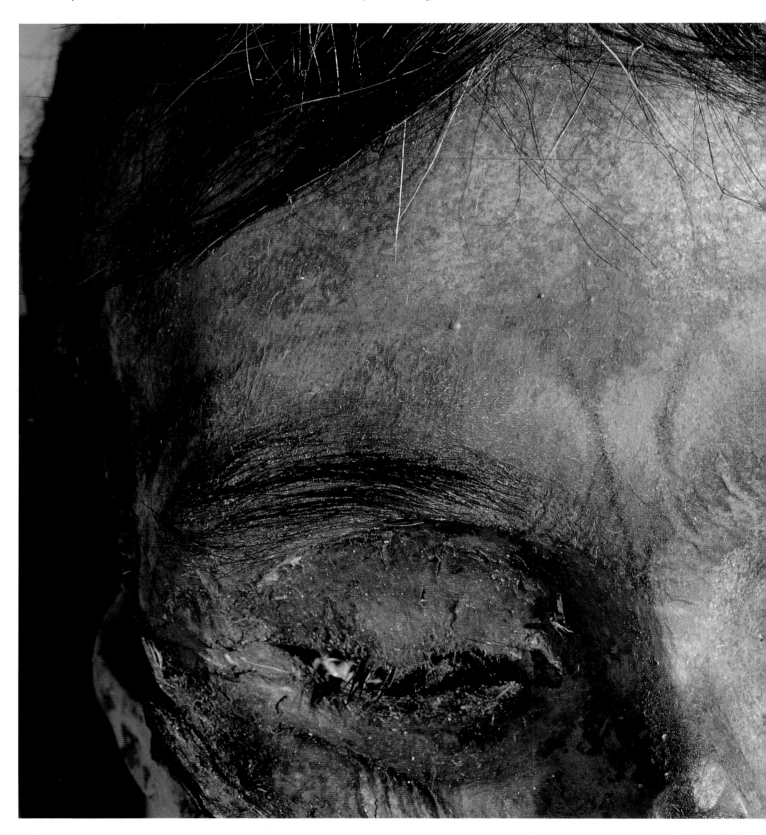

Ultimately, he and his colleagues recovered the remains of five bodies that had been trapped in their house by the sudden ice-surge that had crashed in. Three of the bodies were the skeletal remains of two young girls and a young man. The other two were the mummified remains of a woman in her 20s and a

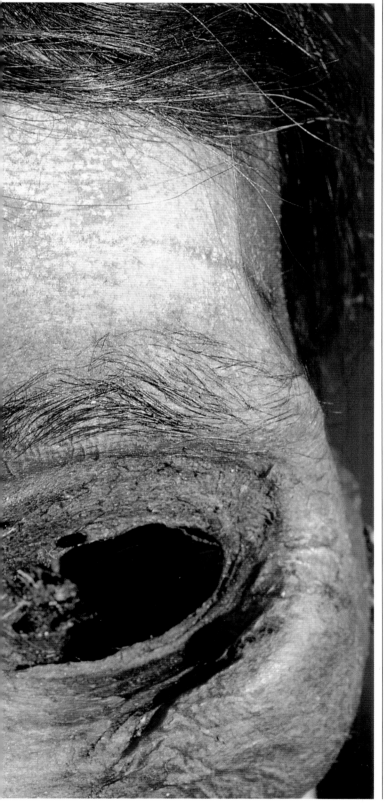

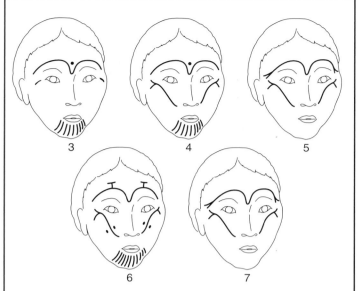

ABOVE: Different patterns of facial tattoos found at Qilakitsoq.

LEFT: This close-up of one of the mummies at Qilakitsoq shows the remarkable preservation achieved by 500 years of deep freeze.

woman in her 40s, which had presumably been preserved by summer meltwater penetrating the house and permanently freezing them. Probably the three young people had been killed closer to the surface and had not been permanently frozen; thus only their bones had survived the centuries.

The two mummified bodies were autopsied, with the full permission of the modern Inupiat community still living in the vicinity. It appears that they had been killed almost instantly by the weight of ice and house. Both of their stomachs were empty and their bladders distended, suggesting that they had been killed during the night. Neither of them was clothed.

The women had been in good health, although there was evidence on the bones of occasional periods when food was scarce. They had suffered from atherosclerosis, caused by eating too much meat and fat (their diet was rich in whale and seal blubber), and from anthracosis (black lung), caused by inhaling too much smoke from the house fires. One of the women had also suffered from pneumonia and perhaps trichinosis, a parasitic infection of the muscles possibly resulting from ingesting raw polar-bear meat. Hair samples were analysed, and these showed higher levels of lead and mercury than in the Greenland mummies. After the autopsies and analyses had been completed, all the bodies were returned to Barrow where they were reinterred.

Besides the bodies, Dekin's team recovered numerous artefacts still in their original locations. For example, winter hunting equipment — snow goggles, ice picks and harpoons — was stored in the entrance tunnel to the house. Small alcoves contained summer fishing equipment such as pieces of netting. The kitchen section of the house contained cooking equipment. ∎

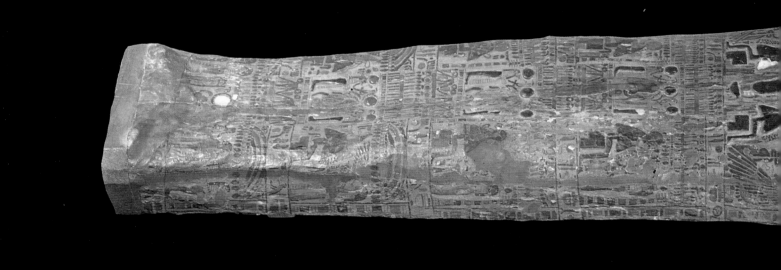

MUMMIES

CHINCHORRO–THE OLDEST MUMMIES IN THE WORLD

Living in the driest place on earth, the Atacama Desert, where virtually no rain ever falls, the Chinchorro were no strangers to natural mummification. Cadavers in this hyperarid climate dried out and became mummies with no treatment at all. But the Chinchorro people took matters into their own hands, and tried to create more life-like images of the dead.

These early mummies are called Chinchorro because one of the first major collections of them was found near Arica, Chile, at a place called the Chinchorro Beach. The first archaeologist to describe them was the German Max Uhle, who called them "Aborigines of Arica". Since then many more finds have been made between Antofagasta (Chile) and Ilo (Peru). Chinchorro cemeteries and tombs are often found in the places where Chinchorro people lived, near their houses. The largest collection of mummies comes from a group of several cemeteries found at a large bluff called El Morro, near Arica, Chile. Many of them are on display in the local museum.

Close-up of mummy head with wig of human hair.

Between 6000 and 1500 BC there lived a people on the coast of northern Chile and extreme southern Peru who followed a fairly simple lifestyle — except in their treatment of their dead. The Chinchorro people, as they are called, were perhaps the first people in the world who artificially, and very elaborately, mummified their dead.

How were the mummies prepared? In a typical process the cadaver was beheaded, and the limbs were removed from the trunk of the body. The various body parts were then skinned, and the skin set aside for later use. The body cavity was emptied of internal organs and dried with hot coals. The limbs were sliced open and the bones removed to be cleaned and dried. The brain was removed from the skull. Once all these parts had been disarticulated and prepared, the body was then reassembled.

Bones were reinforced by being lashed to sticks, and were replaced in the limbs. Sticks were placed inside the body trunk to give it internal support, and the cavity was filled with grass and ashes. Some sticks ran the length of the legs and up through the trunk and into the skull to give the entire mummy internal support.

The reassembled body was then covered with a paste made

from white ash, and modelled to resemble an intact human body. Even genitals were re-created. Over this artificial "flesh", sections of the skin were placed back in their original locations, especially on the skull. Even the scalp and hair of the dead individual were put back on the head and secured in place. Finally, the entire mummy was coated with a nearly black paint made of manganese. Facial features were painted on. And sometimes the completed mummy was given items of clothing to wear.

Other types of mummy were prepared, not by cutting the body into parts, but by making incisions in the body. While the head was removed, the body was prepared by removing internal organs and major muscles, and drying the body cavities with hot coals. Reinforcing sticks were inserted into the body by sliding them

An artificially mummified Chinchorro child coated with black paint.

under the skin and into body cavities. Sometimes the skin was rolled down off the limbs, much like a pair of stockings, and then rolled back up after the muscles were replaced with grass stuffing. The heads were replaced, and provided with artificial flesh and human skin. Again the bodies were covered with an ash paste, and the bodies painted either black or red. In some cases preparation was slightly less elaborate: the cadavers were smoked to preserve them, and then covered with a thick layer of mud.

Who were these people who paid so much attention to their dead? Until recently, while much attention was paid to "dead" Chinchorro people, little attention was paid to how the Chinchorro had lived. Unlike other cultures that produced artificial mummies — many of them great and complex civilizations — these people lived a simple life of hunting and gathering in very small communities. They lived near the Pacific coast in small river valleys where they had access to fresh water. In a climate where rainfall is so rare, fresh water is a critical resource.

Recently an important Chinchorro site was discovered during the construction of a new school in Ilo, Peru. Not only did this site contain a Chinchorro cemetery, but also houses, living areas and trash left behind by Chinchorro people. The site, Villa del Mar, provides a rare glimpse into the lives of the Chinchorro people. The archaeologist Karen Wise, who directed excavations at the site, found that the people ate a diet that consisted of ocean fish, marine birds, sea mammals, shellfish and a few land animals, supplemented by wild plants. Their tools were of chipped stone, using raw materials found in the nearby region. They made fishhooks out of bone, cactus spine and mussel shell. They made their clothes out of the pelts of birds and mammals, and also out of wild reeds that they chewed to soften them; they were put together by twining, a process more simple than true weaving.

Clearly, the ocean was important to the Chinchorro people. They got most of their food from it, and many of their tools were made for fishing, shellfishing, and marine hunting. Many Chinchorro mummies are found buried with fishhooks, bone pries and net bags for shellfish collecting.

In many ways the Chinchorro people were typical of hunter-gatherers who lived throughout the Andean region at the time, during what archaeologists call the Archaic Period. They moved often from one place to another, in search of food, and they did not make pottery or use metals. But the Chinchorro are unique among all the cultures of the time in their mummification practices.

Why did the Chinchorro mummify their dead? While it is impossible to know what they had in mind, we do know that some of the mummies were painted and repainted. Perhaps they were taken out and displayed for important rituals. Given the reinforcing that was added to them, they may even have been stood up in a vertical position.

We do not know why these early fishermen gave up the process of mummifying their dead, but sometime before 1000 BC they abandoned the practice. New mortuary customs replaced the old techniques as these people began to settle into villages occupied year-round, and as they began producing their own foods through agriculture. But the legacy of the ancient Chinchorro remains today in the existence of their remarkable mummies. ■

A red Chinchorro mummy of a subadult male.

MAKING MUMMIES

The most important part of the personality to survive after death — certainly for a non-royal Egyptian during the Old Kingdom — was the *ka*, a concept which can best be summed up as the "life force" of an individual. The *ka* was integral with the body during life and, although separated from the body at death, continued to live on earth, within the tomb (sometimes called the "house of the *ka*" by the Egyptians), and needed both a continual supply of food and drink and a physical host. Substitutes in which the *ka* could dwell included statues placed within the tomb, but the ideal was the body itself.

In the Predynastic Period (before c. 3000 BC) burial for most people consisted of a simple interment in a contracted foetal position in a sand-filled pit in the desert. This modest provision was, accidentally, the most effective means of preserving a dead human body used by the Egyptians, as the dry, desiccating desert sands

The Egyptian mummy has come to characterize archaeology itself in the eyes of the public. Certainly, one of the most remarkable aspects of Egyptian beliefs regarding the afterlife was the continued importance of the physical part of the persona — the body — for the well-being of the spiritual part.

acted as a natural blotting paper, "wicking" away the body fluids released during decomposition and aiding the natural drying-out and preservation of the body. The chance discovery of such bodies (for instance, during later grave-digging in the cemetery) may have helped to develop or reinforce religious ideas that linked the spiritual survival of the personality after death to the physical survival of the body.

Paradoxically, once the Egyptians took measures to shelter and protect the body (as they would have seen it) in coffins and elaborate tombs, the loss of contact with the desert sands meant that decomposition was assured. The Egyptians solved this particular problem not, as might be thought logical, by abandoning the elaborate trappings of burial and returning to the desert, but by using artificial methods to preserve the body.

The earliest method that seems to have been used, and the standard technique for treating high-ranking bodies of the First to the Third Dynasties (c. 3000-2575 BC), was to wrap the body tightly with strips of resin-soaked linen. By the end of this early phase of mummy-making it was not unusual to model the impregnated bandages, sometimes with the help of additional padding, to resemble the features of the body, a technique further developed during the Old Kingdom (ending with the Sixth Dynasty in c. 2152 BC) with the use of a plaster "skim" on top of the outer wrappings for more delicate rendering of the features. These techniques, although they produced an outwardly acceptable appearance, did little to halt the decomposition within; in effect the Old Kingdom mummy was a convincing "shell" containing an unhappy collection of bones.

Attempts to tackle this problem from, as it were, within seem to have begun in the Fourth Dynasty. The tomb

The jackal-headed god Anubis was concerned with the transition from this life to the next, and became the patron deity of mummification.

The Egyptians placed the internal organs which they removed from the body into vessels called canopic jars, one each for the liver, lungs, stomach and intestines.

of Queen Hetepheres, mother of King Khufu (builder of the great pyramid at Giza), contained a simple alabaster box divided vertically into four sections which contained wrapped packages of the Queen's internal organs. Clearly the Egyptians had realized that the removal of the soft viscera of the chest and abdomen was the first step in any serious attempt to preserve the body itself rather than its mere external appearance; these parts were the first to rot and their removal allowed the newly emptied body cavity to be cleansed and dried. The standard technique for the removal of the viscera was by means of a large surgical incision in the abdomen. Once removed, the internal organs could not be discarded since they were still part of the deceased's physical persona, but were carefully preserved and placed in a so-called "canopic" chest like that of Hetepheres, or in four canopic jars — one each for the stomach, intestines, lungs and liver. The heart was considered the seat of the intellect and was left in place, as were the

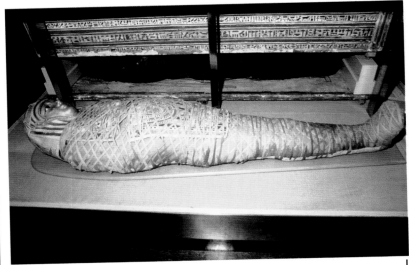

The intricate bandaging of later mummies produced a pleasing appearance but inferior preservation.

The naturally desiccated bodies of simple desert burials may have given the Egyptians the idea of artificially preserving more elaborate entombments.

kidneys. The void left by the removal of the internal organs was filled, usually with resin-soaked linen, and the body wrapped. Sometimes, in addition to the modelling of facial features, male mummies were endowed with sexual organs modelled in linen.

The most important substance used in the mummification process was natron, a naturally occurring salt (a combination of sodium carbonate and sodium bicarbonate with traces of sodium chloride and sodium sulphate) with effective drying and antiseptic properties. Natron was regarded by the Egyptians as a particularly effective purifying substance and was found in a number of places in Egypt, especially the Wadi en-Natrun in the desert to the west of the Nile Delta. Exactly how natron was used in the mummification process is a matter of debate; it would have been most effective if piled on top of, and used to fill the body cavity of, the body as a dry powder. It is likely that most New Kingdom mummies were treated in this way and left for most of the 70 days mentioned in the texts of that period as the interval for preparation of the body that elapsed between death and burial. It is also possible that natron was sometimes used in liquid form (Hetepheres' packages of internal organs had been soaked in a 3% natron solution), but this would have been less effective and would have required a longer period of immersion than the "dry" method — this may account for the 273 days recorded as the preparation time of the body of Queen Meresankh III. It may also be that the generally unsatisfactory results produced by the natron solution method are one reason why well-preserved mummies from the Old Kingdom are so rare, another being the limited clientele (basically the king and favoured members of the royal family and courtiers) who benefited from the experimental attentions of mummy-makers of that period.

The most successful period for the production of good-quality mummies was the New Kingdom and its aftermath (Eighteenth to Twenty-first Dynasties — c. 1550-945 BC). Not only were the organs of the body cavity regularly removed, but so was the brain, usually via a passageway through the nose produced by the breaking of the ethmoid bone, but sometimes from the back of the neck after the dislocation of the atlas vertebra. Molten resin was often liberally poured into any voids within the body, and the "defleshing" of the body by removing the muscle-tissue by means of a number of small incisions was occasionally practised at this time. One of the first mummies to have the muscles removed and replaced by a padding of sawdust, sand or mud was that of King Amenhotep III. However, these mummies suffered from a common problem with this method, the shrinking of the skin over a too-generous packing beneath, with a resultant and unpleasant bursting.

In the Graeco-Roman period mummification, though still practised, declined greatly in skill and technique. Surgical removal of internal organs was abandoned in favour of the quicker and cheaper method of pumping the body full of resin and covering it with the same substance. The blackened appearance of these resin-soaked cadavers gave the name to all preserved bodies, *mummiya* being the Arabic term for bitumen or pitch. ■

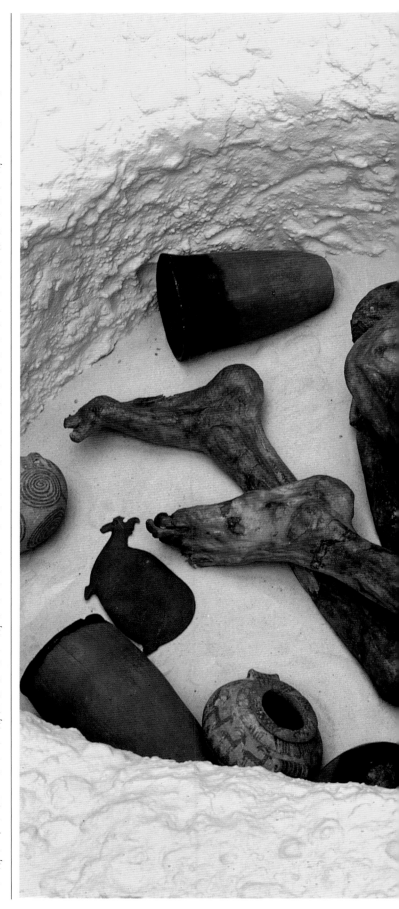

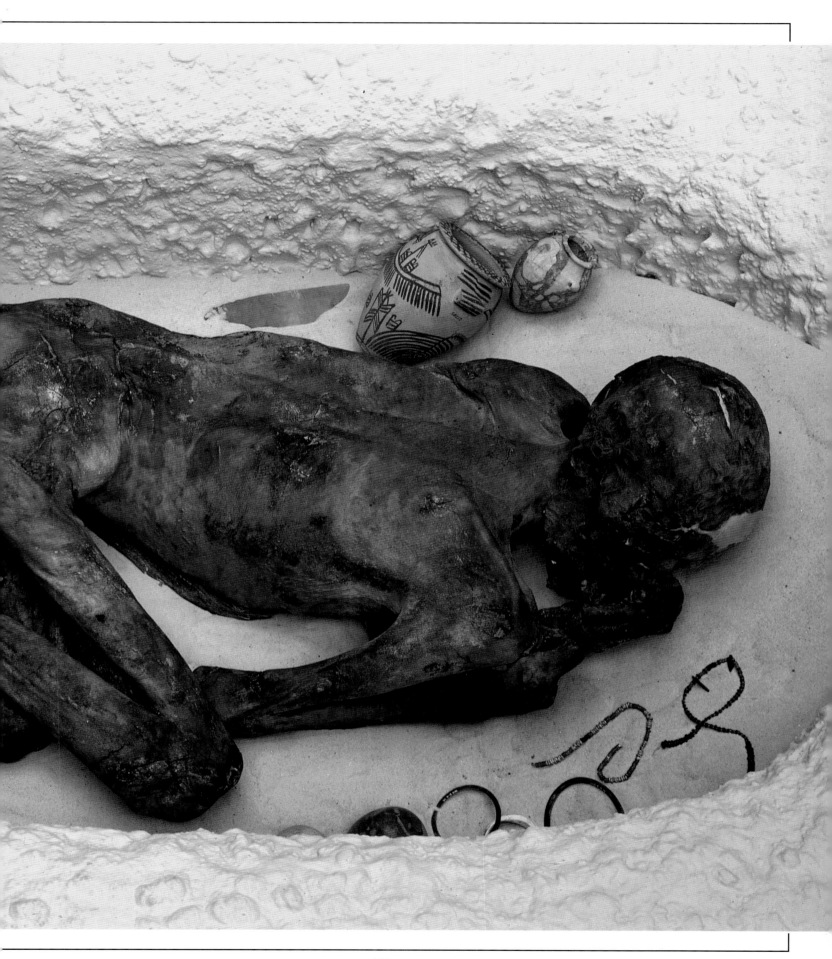

MUMMIES AND MEDICINE

In the eighteenth and especially nineteenth centuries, when Egypt became a popular destination for the more adventurous traveller, mummies were a popular souvenir; the subsequent unwrapping and examination of this memento of a visit to Egypt proved a popular, if ghoulish, entertainment for the folks back home. Sometimes the justification for such "mummy-parties" was their value to science; in the early nineteenth century Thomas Pettigrew, surgeon to the Duke of Kent, made a practice of unwrapping mummies for the edification of large public audiences.

Today many people would find the use of a fellow human being in such a manner, no matter how long dead, unacceptable and might not even be happy to see the bodies (or parts of bodies) of the ancient deceased propped up in museum cases to be gawped at. However, those mummies which have survived in museums, and those excavated in more recent times to prevent their loss or destruction, can be examined in ways that produce maximum information about the lifestyles and health record of the Ancient Egyptians, while respecting them as individuals and people like ourselves.

The first serious practitioner of examining mummies as a means of discovering more about mummification techniques and the health of the people who had been mummified was Elliot Smith, Professor of Anatomy at Cairo and later Dean of the Medical School at Manchester, who worked with a substantial number of bodies from Egypt and Nubia in the early part of the twentieth century.

Because of the concern of the early Egyptians to preserve the bodies of their dead, Egypt is the most important source of ancient bodies that survive not just as skeletons but with much of the other physical tissue intact. It is hardly surprising that we know much more about the health, and other medical-related topics, of the Egyptians than about most ancient peoples. Through the examination of well preserved bodies, questions can be asked to try to solve specific archaeological problems; the relationships between members of the Egyptian royal family in the late Eighteenth Dynasty is one such problem (see p.190) for which the major limit to reaching a satisfactory conclusion is the absence of the bodies of key individuals. Apart from the question of who he

The interest of people in the West in mummies seems to have been initially stimulated by a belief in the efficacy of powdered mummy (bituminous drug) as a medicine for various ills, which was prescribed from the sixteenth century onwards as a cure for a wide variety of ailments.

was related to, the examinations of Tutankhamen's body in 1926 and 1968 revealed that the young king died aged around eighteen years old (estimated through the examination of the joints of the humerus), had wide sinuses (the result of living in a hot, dry climate), and stood about 1.68 m (5 ft 6 in) tall; the latter examination suggests that he died neither of tuberculosis nor a blow to the head (both of which had been suggested after the initial examination) — in fact there is no obvious evidence of cause of the death on Tutankhamen's body.

More general conclusions about the wider population of Egypt can be made from studying the bodies of less illustrious individuals. The use of multi-disciplinary teams of individual specialists to study different aspects of the palaeopathology of a particular body was an important development in mummy studies during the 1970s. This has affected the ways in which mummies in museum collections are studied and how fieldwork is planned, with many excavations of cemetery sites now including specialists in biological sciences.

Radiograph of the feet of King Ramesses II.

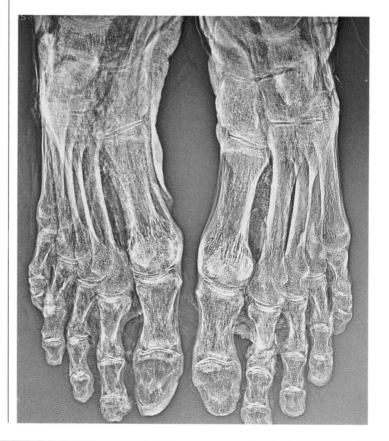

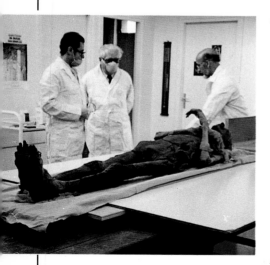

The badly damaged mummy of King Ramesses II undergoing restoration in Paris.

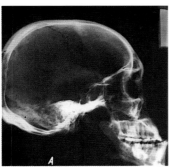

ABOVE AND LEFT: Examination of Egyptian mummies by X-ray can give much information about ancient pathology.

loides worms and Bilharzia; many of these infestations still affect the modern rural population of Egypt.

Specialists from outside the close confines of medical science and surgery can also be recruited for their expertise; for example, in the study of the fingerprints of Egyptian mummies. One particularly interesting technique is the reconstruction of the appearance of the heads and faces of long-dead Egyptians; this is done by using the underlying bone structure of the skull as the base on which to rebuild the soft tissues, in model form, to recreate what might be a close resemblance to the appearance in life of the subject.

Looking inside the bundle

Today the surgical table has been replaced by the body-scanner as the place where research on mummies is carried out.

The use of modern non-invasive techniques for the examination of Egyptian mummies is itself a century old. In 1898 the British Egyptologist Flinders Petrie, with his typical eagerness to embrace new analytical methods for archaeological research, used X-rays to examine Egyptian mummies only a few years after the discovery of this form of radiation by Roentgen. This method of seeing inside the wrappings of a mummy has produced interesting results without the destruction of the body. Work of this kind commonly reveals that the ancient embalmers were often less than diligent in preserving the body handed over to their care; odd jumbles of bones or the presence of a cat's body inside the mummy-wrappings purportedly of a child were invisible to relatives presented with a finished package supposedly containing a mummified relative.

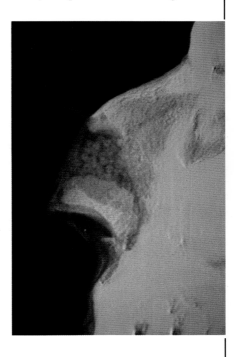

Scan of the nose of Ramesses II, showing a small bone inserted to maintain its shape.

A more recent elaboration of simple X-raying is the use of computed tomography (CT) scanning. With this technique the scanner produces images of thin "slices" through the body being examined; these "slices" may then be manipulated by computerized imaging equipment to produce a three-dimensional image of the whole body. This is a substantial improvement on simple two-dimensional X-ray examination which produces an image on which everything viewed is superimposed in an often unclear manner. With CT scanning the nature and relative position of the internal organs, and indeed everything left inside the mummy-wrappings, can be clearly distinguished. The imaging produced by CT scanning is so detailed that the examination of individual, information-producing parts of the body can be made without the unwrapping and inevitable destruction of the body. ∎

Some of the results of such work confirm what one might suspect about the health of the Ancient Egyptians. The ever-present sand blowing off the desert found its way into the major staple of the Egyptian diet — bread — resulting in obvious wear on the teeth. Sand pneumoconiosis, a common problem for desert-dwelling people who suck in sand with every breath, is also detectable through characteristic scarring of the lungs. If sand is the unwelcome result of living near the desert, the agricultural land of the Nile Valley also brought its problems, not least in parasites that flourish in infected water such as Guinea worms, Strongy-

THE DEIR EL-BAHRI CACHE

By 1870 the role of the Valley of the Kings as the burial place of the New Kingdom pharaohs had been established and many of the tombs cleared and their owners identified, although few contained much more than broken fragments of the luxurious trappings that once filled these underground vaults. During the 1870s a number of antiquities appeared on the international antiquities market whose origin was clearly a royal tomb. The Director of Egypt's Antiquities Service, August Mariette, was offered, and bought, two papyri from the tomb of a Queen Henuttawy, while about the same time a contact of the Egyptologist Gaston Maspero was offered a papyrus made for a Queen Nodjmet, and Maspero himself was shown yet another from the burial of the High Priest of Amen, Pinudjem II. *Shabtis* (small funerary statuettes) of Pinudjem II also started to appear on the antiquities market. It seemed likely that all these objects had a common origin in a royal family tomb, and Maspero decided to track down this tomb, aided by Charles Wilbour, an American

The royal tombs in the Valley of the Kings belong to one of the most important single cemeteries of the ancient world; they are the places where the rulers of Egypt in the New Kingdom (c. 1550-1070) planned to spend eternity. Today almost all of these tombs are empty of their original occupants and original contents — Tutankhamen being the only exception. But the history of the use of the Valley of the Kings in ancient times, and its modern rediscovery, is by no means as straightforward as one might think.

mature student of his who went down to Luxor posing as a rich tourist. In Luxor, Wilbour discovered that a certain Ahmed abd er-Rassul had good-quality antiquities for sale and was shown papyri and, a little later, leather mummy bindings embossed with the name of the High Priest of Amen, Pinudjem I. The abd er-Rassul family had recently built a new house at Gurna, the village on the west bank at Thebes said to be built over many ancient tombs. Ahmed abd er-Rassul and his brother Hussein were arrested and "encouraged to talk", and their role in the appearance of these antiquities became clearer.

With Maspero absent, the Egyptologist Emile Brugsch investigated the matter; he was taken to Deir el-Bahri, a great natural bay in the eastern face of the Theban mountain, best known for the temple of Queen Hatchepsut at its base and the tombs which honeycomb its sloping flanks. Here a narrow shaft was identified, at the bottom of which a passageway led to a chamber 5 m (17 ft) square, filled with coffins belonging to, among others, the kings Ahmose, Tuthmosis I-III, Ramesses I, Seti I and Ramesses II. A second room contained the coffins of the family of Pinudjem I. After two days of hard work the tomb was cleared and its voluminous contents packed aboard the Museum's own steamer, which set off northwards for Cairo where the itinerant kings and queens of Ancient Egypt would find their latest resting place in the Egyptian Museum.

Robberies and reburials

It seems that the tomb of the cache had been discovered by the abd er-Rassul family in 1871. The tomb itself had probably originally belonged to an Eighteenth-Dynasty queen called Inhapy, but had later been used for the burial of the family of Herihor — the effective ruler of southern Egypt during the latter part of the reign of King Ramesses XI (c. 1080 BC). This was a time of internal disruption in Egypt as its unity began to disintegrate at the end of the New Kingdom. Herihor's descendants, the high Priests of Amen at Thebes, did not claim the throne, but were the effective rulers of southern Egypt; they included among their number both Pinudjem I and Pinudjem II. One result of this instability seems to have been robbery in the royal necropolis, a problem which appears to have plagued the west bank at Thebes during the Twentieth Dynasty (c. 1196-1070). Egyptian records from the late New Kingdom include the reports of commissions

LEFT: Some of the most famous pharaohs from Ancient Egypt, like Seti II, father of Ramesses II, were found in caches hidden in Western Thebes.

RIGHT: Priests hid the bodies of New Kingdom pharaohs in secret niches in Western Thebes.

of enquiry set up to investigate reported robberies from royal tombs; these "tomb robbery papyri" paint a picture of the active robbery of tombs by workmen who should have been working on the current royal tomb, protected by corrupt local officials. It seems that one practical effect of the discovery of plundered tombs was the removal of bodies of kings and queens who still remained undestroyed by the robbers and their reburial in other tombs, sometimes as large collections of royal mummies. This appears to have been the reason why so many royal mummies were found in one tomb along with the descendants of Herihor — texts on coffins and mummies of the royal bodies from the Valley of the Kings show that they were moved to the tomb of Inhapy during the reign of Pinudjem II. Some of these bodies had at some stage been taken to the tomb of Seti I, presumably for restoration, after robbery. The latest royal burial in the tomb was that of Pinudjem II himself after his death around 969 BC. The earlier royal burials had been robbed of their rich trappings before reburial — this is why the objects that the abd er-Rassuls had been selling were from the burials of Herihor's family, not those of the earlier kings and queens whose bodies are, nevertheless, the richest treasure to come from the tomb.

A second cache of royal mummies was discovered soon afterwards by Victor Loret, who became Director of the Antiquities Service in 1898 and immediately began to excavate in the southernmost part of the Valley of the Kings. Loret quickly discovered the tombs of both Tuthmosis III and his son Amenhotep II. Important as these tombs were, their immediate interest was based on their containing another, though smaller, cache of royal burials, including those of Amenhotep II himself, Seti II, Tuthmosis IV, Amenhotep III and Queen Tiy. The kings and queens within Amenhotep II's tomb had also been interred there during the reburials of the reigns of the Pinudjems and with the Deir el-Bahri cache, make up the roll-call of most of the predominant monarchs of Egypt's New Kingdom. ■

RIGHT: The mummified body of King Ramesses II.

BELOW: The proceedings of a late New Kingdom court of enquiry into royal tomb robberies have been preserved in the form of papyri.

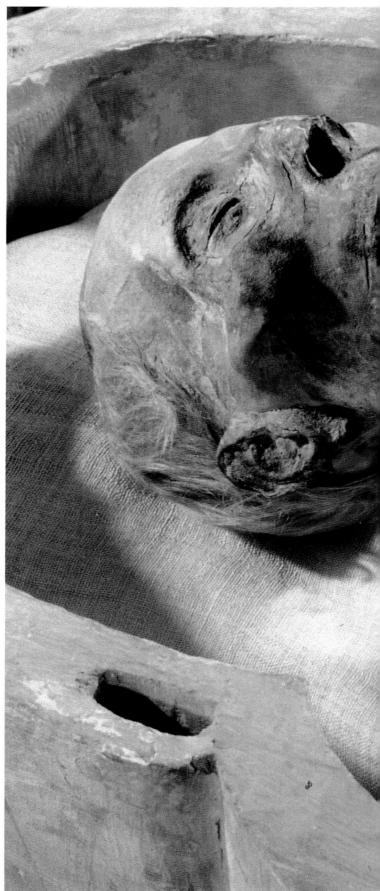

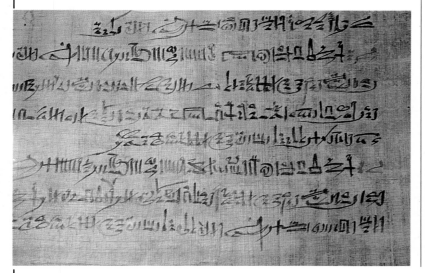

THE FAMILY OF TUTANKHAMEN

When King Amenhotep IV (son of Amenhotep III and Queen Tiy) changed his name to Akhenaten, made the worship of the sun-disc, the Aten, the state religion, and moved his capital to the virgin site of Amarna, he was already married to Nefertiti who had given birth to three daughters by Year 4 of his reign as Akhenaten. Three further daughters followed, but only two of these children seem to have survived their father, Meretaten and Ankhesenpaaten. Akhenaten had other wives besides Nefertiti, the most prominent of whom was a woman called Kiya who seems to have been held in special favour by the king, although she disappears from the archaeological record after Year 11 of Akhenaten's reign. The name of Nefertiti ceases to be inscribed on Amarna monuments after Year 14, at the same time as the appearance of a co-regent for Akhenaten. This co-regent is almost certainly the short-lived ruler called Smenkhkare who followed Akhenaten, and preceded Tutankhamen, on the throne after Akhenaten's death in his Year 17. According to which account of the period one chooses to believe, Smenkhkare was either a young man of royal blood, pos-

The tomb of Tutankhamen is one of the most astounding archaeological discoveries of this or any other century. The vast archaeological riches of the tomb are well known, but despite the fame of this young king of the Egyptian Eighteenth Dynasty one of the simplest questions about the king — who were his parents? — is one of the most difficult to answer. Untangling the complex relationships within Tutankhamen's family still presents one of the knottiest problems in Egyptology. Lost bodies, discovered bodies and the tantalizing evidence of royal tombs present a confusing picture.

sibly the son of Akhenaten, or Nefertiti herself, having changed her name and adopted a more active royal role for herself late in the reign of her husband and eventually succeeding him. Smenkhkare seems to have been married to Meretaten, eldest daughter of Akhenaten, but the couple appear to have died childless.

Akhenaten himself was probably buried in the tomb he had prepared in the desert close to Amarna, but this tomb was subsequently robbed and desecrated in a deliberate fashion; the body of the king was probably destroyed at this time. The final resting places of Nefertiti and of Kiya are not known.

Tomb KV55

In 1907 a team led by the American Theodore Davis was working in the Valley of the Kings. They discovered a small rock-cut tomb intended for someone connected to the Amarna royal family. The burial had been hasty, then ransacked, then damaged by water-seepage. Much of the burial equipment carried the names of Amenhotep III and Tiy, especially fragments of a gilded shrine which surrounded the original burial and bore the name of the queen. Davis concluded, probably correctly, that the original intended occupant of the tomb was indeed Tiy. It is likely that, after she had died at Amarna and been buried there, Tiy's body with burial equipment was reinterred in the Valley of the Kings as a much-revered family figure after Amarna itself had been abandoned, possibly by Tutankhamen. The body of Tiy has been tentatively identified as one of those found in the cache from the tomb of Amenhotep II (see p. 190) and may have been removed

The coffin found in Tomb KV55 in the Valley of the Kings, made for a lady but containing a young man.

ABOVE: Queen Nefertiti, wife of Akhenaten and mother of Ankhesenpaaten.

RIGHT: The solid gold inner coffins of Tutankhamen's tomb mark, technically and artistically, one of the high-points of Egyptian civilization.

OVERLEAF: Elaborate gold coffin of Tutankhamen.

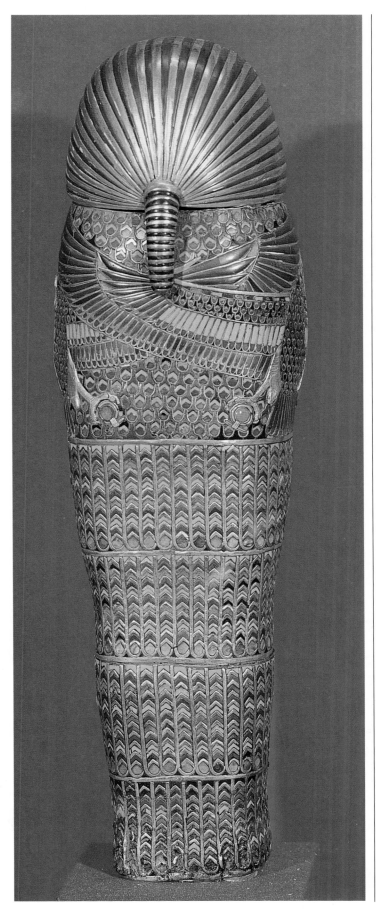

there for safety when KV55 was accidentally cut into during the construction of the tomb of Ramesses IX. However, the coffin found within KV55, while in Amarna style and clearly made for a royal lady, had been altered so that the inscriptions it bore indicated a male, not female, occupant and someone whose name in the royal cartouches had been carefully removed. The body within the coffin, originally declared to be of a woman, has since been determined as a man who died around the age of twenty — clearly too young to be Akhenaten himself. Just as the tomb may have been used for the burial of more than its original occupant, so the coffin (made for any one of the more important wives or daughters of Akhenaten) may have been pressed into service for an unexpectedly deceased man and altered accordingly, only to be desecrated at a later stage. It is now generally believed that the coffin was originally made for Kiya, but the young man who was actually buried in it was Smenkhkare.

The tomb of Tutankhamen

The discovery of the tomb of Tutankhamen in 1922 provided a number of clues to relationships within the Amarna royal family, the most important being the body of the king himself. But Tutankhamen's tomb also provides a number of surprising additions and absences within the tomb which also throw both light and confusion on the situation. The most obvious absence is, despite the presence of a collection of "heirlooms" bearing the names of various members of the royal family including Amenhotep III, Tiy, Akhenaten and various daughters of Akhenaten, that there is no mention of either Nefertiti or Kiya, the two leading contenders to be Tutankhamen's mother. The surprising additions were two mummified foetuses, probably five months and nine months old respectively, who may well have been the unfortunate progeny of Tutankhamen and his wife Ankhesenpaaten. Tutankhamen died, childless, at about eighteen years old.

The body of Tutankhamen, when examined, was found to

The body of Tutankhamen, unlike the wonderful paraphernalia found inside the tomb, is not particularly well preserved.

ABOVE: The two foetuses from the tomb of Tutankhamen.

RIGHT: The tomb of Tutankhamen contained many representations of the king with his young wife Ankhesenpaaten, daughter of Akhenaten.

be remarkably similar to that found in KV55. Comparison of the skulls showed a distinct resemblance, and the blood groups of the young men matched closely. In all likelihood they were brothers, and if the KV55 body was indeed Smenkhkare then the only conceivable candidate for the father of these two kings must be Akhenaten himself. Theories which suggest that Tutankhamen's father was Amenhotep III (who must therefore have shared the throne with Akhenaten for ten years of the latter's reign) lack any convincing evidence. But who was the mother of Tutankhamen and Smenkhkare? Some scholars have suggested that the reason for the esteem in which Kiya was held ("Greatly Beloved Wife") by Akhenaten was that she had given the king a male heir; this contrasts sharply with his ability to produce only daughters with Nefertiti. That male heir, born just before Akhenaten came to the throne himself, would have been Smenkhkare, while the birth of Tutankhamen (which can be placed around Year 10 or 11 of Akhenaten's reign) coincides closely with the disappearance of Kiya — her death in childbirth might not be an impossible speculation. ■

THE MUMMIES OF THE NORTHERN FUJIWARA

Hiraizumi was the capital of the Northern Fujiwara who ruled northern Honshu as a semi-independent kingdom in the twelfth century AD. The Konjikidō was completed in 1124 by the first Fujiwara chieftain Kiyohira as a private chapel within the Chūsonji temple. Except for the roof tiles, the outside of the building is covered with gold leaf, giving rise to its name "Konjikidō" or "Gold Coloured Hall". Gilt statues of the Amida Buddha and his attendants sit on the central altar. But the Konjikidō is more than just an Amida hall for it also contains the mummified remains of the four generations of the Northern Fujiwara.

Marco Polo's description of the golden roofs and walls of medieval Japan had a potent effect on the European imagination, and when Columbus set off to cross the Atlantic in 1492 it was in the hope of finding Polo's fabled kingdom of Zipangu. Of course Marco Polo never actually visited Japan, and his account of that country was widely exaggerated. Nevertheless, there is one building that may have served as a stimulus for his story — the Konjikidō Hall in Hiraizumi.

Mummification has always been quite rare in Japan. The few examples of the custom that do exist are mostly Buddhist priests who underwent self-mummification by gradually reducing their intake of food and water. Although after death these mummies were subjected to various drying procedures, their internal organs were not usually removed and they did not undergo the elaborate embalming techniques found in other parts of the world. The Fujiwara mummies are unusual in that they are the only example from Japan of the mummification of political rather than religious figures. Furthermore, while direct evidence is absent, it seems likely that the bodies of the four Fujiwara leaders underwent some sort of deliberate embalming process of a type not employed for the mummies of Buddhist monks.

The mummies of the Konjikidō Hall were subjected to analysis by a multi-disciplinary team in March 1950, and the results were published in the summer of that same year. This was the first and so far the only scientific study of these bodies, and the project must be counted as a notable achievement at a time when Japan was still recovering from the ravages of the Second World War. Detailed descriptions and measurements of the mummies were made, X-rays taken, and the blood type of each body determined.

Analysis was also made of the seeds, fabrics and other materials found in the coffins, and of the position of each mummy inside the altar of the Konjikidō.

Of the four mummies, one was only a decapitated head. This had belonged to the last chieftain, Yasuhira, who had been beheaded after the fall of Hiraizumi to the Kamakura shogunate in 1189. Yasuhira's head bore clear traces of sword cuts and punctures. Although their internal organs had been devoured by rats, most of the mummies were otherwise in a good state of preservation. The least well preserved was the first chieftain, Kiyohira, who had died in 1128. Evidence of pathologies was found on several of the mummies, with both Kiyohira and his grandson Hidehira showing signs of having suffered from disease of the spinal column. Hidehira and his father Motohira would both have been rather obese while they were alive. The estimated ages at death of the four mummies all matched the available historical information as closely as

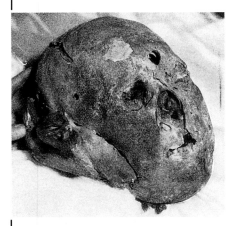

ABOVE: Mummified head of Yasuhira; his right ear has been cut off.

RIGHT: Investigations of the third chieftain, Hidehira, being conducted in 1950.

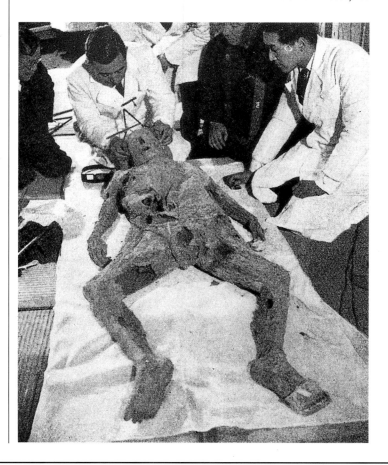

Central altar of the Konjikido Hall. The mummies are housed in special containers at its base.

could be expected.

One of the main points of debate regarding the Northern Fujiwara has long been their ethnic or racial identity. From the eighth century AD the Japanese state based in the Nara-Kyoto region began full-fledged military expansion into the northeast. The people of the latter region were called *Emishi* or other derogatory names meaning "eastern barbarians". This terminology was clearly influenced by Chinese concepts of a civilized core surrounded in all cardinal directions by peripheral barbarians. Such thinking persisted as late as the sixteenth century, when Iberian merchants arriving from Southeast Asia were called *Namban* or "southern barbarians". It is therefore possible that the Emishi could simply have been provincial Japanese who opposed the Japanese state and were designated barbarians in order to prove that, like China, Japan was now civilized enough to have such barbarians at its borders. Alternatively, the Emishi may really have been a quite separate ethnic group — presumably related to the Ainu who are known to have inhabited Hokkaido and neighbouring islands from at least the medieval period.

The Northern Fujiwara were the most powerful Emishi rulers with an extensive kingdom based on trade, horses and gold. Kiyohira referred to himself as the "head of the eastern barbarians", but his father is known to have been a high-ranking Kyoto aristocrat who was dispatched to the provinces. What, then, could the actual skeletons of the Northern Fujiwara tell us about their ethnic identity? Were they Japanese or Ainu?

Although there was considerable variation in skull dimensions between the four mummies, with Hidehira having a particularly long face, the results of the 1950 investigation clearly showed that the Northern Fujiwara were anatomically much closer to modern Japanese than to the Ainu. This confirms the historical data that the family was originally of Kyoto origin, but it leaves open the historical question of why a family of such pedigree should have chosen to associate itself with the "barbarians" of the east.

One remaining problem concerns the origins of the mummification techniques used on the Konjikidō corpses. The nineteenth-century Japanese explorer Mamiya Rinzō described the mummification of Ainu chiefs on Sakhalin, and prehistoric mummies have also been found in the Aleutian Islands. Many scholars have concluded that it was influence from such northern peoples that led to the custom of mummification being adopted by the Northern Fujiwara. The problem with this argument, however, is that no mummies are known from neighbouring Hokkaido. At present, therefore, the roots of the tradition of mummification that flourished briefly in northeast Japan in the twelfth century remain a mystery. ■

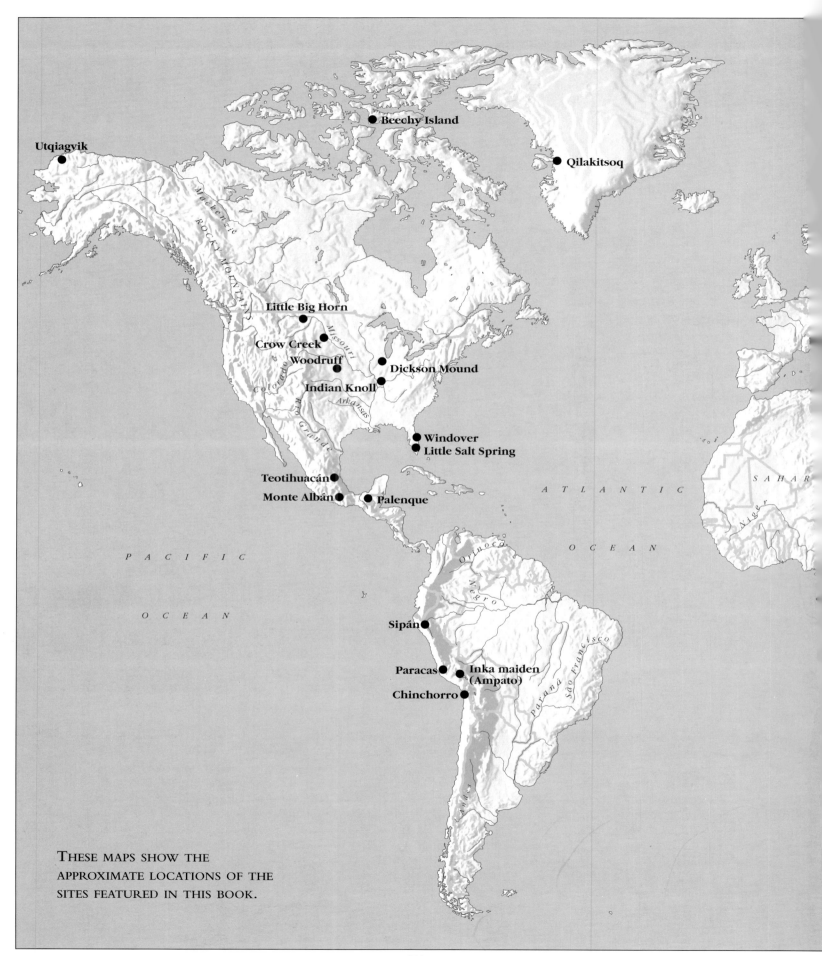

Utqiagvik

Beechy Island

Qilakitsoq

ROCKY MOUNTAINS

Mackenzie

Little Big Horn

Crow Creek

Woodruff

Missouri

Colorado

Rio Grande

Arkansas

Dickson Mound

Indian Knoll

Windover
Little Salt Spring

Teotihuacán

Monte Albán

Palenque

ATLANTIC

SAHAR

Niger

PACIFIC

OCEAN

OCEAN

Orinoco

Negro

Sipán

Paracas

Inka maiden
(Ampato)

Chinchorro

Paraná

São Francisco

Andes

THESE MAPS SHOW THE
APPROXIMATE LOCATIONS OF THE
SITES FEATURED IN THIS BOOK.

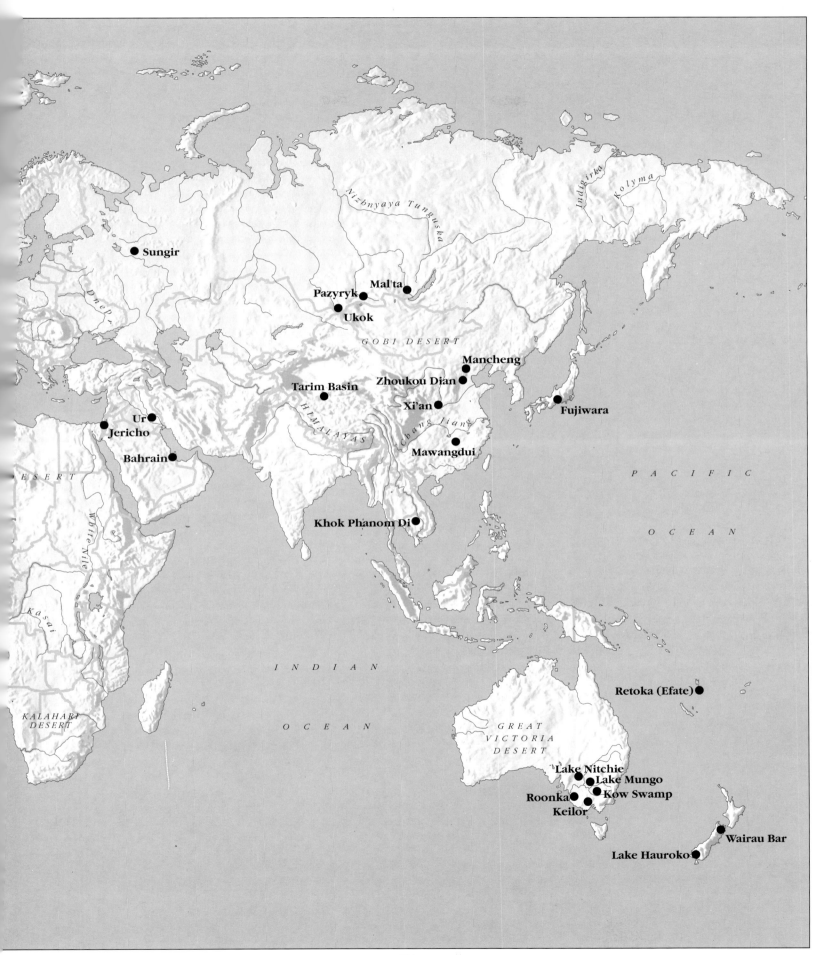

Sungir

Mal'ta

Pazyryk

Ukok

GOBI DESERT

Mancheng

Zhoukou Dian

Tarim Basin

Xi'an

HIMALAYAS

Chang Jiang

Fujiwara

Ur

Jericho

Mawangdui

Bahrain

PACIFIC

OCEAN

DESERT

White Nile

Khok Phanom Di

Kasai

KALAHARI
DESERT

INDIAN

OCEAN

Retoka (Efate)

GREAT
VICTORIA
DESERT

Lake Nitchie

Lake Mungo

Kow Swamp

Roonka

Keilor

Wairau Bar

Lake Hauroko

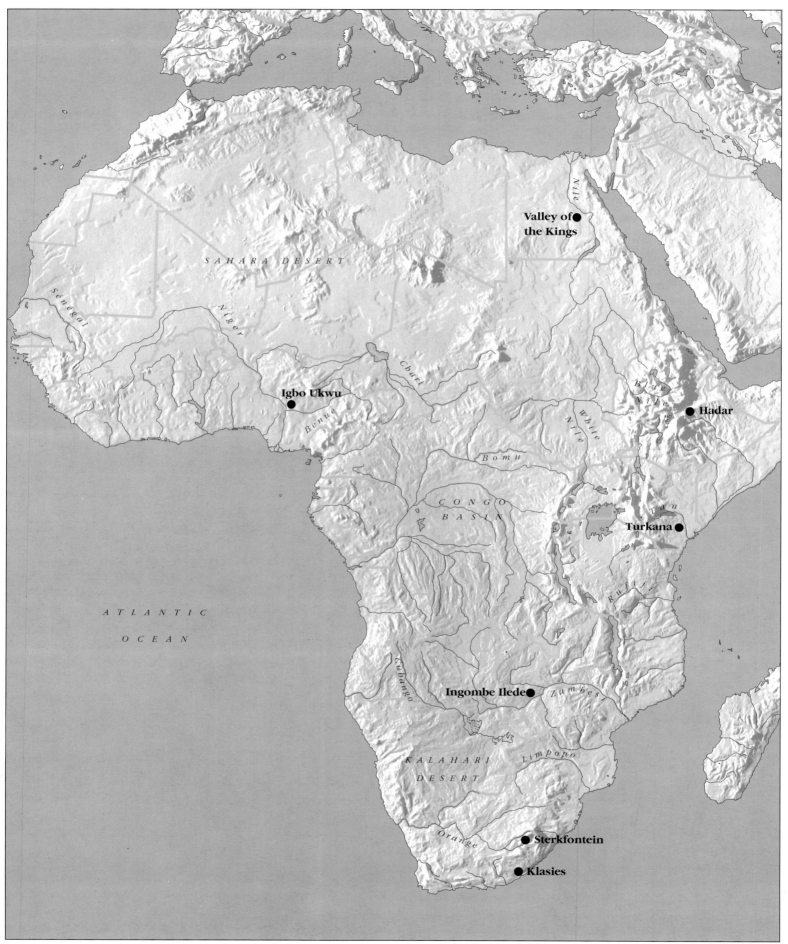

SAHARA DESERT

Valley of
the Kings ●

Nile

Senegal

Niger

Chari

Blue Nile

Igbo Ukwu ●

Benue

Bomu

White Nile

Hadar ●

CONGO
BASIN

Tana

ATLANTIC

OCEAN

Turkana ●

Rufiji

Cubango

Ingombe Ilede ●

Zambesi

KALAHARI
DESERT

Limpopo

Orange

Sterkfontein ●

Klasies ●

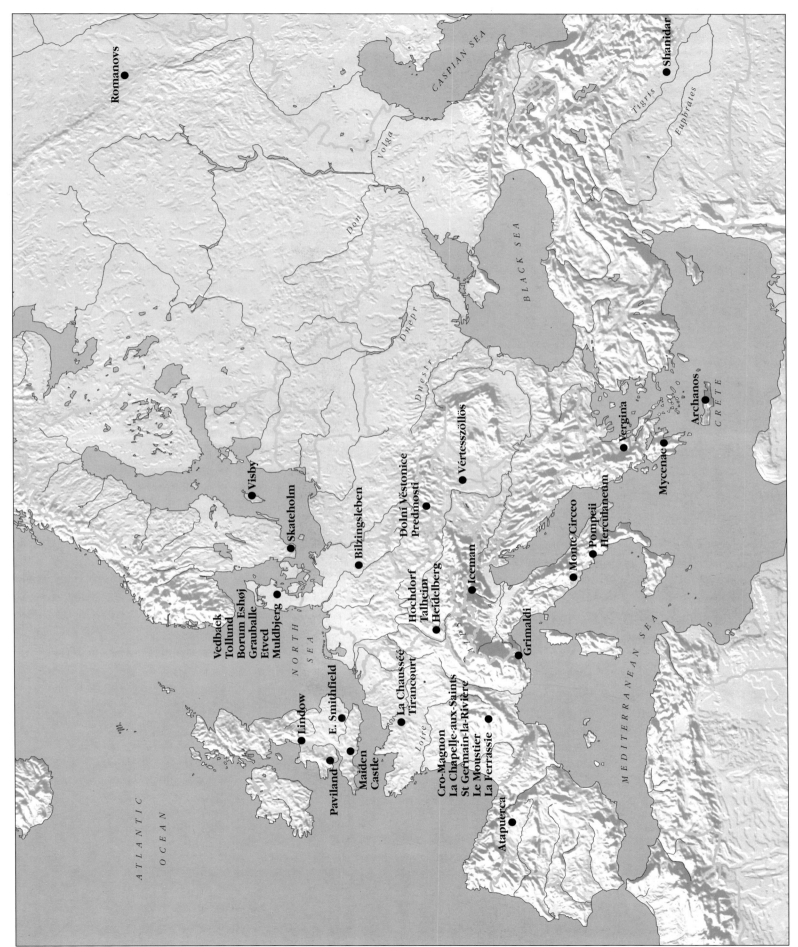

Romanovs

Shanidar

CASPIAN SEA

Volga

Don

BLACK SEA

Dnepr

Dniestr

Tigris

Euphrates

Visby

Skateholm

Bilzingsleben

Dolní Věstonice
Předmostí

Vértesszöllös

Archanos

Vergina

CRETE

Mycenae

Vedbaek
Tollund
Borum Eshøj
Grauballe
Etved
Muldbjerg

NORTH
SEA

Monte Circeo

Pompeii
Herculaneum

Hochdorf
Talheim
Heidelberg

Iceman

Lindow

E. Smithfield

La Chaussée
Tirancourt

A L P S

Grimaldi

Paviland

Maiden
Castle

Loire

Cro-Magnon
La Chapelle-aux-Saints
St Germain-la-Rivière
Le Moustier
La Ferrassie

M E D I T E R R A N E A N   S E A

Atapuerca

ATLANTIC
OCEAN

BIBLIOGRAPHY

PREFACE

Brothwell, D. 1986. *The Bog Man and the Archaeology of People*, British Museum Press: London.

Cockburn, A. & Cockburn, E. (eds) 1980. *Mummies, Disease and Ancient Cultures*, Cambridge University Press: Cambridge.

Spindler, K. *et al.* (eds.) l995. *Human Mummies. A Global Survey of their Status and the Techniques of Conservation*, Springer-Verlag: New York.

BONES

1. LUCY: OUR MOST FAMOUS RELATIVE

Johanson, D. C. 1996. "Face-to-face with Lucy's family", *National Geographic* 189, pp. 96-117.

Johanson, D. & Edey, M. 1981. *Lucy: The Beginnings of Humankind*, Simon & Schuster: New York.

2. THE TURKANA BOY

Leakey, R. & Walker, A. 1985. "*Homo erectus* unearthed", *National Geographic* 168, pp. 625-9.

Walker, A. & Leakey, R. (eds) 1993. *The Nariokotome* Homo Erectus *Skeleton*, Harvard University Press: Cambridge, MA.

3. BEFORE THE NEANDERTHALS: THE FIRST EUROPEANS

Bahn, P. G. 1996. "Treasure of the Sierra Atapuerca", *Archaeology* 49 (91), pp. 45-8.

Carbonell, E. *et al.* 1995. "Lower Pleistocene hominids and artifacts from Atapuerca-TD6 (Spain)", *Science* 269, pp. 826-30.

Cook, J. *et al.* 1982. "A review of the chronology of the European Middle Pleistocene hominid record", *Yearbook of Physical Anthropology* 25, pp. 19-65.

Kraatz, R. 1989. "A review of recent research on Heidelberg Man, *Homo erectus heidelbergensis*", in *Ancestors: The Hard Evidence* (ed. E. Delson), Alan R. Liss: New York. pp. 268-71.

4. PEKING AND JAVA MAN

Huang Wanpo *et al.* 1995. "Early *Homo* and associated artifacts from Asia", *Nature* 378, pp. 275-8.

Sémah, F. (ed.) 1991. "100 Years of hominid discovery in Java"; collection of papers in *Bulletin of the Indo-Pacific Prehistory Association* 11.

Shapiro, H. L. 1974. *Peking Man: The Discovery, Disappearance and Mystery of a Priceless Scientific Treasure*, Allen & Unwin: London.

5. EARLIEST AUSTRALIANS

Flood, J. 1995. *Archaeology of the Dreamtime*, 3rd ed., Angus & Robertson: Sydney.

6. HUMAN SACRIFICE AT ARCHANES-ANEMOSPILIA

Catling, H. W. 1979-80. "Archaeology in Greece 1979-80", *Archaeological Reports* 26, pp. 50-51.

Hughes, D. D. 1991. *Human Sacrifice in Ancient Greece*, Routledge: London.

GRAVES

7. THE PUZZLE OF NEANDERTHAL BURIAL

Defleur, A. 1993. *Les sépultures moustériennes*, CNRS: Paris.

Solecki, R. S. 1971. *Shanidar: The First Flower People*, Alfred A. Knopf: New York.

Stringer, C. & Gamble, C. 1993. *In Search of the Neanderthals*, Thames & Hudson: London & New York.

Trinkaus, E. & Shipman, P. 1992. *The Neanderthals: Changing the Image of Mankind*, Alfred A. Knopf: New York.

8. LATE ICE AGE BURIALS OF EURASIA

Binant, P. 1991. *La Préhistoire de la Mort: les premières sépultures en Europe*, Editions Errance: Paris.

Jelínek, J. 1992. "New Upper Palaeolithic burials from Dolní Vestonice", in *5 Million Years, the Human Adventure* (ed. M. Toussaint), *ERAUL (Etudes et Recherches Archéologiques de l'Université de Liège)* 56, pp. 207-28.

9. JERICHO SKULLS

Kenyon, K. 1982. *Excavations at Jericho* 3, British School of Archaeology in Jerusalem: London.

Mellaart, J. 1975. *The Neolithic of the Near East*, Thames & Hudson: London.

Rollefson, G. 1983. "Ritual and ceremony at neolithic Ain Ghazal (Jordan)", *Paléorient* 9 (92), pp. 29-38.

10. LA CHAUSSÉE-TIRANCOURT

Joussaume, R. 1987. *Dolmens for the Dead*, Batsford: London.

Masset, C. 1993. *Les Dolmens: Sociétés Néolithiques, Pratiques Funéraires*, Editions Errance: Paris.

Mohen, J-P. 1989. *The World of Megaliths*, Cassell: London.

Scarre, C.J. 1984. "Kin groups in megalithic burials", *Nature* 311, pp. 512-13.

11. THE TALHEIM NEOLITHIC MASS BURIAL

Bogucki, P. 1996. "The spread of early farming in Europe", *American Scientist* 84(3), pp. 242-53.

Keeley, L. 1996. *War Before Civilization*, Oxford University Press: New York.

Wahl, J. & König, H. G. 1987. "Anthropologisch-traumatologische Untersuchung der menschlichen Skelettreste aus dem bandkeramischen Massengrab bei Talheim, Kreis Heilbronn", *Fundberichte aus Baden-Württemberg* 12, pp. 65-193.

12. MASS BURIALS IN NORTH AMERICA

Fagan, B. 1995. *Ancient North America* (2nd ed.), Thames & Hudson: London & New York.

Wedel, W. 1986. *Central Plains Prehistory*, University of Nebraska Press: Lincoln.

Zimmerman, L. 1985. *Peoples of Prehistoric South Dakota*, University of Nebraska Press: Lincoln.

13. MASS GRAVES: VISBY AND EAST SMITHFIELD

Hawkins, D. 1990. "The Black Death and the new London cemeteries of 1348", *Antiquity* 64, pp. 637-42.

Thordeman, B. (ed.) 1939-40. *Armour from the Battle of Wisby 1361*, Stockholm.

Thordeman, B. 1946. *Invasionen paa Gotland 1361*, Copenhagen.

14. THE TRAGIC END OF THE ROMANOVS

O'Conor, J. F. 1972. *The Sokolov Investigation of the Alleged Murder of the Russian Imperial Family*, Souvenir Press: London / Speller & Sons: New York.

Radzinsky, E. 1992. *The Last Tsar*, Doubleday: New York / Hodder & Stoughton: London.

CEMETERIES

15. SCANDINAVIAN MESOLITHIC BURIALS

Larsson, L. 1993. "The Skateholm Project: Late Mesolithic coastal settlement in southern Sweden", in *Case Studies in European Prehistory* (ed. P. Bogucki), CRC Press: Boca Raton, pp. 31-62.

Grøn, O. & Skaarup, J. 1991. "Møllegabet II - a submerged Mesolithic site and a `boat burial` from Aerø", *Journal of Danish Archaeology* 10, pp. 38-50.

16. MURRAY VALLEY CEMETERIES

Flood, J. *Archaeology of the Dreamtime*, 3rd ed., Angus & Robertson, Sydney.

17. THE ROYAL CEMETERY AT UR

Woolley, L. 1934. *Ur Excavations II: The Royal Cemetery*, 2 vols, British Museum: London.

Woolley, L. & Moorey, P. R. S. 1982. *Ur "of the Chaldees"*, revised ed., Herbert Press: London.

18. THE CEMETERY AT KHOK PHANOM DI

Higham, C. & Thosarat, R. 1994. *Khok Phanom Di: Prehistoric Adaptation to the World's Richest Habitat*, Harcourt Brace College Publishers: Fort Worth, Texas.

19. BATTLE CEMETERIES

Pritchett, W. K. 1985. *The Greek State at War*, IV, University of California Press: Berkeley.

Sharples, N. M. 1991. *Maiden Castle: Excavations and Field Survey 1985-6*, English Heritage: London.

Sharples, N. M. 1991. *The English Heritage Book of Maiden Castle*, Batsford: London.

Wheeler, R. E. M. 1943. *Maiden Castle, Report of the Research Committee of the Society of Antiquaries* XII: Oxford.

20. THE PARACAS NECROPOLIS

Paul, A. (ed.) 1991. *Paracas Art and Architecture: Object and Context in South Coastal Peru*, Iowa (especially articles by Paul [2], Daggett and Silverman).

Tello, J. C. & Mejía Xesspe, T. 1979. *Paracas, Segunda Parte: Cavernas y Necrópolis*, Universidad Nacional Mayor de San Marcos.

21. THE TEMPLE OF QUETZALCOATL AT TEOTIHUACÁN

Cabrera Castro, R., Sugiyama, S. & Cowgill, G. L. 1991. "The Templo de Quetzalcoatl Project at Teotihuacán: A Preliminary Report", *Ancient Mesoamerica* 2(1), pp. 77-92.

Cabrera Castro, R., Cowgill, G., Sugiyama, S. & Serrano, C. 1989. "El Proyecto Templo de Quetzalcoatl", *Arqueología* 5, INAH: Mexico, pp. 51-79.

Carlson, J. B. 1993. "Rise and Fall of the City of the Gods", *Archaeology* 46(6), pp. 58-69.

Sugiyama, S. 1989. "Burials Dedicated to the Old Temple of Quetzalcoatl at Teotihuacán, Mexico", *American Antiquity* 54, pp. 85-106.

22. INGOMBE ILEDE

Fagan, B. M., Phillipson, D. W. & Daniels, S. G. 1969. *Iron Age Cultures in Zambia (Dambwa, Ingombe Ilede and the Tonga)*, II, Chatto & Windus: London.

Phillipson, D. W. & Fagan, B. M. 1969. "The date of the Ingombe Ilede burials", *Journal of African History* 10, pp. 199-204.

23. VOICES OF THE SEVENTH CAVALRY

Fox, R. A. 1993. *Archaeology, History, and Custer's Last Battle*, University of Oklahoma Press: Norman.

Scott, D. D., Fox, R. A., Connor, C. A. & Harmon, D. 1989. *Archaeological Perspectives on the Battle of the Little Big Horn*, University of Oklahoma Press: Norman.

TOMBS

24. THE SHAFT GRAVES OF MYCENAE

Dickinson, O. T. P. K. 1977. *The Origins of Mycenaean Civilisation*, Studies in Mediterranean Archaeology 49: Göteborg.

25. DANISH BRONZE AGE LOG COFFIN BURIALS

Glob, P. V. 1974. *The Mound People*, Faber & Faber: London.

Jensen, J. 1982. *The Prehistory of Denmark*, Methuen: London.

26. TOMBS IN THE PERSIAN GULF

Bibby, G. 1971. *Looking for Dilmun*, Alfred A. Knopf: New York.

Cleuziou, S. & Vogt, B. 1983. "Umm an-Nar burial customs, new evidence from Tomb A at Hili North", *Proceedings of the Seminar for Arabian Studies* 13, pp. 37-52.

Moawiyah, I. 1982. *Excavations of the Arab Expedition at Sar el Jisr*, Ministry of Information: Manama, Bahrain.

27. KLASIES RIVER MOUTH CAVE 5

Deacon, J. 1984. "Later Stone Age people and their descendants in southern Africa", in Klein, R.G. (ed.), *Southern African prehistory and paleoenvironments*, A.A. Balkema: Rotterdam, pp. 221-328.

Hall, S. & Binneman, J. N. F. 1987. "Later Stone Age burial variability in the Cape: a social interpretation", *South African Archaeological Bulletin* 42, pp. 140-52.

28. HOCHDORF

Biel, J. 1980. "Treasure from a Celtic tomb", *National Geographic* 157, pp. 428-38.
  1986. *Der Keltenfürst von Hochdorf*, Konrad Theiss: Stuttgart.

Wells, P. S. 1980. "Iron Age Central Europe", *Archaeology* 33(5), pp. 6-11.
  1984. *Farms, Villages, and Cities: Commerce and Urban Origins in Late Prehistoric Europe*, Cornell University Press: Ithaca, NY.

29. PHILIP OF MACEDON

Andronicos, M. 1984. *Vergina: The Royal Tombs and the Ancient City*, Athens.

Exhibition catalogue 1980. *The Search for Alexander: An Exhibition*, National Gallery: Washington.

30. ROYAL BURIALS OF EARLY IMPERIAL CHINA

Cotterell, A. 1981. *The First Emperor of China*, Macmillan: London.

Pirazzoli-t'Serstevens, M. 1982. *The Han Civilization of China*, Phaidon: Oxford.

31. THE LORDS OF SIPÁN

Alva, W. 1988. "Discovering the world's richest unlooted tomb", *National Geographic* 174 (4), pp. 510-49.

Alva, W. 1990. "New tomb of royal splendor", *National Geographic* 177 (6), pp. 2-15.

Alva, W. & Donnan, C. 1993. *Royal Tombs of Sipán*, Fowler Museum of Cultural History: University of California Los Angeles.

32. MONTE ALBÁN, TOMB 7

Caso, A. 1969. *El tesoro de Monte Albán*, Memorias del Instituto Nacional de Antropología e Historia 3, Mexico City.

McCafferty, S. D. & G. G. 1994. "Engendering Tomb 7 at Monte Albán: Respinning an old yarn", *Current Anthropology* 35 (2), pp. 143-66.

Rubín de la Borbolla, D. F. 1969. "La osamenta humana encontrada en la Tumba 7: Appendix", in Caso, pp. 275-324.

33. THE TOMB OF PACAL AT PALENQUE

Greene Robertson, M. 1983. *The Sculpture of Palenque*, I: *The Temple of the Inscriptions*, Princeton University Press: Princeton, NJ.

Ruz Lhuillier, A. 1952. "Estudio de la Cripta del Templo de las Inscripciones en Palenque", Tlatoani, Boletín de la Sociedad de Alumnos de la Escuela Nacional de Antropología e Historia, Mexico, I (5, 6), pp. 2-28.
  1953. "The Mystery of the Temple of the Inscriptions" (trans. J. Alden Mason), *Archaeology* 6 (1), pp. 3-11.

34. IGBO-UKWU

Shaw, T. 1970. *Igbo-Ukwu*, 2 vols, Northwestern University Press: Evanston, IL.

Shaw, T. 1978. *Nigeria. Its archaeology and early history*, Thames & Hudson: London & New York.

35. EARLY PACIFIC ISLANDERS

Bellwood, P. 1978. *Man's Conquest of the Pacific*, Collins: Auckland.

Trotter, M. & McCulloch, B. 1989. *Unearthing New Zealand*, GP Books: Wellington.

CORPSES

36. DISCOVERING THE ORIGINS OF NEW WORLD HUMANS

Clausen, C. J. *et al.* 1979. "Little Salt Spring, Florida: a unique underwater site", *Science* 203, pp. 609-14.

Doran, G. H. 1992. "Problems and potential of wet sites in North America: the example of Windover", in *The Wetland Revolution in Prehistory* (ed. B. Coles), Prehistoric Society / WARP: Exeter, pp. 125-34.

Doran, G. H. *et al.* 1986. "Anatomical, cellular and molecular analysis of 8,000-yr-old human brain tissue from the Windover archaeological site", *Nature* 323, pp. 803-6.

37. THE ICEMAN

Bahn, P.G. 1995. "Last days of the Iceman", *Archaeology* 48 (3), pp. 66-70.

Spindler, K. 1994. *The Man in the Ice*, Weidenfeld & Nicolson: London.

38. PAZYRYK AND THE UKOK PRINCESS

Polosmak, N. 1994. "A mummy unearthed from the Pastures of Heaven", *National Geographic* 186 (4), pp. 80-103.

Rudenko, S. 1970. *Frozen Tombs of Siberia: The Pazyryk Burials of Iron Age Horsemen*, University of California Press: Berkeley & Los Angeles / Dent: London.

39. LOST CAUCASOIDS OF THE TARIM BASIN

Allen, T. B. 1996. "The Silk Road's Lost World", *National Geographic* 189(93), pp. 44-51.

Mair, V. (ed.) 1995. "The mummified remains found in the Tarim Basin", collection of papers in *The Journal of Indo-European Studies*, 23(3-4).

40. HERCULANEUM AND POMPEII

Gore, R. 1984. "After 2,000 years of silence the dead do tell tales at Vesuvius", *National Geographic* 165, pp. 556-613.

41. INKA MOUNTAIN SACRIFICES

McIntyre, L. 1957. *The Incredible Incas and Their Timeless Land*, National Geographic Society.

Reinhard, J. 1992. "Sacred Peaks of the Andes", *National Geographic* 181 (3), pp. 84-111.

Reinhard, J. 1996. "Peru's Ice Maidens: Unwrapping the Secrets", *National Geographic* 189 (6), pp. 62-81.

Schobinger, J. 1995. *Aconcagua: Un enterratorio incaico a 5.300 metros de altura*, Inca Editorial: Mendoza, Argentina.

42. BOG BODIES OF BRITAIN AND DENMARK

Glob, P. V. 1969. *The Bog People*, Faber & Faber: London.

Stead, I. M., Bourke, J. B. & Brothwell, D. 1986. *Lindow Man: The Body in the Bog*, British Museum Press: London.

Turner, R. C. & Scaife, R. G. (eds) 1995. *Bog Bodies. New Discoveries and New Perspectives*, British Museum Press: London.

van der Sanden, W. 1996. *Through Nature to Eternity*, Batavian Lion International: Amsterdam.

43. THE FRANKLIN EXPEDITION

Beattie, O. & Geiger, J. 1987. *Frozen in Time*, Bloomsbury: London / Dutton: New York.

44. MUMMIES IN THE FAR NORTH

Dekin, A. A. 1987. "Sealed in time: ice entombs an Eskimo family for five centuries", *National Geographic* 171 (6), pp. 824-36.

Hart Hansen, J. P., Meldgaard, J. & Nordqvist, J. (eds) 1991. *The Greenland Mummies*, British Museum Press: London / Smithsonian Institution Press: Washington.

MUMMIES

45. CHINCHORRO MUMMIES

Arriaza, B. T. 1995. *Beyond Death: The Chinchorro Mummies of Ancient Chile*, Smithsonian Institution Press: Washington & London.

Arriaza, B. T. 1995. "Chinchorro Bioarchaeology: Chronology and Mummy Seriation", *Latin American Antiquity* 6 (1), pp. 35-55.

Arriaza, B. T. 1995. "Chile's Chinchorro Mummies", *National Geographic* 187 (3), pp. 68-89.

46. MAKING MUMMIES

Adams, B. 1984. *Egyptian Mummies*, Shire Egyptology: Princes Risborough.

Andrews, C. 1984. *Egyptian Mummies*, British Museum Publications: London.

D'Auria, S., Lacovara, P. & Roehrig, C. 1988. *Mummies and Magic: The Funerary Arts of Ancient Egypt*, Boston.

Harris, J. E. & Weeks, K. 1973. *X-raying the Pharaohs*, Macdonald: London.

Spencer, A. J. 1982. *Death in Ancient Egypt*, Penguin: Harmondsworth.

47. MUMMIES AND MEDICINE

David, A. R. (ed.) 1979. *Manchester Museum Mummy Project*, Manchester University Press: Manchester.
      (ed.) 1986. *Science in Egyptology*, Manchester Univerity Press: Manchester.

Goyon, J.-C. & Josset, P. 1988. *Un Corps pour l'éternité: Autopsie d'une momie*, Le Léopard d'Or: Paris.

48. THE DEIR EL-BAHRI CACHE

Harris, J. E. & Wente, E. 1980. *X-Ray Atlas of the Royal Mummies*, Chicago University Press: Chicago.

Maspero. G. 1881. *La Trouvaille de Deir el Bahari*, Cairo.
      1889. *Les Momies Royales de Deir el Bahari*, Cairo.

Smith, G. E. 1912. *Cairo Catalogue: Royal Mummies*, Imprimerie de l'Institut français d'Archéologie Orientale: Cairo.

49. THE FAMILY OF TUTANKHAMEN

Carter, H. 1923-33. *The Tomb of Tut.ankh.amen*, Cassell: London.

Desroches-Noblecourt, C. 1965. *Tutankhamen*, Penguin: Harmondsworth.

Harrison, R. G, & Abdalla, A. G. 1972. "The remains of Tutankhamun", *Antiquity* 46, pp. 8-14.

Reeves, N. 1988. "New light on Kiya from texts in the British Museum", *Journal of Egyptian Archaeology* 74, pp. 91-101.
      1990. *The Complete Tutankhamun*, Thames & Hudson: London & New York.

50. THE MUMMIES OF THE NORTHERN FUJIWARA

Sakurai, K. & Ogata, T. 1980. "Japanese mummies", in *Mummies, Disease and Ancient Cultures* (ed. A. & E. Cockburn), Cambridge University Press: Cambridge, pp. 211-23.

INDEX

A

abd er-Rassul, Ahmed & Hussein 188, 190
Aborigines, Australian 26-9, 66-7
Acheulean tradition 19
Adovasio, James 138
adzes 47, 132
Agamemnon, King 92, 95
Ahmose, King 188
Aigai (Macedonia) 110-13
Ain Ghazal (Jordan) 42, 44-5
Ainu 199
Akalamdug, King 70
Akhenaten (Amenhotep IV), King 192, 196
Aleutian Islands 199
Alexander the Great 77, 111
Alva, Walter 118
Amarna (Egypt) 192
Amenhotep II, King 190, 192
Amenhotep III, King 184, 190, 192, 196
Amenhotep IV, King see Akhenaten
Americans, Native, Battle of the Little
    Big Horn 88-9; mass burials 50-1;
    origins of 138-9
Amida Buddha, statue of 198
Ampato (Peru) 160
ancestor cult 44-5
Anderson, Anna 59; J.D.W. 86
Andronicos, Manolis 110-13
Androutsos, Odysseus 77
Ankhesenpaaten 192, 196
Anozie family 130
Aramis (Ethiopia) 17
Archanes-Anemospilia (Crete) 30-1
Ardipithecus ramidus 17
Arena Blanca (Peru) 79
Arica (Chile) 180
armour 53, 110-11, 112
Arrhidaios 113
arrows & arrowheads, Athens 77; Iceman
    144; Mycenae 95; Pazyryk 150;
    Scandinavia 64, 65
Arsuaga, Juan Luis 20
ash, in coffins 55
Atapuerca (Spain) 15, 20-1
Athens (Greece) 77
Aurignacian burials 38-9
Australia, cemeteries 66-7; human
    origins 26-9
Australopithecus afarensis 14-16
Australopithecus africanus 16
Australopithecus anamensis 16
Avdonin, Aleksandr 58
axes (see also handaxes), Iceman 141;
    Indian Knoll 51; La Chaussée-Tiran-
    court 47; Pazyryk 150; Skateholm 62;
    Talheim 49; Ur 68
Ayia Triadha (Crete) 31
Aztecs 125

B

backpack, wooden 144
Bader, Otto 39
Bahrain 100-2
bark cloth 86, 132
Barrow (Alaska) 174-7
barrows see tumuli
baskets 79, 101
Batres, Leopoldo 82
battle graves, Crow Creek 50; Greek 76-
    7; Little Big Horn 88-9; Maiden
    Castle 74-6; Roman 77; Talheim 48-9;
    Visby 52-4
beads (see also necklaces; pendants),
    Dilmun 101; Hochdorf 108; Igbo-Ukwu
    130, 131; Indian Knoll 51; Ingombe
    Ilede 86; Khok Phanom Di 72, 73;
    Klasies River Mouth Cave 104-5; La
    Chaussée-Tirancourt 47; Magan 102;
    Murray Valley 66; Mycenae 95; New
    Hebrides 133; Palenque 127; Sipán
    118, 120, 121; Sungir 39-40; Teoti-
    huacán 84; Vedbaek 62; Woodruff
    Ossuary 51
Beattie, Owen 170-1
Beechy Island (Canada) 170-1
Benteen, Capt. Frederick 88
Biel, Jorg 107
Bilzingsleben (Germany) 20
Binneman, Johan 104, 105
Black, Davidson 22
Black Death 52, 54-5
Blanc, Alberto 35
boats 65, 158
bog bodies 164-9
bones, animal (see also meat), in bur-
    ials 35, 36, 40, 64, 65, 86; carved
    124-5
books 114-15
Borgbjerg (Denmark) 99
Borre Fen (Denmark) 169
Borum Eshøj (Denmark) 98-9
Boule, Marcellin 34
Bouyssonie, Amédé & Jean 34
Bowler, Jim 27
bows 141-4, 150
bracelets (bangles; wristlets), Egtved
    96; Igbo-Ukwu 130, 131; Ingombe Ilede
    86; Mal'ta 40; Nan Douwas 132; New
    Hebrides 133; Paviland Cave 39;
    Pompeii 158; Sungir 39-40
Braine, William 170, 171
brains 99, 139, 140, 141
Bray, Donald 170
Bronze Age burials, Denmark 96-9
bronzes 130-1
Broom, Robert 16
Brown, Peter 28

Brugsch, Emile 188
bucket 99
Buckland, William 38
burial, earliest deliberate 15, 21, 34-6

C

Cahokia (USA) 51
Cannae (Italy) 77
cannibalism 24-5, 35, 133, 170
canoe 65
canopic jars 183
Carbonell, Eudald 20
Carlson, John 84
Caso, Alfonso 122, 123, 124-5
Cassius Dio 154
Cavernas burials 78-80
celts 127, 129
Cerro Colorado (Peru) 78-9
Cerro el Toro (Argentina) 160
Cerro el Plomo (Chile) 160
Chairon 77
Chaironeia (Greece) 77
Chan Bahlum II, King 129
Chaplin, J.H. 86
charcoal, in burials 40, 105, 114
chariots 114
Chinchorro Beach (Chile) 180-1
Clausen, Carl 139
clothing, Aboriginal burials 67; bog
    bodies 168-9; Chinchorro mummies 180,
    181; Danish bronze age burials 96-7,
    98; Franklin expedition victims 171;
    Iceman 145; Inka sacrifice victims
    160; Maori burial 133; Mawangdui
    tombs 115; Paracas mummies 80;
    Pazyryk burials 150; Pompeii victims
    156; Sipán tomb 120, 121; Sungir Ice
    Age burial 40; Tarim Basin mummies
    152; Thule culture mummies 174; Ur
    royal tombs 71; Windover Pond burials
    138
Clytemnestra 92
coffins, Danish Bronze Age burials 96-9;
    East Smithfield 55; Egypt 182, 188,
    190, 196; Franklin expedition victim
    170; Fujiwara 198; Mawangdui 114;
    Murray Valley 66; Pazyryk 147-50;
    Sipán 119-20, 121; Wairau Bar 132
Cohuna (Australia) 26, 28
combs 96, 99, 108
Coobool Creek (Australia) 66
copper 101
coppersmith 145
Cornelius Tacitus 154
cremations, Australia 27, 66-7;
    Greece 76-7; Macedonia 111-12, 113
Crete 30-1

Cro-Magnon (France) 39
Cro-Magnon Man 20
Crow Creek (USA) 50
Cueva Morín (Spain) 39
Custer, Lt. Col. George Armstrong 88-9

D

daggers & knives 30, 39, 62, 95, 98, 144, 150
Darion (Belgium) 49
Dart, Raymond 16
Davis, Theodore 192
death, causes of (see also disease; sacrifice), Athenian battle victims 77; Australopithecines 16; Crow Creek burials 50; Franklin expedition 170-1; Herculaneum victims 158; Klasies River Mouth burial 104; Little Big Horn victims 89; Maiden Castle burials 74, 76; Pazyryk burial 150; Pompeii victims 154, 156, 158; Romanov family 56-9; Talheim burials 48-9; Thule mummies 176-7; Turkana Boy 19; Tutankhamen 186; Visby burials 53-4
Deir el-Bahri (Egypt) 188-90
Dekin, Albert 176-7
Delion, battle of 77
Demidova 59
dentistry 59, 89
Dian, Kings of 115
Dickson Mound (USA) 51
diet, Aborigines 27; Australopithecus afarensis 15; bog bodies 169; Chinchorro culture 181; Crow Creek burials 50-1; Dilmun burials 101; Ertebølle culture 62; Heidelberg man 21; Iceman 141; Little Big Horn casualties 89; Minoan priest 31; Natufian culture 42; Thule mummies 174, 177; Wairau Bar burials 133
Dilmun (Bahrain) 100-1
Dinka people 18
Diomedes, villa of 158
disease (see also Black Death; death, causes of; genetic research; medicine; surgery), Aborigines 29, 66; Americans, Native 50, 51; Australopithecus afarensis (Lucy) 14; bog bodies 168; Egyptian mummies 187; Franklin expedition members 170, 171; Fujiwara 198; Iceman 141; Inka sacrifice victim 162; Little Big Horn casualties 89; Minoan priestess 31; Monte Albán burial 124; Neanderthal burial 35; Thule mummies 174, 177; Turkana Boy 19

Dmanisi (Caucasus) 21
dog burials, Mancheng 114; Pompeii 156, 158; Sipán 119; Skateholm 62, 64, 65
Dolní Vestonice (Moravia) 40
Dooley, Stephen 164
Doran, Glen 139
Dosal, Pedro 82
Dubois, Eugène 19, 22
Duff, Roger 132
Durotriges 76

E

earring 96
East Smithfield (London) 52, 54-5
Egtved (Denmark) 96-8, 99
El Morro (Chile) 180
embalming (see also mummies; mummification) 147, 151, 198
Emishi 199
Eros 158
Ertebølle culture 62-5
Eurydice, Queen 113
excarnation 50, 67, 76, 132
exposure see excarnation
Eyles, Jim 132

F

face masks 95, 127
facial reconstruction, Egyptian mummies 187; Little Big Horn casualty 89; Minoan priests 31; Mycenaean burials 94; Philip of Macedon 113; Romanovs 59
Fagan, Brian 86
Fagg, William 131
fingerprints 169, 187
Fiorelli, Giuseppe 154
fish-hooks 51, 108, 132, 181
flowers, in burials 36, 98
foetuses, mummified 196
footprints 15, 16
Fox, Richard 88
Franklin, Sir John 170-1
Franklin expedition 170-1
Fujiwara 198-9
furniture, Guldhøj 99; Hochdorf 108; Igbo-Ukwu 131; Macedonia 111-12; Pazyryk 150; Pompeii 156

G

Garanger, José 133
genetic research (see also kinship groups), American Indian burials 138-

9; Iceman 140; Khok Phanom Di burials 73; La Chaussée-Tirancourt burials 46, 47; Magan burials 102; Romanov family 59; Tarim Basin mummies 152
gift exchange systems 104, 105
Glob, Peter 168
gold grave goods, Borgbjerg 99; Hochdorf 108; Ingombe Ilede 86; Inka sacrifices 160; Macedonia 110-12, 113; Mancheng 114; Monte Albán 122; Mycenae 92, 94-5; Paracas 80; Pazyryk 150; Pompeii 158; Sipán 118, 120-1; Ur 68, 70-1
Golden, Pte. Patrick 89
Gotland (Sweden) 52-3, 65
grass & reed objects, Chinchorro mummies 181; Iceman 140, 141, 144-5
Grauballe Man 168, 169
grave robbers see looting
Gravettian burials 40
Gray, Tom 14
Greek battle graves 76-7
Grimaldi Cave (Italy) 40
Grinvold, Hans & Jokum 174
Grogh, Erich 160
Grotte des Enfants (Italy) 39
Guldhøj (Denmark) 99
Gundestrup (Denmark) 169
Gurna (Egypt) 188

H

Hadar (Ethiopia) 14, 15, 16
Hall, Simon 105
Hallstatt burials 106-9
handaxes 19, 34
Hannibal 77
harpoons 177
Hart Hansen, J.P. 174
Hartnell, John & Thomas 170, 171
Hauser, Otto 34
'Heidelberg Man' 20, 21
helmets, copper 71
Henuttawy, Queen 188
Herculaneum (Italy) 154, 158
Herihor family 188, 190
Hetepheres, Queen 183, 184
Heuneberg (Germany) 106, 109
hide, in burials 98, 99
Hidehira 198, 199
Hiraizumi (Japan) 198
Hochdorf (Germany) 106-9
Hohenasperg (Germany) 106, 109
Hohmichele (Germany) 106
Hokkaido (Japan) 199
Homo erectus 18-19, 22-5, 26
Homo ergaster 19, 25
Homo habilis 19, 25

horse burials 114, 150
horse trappings 110, 150
Houghton, Philip 132
Huayna Pichu (Peru) 163
Huldre Fen (Denmark) 169

I

Ice Age 21, 38–40
ice picks 177
Iceman 140–5
Igbo-Ukwu (Nigeria) 130–1
Ilo (Peru) 181
Indian Knoll (USA) 50–1
Indians, American *see* Americans, Native
Ingombe Ilede (Zambia) 86–7
Inhapy, Queen 188, 190
Inka sacrifices 160–3
Ipatiev, house of 56
iron age burials, bog bodies 164–9;
    Hochdorf 106–9; Maiden Castle 74–6;
    Pazyryk 146–51

J

jade grave goods 114, 115, 122, 127, 129
Java Man 22, 24–5
Jeraly (Australia) 67
Jericho (Jordan) 42–5
jewellery (*see also* beads; bracelets;
    earring; necklaces; pendants; rings),
    Dilmun burials 101; Ingombe Ilede
    burials 86; Magan burials 102; Myce-
    naean burials 94–5; Romanov family 57;
    Sipán 120; Ur royal burials 68, 71
Johanson, Donald C. 14, 16

K

Kallimachos, General 76
Kanapoi (Kenya) 16
Keilor (Australia) 26
Kenniff Cave (Australia) 27
kettle, bronze 108
Kharitonov 59
Khok Phanom Di (Thailand) 72–3
Kimeu, Kamoya 18
King William Island (Canada) 170
kinship groups (*see also* genetic re-
    search), Egypt 196; Khok Phanom Di
    72–3; La Chaussée-Tirancourt 46, 47;
    Magan 102; Skateholm 62
Kiya, Queen 192, 196
Kiyohira 198, 199
Klasies River Mouth (S. Africa) 104–5
knives *see* daggers & knives

Konjikido Hall (Hiraizumi, Japan) 198–9
Koryakova, Ludmila 58
Kostenki (Russia) 39
Kow Swamp (Australia) 26-8, 65
Kroeber, Alfred 78
Kyoto 199

L

La Chapelle-aux-Saints (France) 34
La Chaussée-Tirancourt (France) 46–7
La Ferrassie (France) 34–5
Laetoli (Tanzania) 15, 16
Lake Garnpung (Australia) 28
Lake Mungo (Australia) 27–8
Lake Nitchie (Australia) 66
Lake Turkana (Kenya) 18–19
Lakedaimonians 77
lapis lazuli 68, 70
Larsson, Lars 62, 64, 65
Le Moustier (France) 34
Leakey, Maeve 16; Richard 18
leather (*see also* clothing; hide; seal-
    skin), Iceman 140, 141, 145;
    Pazyryk tombs 146, 147, 150; Tarim
    Basin mummies 152
Leclerc, Jean 46
Lell, Corp. George 89
Li Cang 115
Liebfried, Renate 107
Lindow Man 164–8, 169
Lindsay Island (Australia) 67
Linear Pottery Culture 48–9
Lithberg, Nils 53
Little Big Horn, battle of 88–9
Little Salt Spring (USA) 139
Liu Sheng, King 114
Livy 77
Longchamps (Belgium) 49
Longgupo Cave (China) 25
looting, Danish bronze age burials 99;
    Dilmun 101; Egypt 188–9; Macedonia
    110; Nan Douwas 132; Pazyryk 147,
    150; Sipán 118; Teotihuacán 84; Ur 71
Lop Nur (China) 152
Loret, Victor 190
Loulan (China) 152
'Lucy' 14–17
lyres 70

M

McCafferty, Geoffrey & Sharisse 124,
    125
Macedonian burials 77, 110–13
Machatas 113

Machu Picchu (Peru) 162–3
Macintosh, N.W.G. 26
Magan 101–2
Magdalenian burials 40
Maiden Castle (England) 74–6
Mal'ta (Russia) 40
Mancheng (China) 114
Mann, Packer Frank 89
Maori burials 132–3
Marathon (Greece) 76–7
Mariette, August 188
Marinatos, Prof. 77
Mary Island (New Zealand) 133
Maska, Karel 40
Maspero, Gaston 188
Masset, Claude 46
Mawangdui (China) 114–15
Maya culture 126–9
Mbara 86–7
mead 108
meals, funerary 64, 93, 98, 101
meat, with burials 74, 76, 101, 132, 150
medicine (*see also* surgery) 186–7
megalithic tombs 46–7
Mejia Xesspe, Toribio 78, 79
Meldgaard, Jørgen 174
Menander, House of 156, 158
Meresankh III, Queen 184
Meretaten 192
Meskalamdug, King 70, 71
mesolithic burials 62–5
Minoan sacrifice 30–1
mirrors 68, 82, 150
Mithras 152
Mixtec burials 122–5
M'Lintock, Capt. Francis 170
Moche burials 118–21
Mojokerto (Java) 25
Mollegabet (Denmark) 65
Mont Lassois (France) 106, 109
Monte Albán (Mexico) 122–5
Monte Circeo (Italy) 35, 36
Mossgiel (Australia) 26
Motohira 198
Mould, Andy 164
Muldbjerg (Denmark) 98
mummies, Chinchorro 180–1; Egypt 182–4,
    186–7, 188–90, 192–6; Inka sacrifices
    162; Japan 198–9; Mycenae 94; Paracas
    78–80; Russia 150–1; Tarim Basin 152–
    3; Thule culture 174–7
mummification 180–1, 182–4, 186, 199
Murray Valley (Australia) 66–7
musical instruments 70, 115
Mycenae, shaft graves 92–5
Mylonas, George 93

N

Nahal Nemar (Israel) 44
Nan Douwas (Caroline Islands) 132
Nan Modal (Caroline Islands) 132
Nariokotome (Kenya) 18, 19
natron 184
Natufian burials 42
Neanderthals 20, 21, 34–6
Nebelgard Fen (Denmark) 169
necklaces (see also beads), Dolní Vesto-
    nice 40; Hochdorf 108; Iceman 145;
    Mal'ta 40; Murray Valley 66, 67;
    Mycenae 94; Nan Douwas 132; New
    Hebrides 133; St Germain-la-Rivière
    40; Sipán 120, 121; Skateholm 64;
    Sungir 40; Teotihuacán 82–4; Vedbaek
    62; Wairau Bar 132
Nefertiti, Queen 192, 196
neolithic burials, Jericho 42–5; La
    Chaussée-Tirancourt 46–7; Talheim 48–9
Nicholas II, Tsar see Romanov family
Nodjmet, Queen 188
Nordqvist, Jørgen 174
Nørlund, Poul 53
Northwest Passage, quest for 170–1

O

obsidian objects 82, 84, 127
ochre, use of, Aboriginal burials 27,
    66, 67; Dolní Vestonice 40; Grimaldi
    Cave 40; Grotte des Enfants 39;
    Jericho 44; Klasies River Mouth Cave
    104–5; Kostenki 39; La Chapelle-aux-
    Saints 34; Paviland Cave 39; Skate-
    holm 64; Sungir 40; Vedbaek 62
Okladnikov, Alexey 35
Oleye (Belgium) 49
oxen burials 71
Ozo burial 131

P

Pääbo, Svante 139
Pacal, King 126–9
Pachacuti, Emperor 163
Palenque (Mexico) 126–9
Papadimitriou, John 93
Paracas (Peru) 78–80
Pardoe, Colin 66, 67
Paul, Anne 80
Pausanias 76, 77, 92
Paviland (Wales) 38–9
Pazyryk burials 146–51
Peiraieus (Greece) 77
Peking Man 22–5

Peloponnesian War 77
pendants 40, 47, 67, 105, 132
Persian Wars 76–7
Petrie, Sir Flinders 187
Pettigrew, Thomas 186
Peyrony, Denis 34
Phila 113
Philip II of Macedon 77, 111, 112–13
Pichu Pichu (Peru) 162
pig burials 133
pins 67, 94, 98, 102, 169
Pinudjem I & II 188, 190
Pithecanthropus erectus 22
plague see Black Death
Plataians 77
Pliny the elder & younger 154
Plutarch 77, 110
Polosmak, Natalya 150
Polybius 77
Polynesian burials 132–3
Pompeii (Italy) 154–8
Pomponius, House of 154
portrait heads, ivory 111, 113
pottery, Archanes-Anemospilia 30, 31;
    bog bodies 169; Dilmun 101; Igbo-Ukwu
    130; Khok Phanom Di 72, 73; La Chau-
    ssée-Tirancourt 47, 48; Magan burials
    102; Maiden Castle 74; Mancheng 114;
    Marathon 77; Mawangdui 115; Monte
    Albán 123; Mycenae 93, 94; Palenque
    127; Sipán 119, 121; Ur 68
Predmostí (Moravia) 40
priests & priestesses, Buddhist 198;
    Egyptian 188, 190; Minoan 31; Roman
    158; at Teotihuacán 84
Pu-abi, Queen 70
Pumasillo (Peru) 163
pyramids, American 82–4, 118–19, 121,
    127–9

Q

Qilakitsoq (Greenland) 174
Qin Shi Huangdi, Emperor 114
Qizilchoqa (China) 152
Quetzalcoatl, Temple of 82–4
quiver 144

R

Ramesses I 188
Ramesses II 188
Ramesses IX 196
Ravensholt (Denmark) 168
razors 68, 86, 99, 108
red ochre see ochre
Reinhard, Johan 160, 162

Reno, Major Marcus 88
Republic Graves (USA) 139
Retoka Island (New Hebrides) 133
rings 31, 95, 98, 127
Rinzo, Mamiya 199
Roman burials 77, 154–8
Romanov family 56–9
Roonka (Australia) 67
Rosing, Jens 174
Roy Mata 133
Rudenko, Sergei I. 146–7
Ruz Lhuillier, Alberto 127
Ryabov, Geli 58

S

sacrifice, animal 31, 71, 162
sacrifice, human (see also bog bodies),
    Ain Ghazal 44; Archanes-Anemospilia
    30–1; Inka mountain top 160–3; New
    Hebrides 133; Palenque 127; Teotihua-
    cán 82, 84; Ur 68, 71
St Germain-la-Rivière (France) 40
Sakellarakis, Evi & Yiannis 30
Sakhalin (Japan) 199
Salcantay (Peru) 163
Sangiran (Java) 25
sceptre 118
Schliemann, Heinrich 76, 92, 95
Schoentensack, Otto 20
Scott, Douglas 88, 89
Scythians 151
seals 31, 71, 101, 115
sealskin 174
Seti I 188, 190
Seti II 190
shabtis 188
shaft graves 92–5
Shanidar (Iraq) 35–6
Sharples, Niall 76
Shaw, Thurstan 130, 131
shells, in burials (see also beads),
    Dilmun 101; Grimaldi Cave 40; Indian
    Knoll 51; Klasies River Mouth Cave
    104, 105; La Chaussée-Tirancourt 47;
    Murray Valley 66; Teotihuacán 84;
    Vedbaek 62
Shizhaishan (China) 115
Shona empire 86
shrines 30–1, 161, 192
silver grave goods, Inka sacrifices 160;
    Macedonian tombs 111, 113; Mancheng
    114; Monte Albán 122; Mycenae 95;
    Pazyryk 150; Sipán 120; Ur 71
Similaun Man see Iceman
Singer, Ronald 105
Sipán (Peru) 118–21
Skateholm (Sweden) 62–4, 65

skulls, Natufian 44-5
Smenkhkare, King 192, 196
Smith, Elliot 186
snow goggles 177
Solecki, Ralph 35-6
spears 40, 74, 77, 95, 110
Spencely, Brian 170
spindle whorls 124
Stais 76
Stamatakis 92
stelae 77, 92, 93, 129
Sterkfontein (S. Africa) 16
stones, painted 104, 105
Strøby Egede (Denmark) 64-5
Subeshi (China) 152
Sumerian burials 68-71
Sungir (Russia) 39-40
surgery, evidence for 78-9, 152
swords 95, 98, 110

T

Taft, Dr Jonathan 89
Talgai (Australia) 26
Talheim (Germany) 48-9
Tarim Basin (China) 152-3
tattoos 141, 150, 174
Taung (S. Africa) 16
Tell Ramad (Syria) 44
Tello, Julio C. 78
temples 82-4, 127-9, 158
Teotihuacán (Mexico) 82-4
Terracotta Army 114-15
Terry, Brig. Gen. Alfred 88
Teutoburger Forest (Germany) 77
textiles (see also bark cloth;
    clothing), Danish bronze age burials
    96, 98; East Smithfield 55; Egyptian
    182, 184; Fujiwara 198; Hochdorf 108;
    Igombe Ilede 86; Ingombe Ilede 120;
    Inka sacrifices 160, 162; Macedonia
    111-12; Mancheng 114; Mary Island
    133; Mawangdui 114-15; Monte Albán
    123; Paracas 78, 79-80; Pazyryk 146,
    147, 150, 151; Sipán 120; Tarim Basin
    152; Windover Pond 138
Thespiai (Greece) 77
Thibrakos 77
Thordeman, Bengt 53
Thorne, Alan 26-8
Thule culture 174
tin cans 171
Tiy, Queen 190, 192, 196
Tlaloc 84
Tocharian problem 153
Tollund Man 168, 169
Tonga, Polynesian burials 132
Tongoa (New Hebrides) 133

tools (see also adzes; axes; handaxes;
    obsidian; weapons), Atapuerca 21;
    Bilzingsleben 20; Chinchorro 181;
    Grimaldi Cave 40; Heidelberg 20;
    Iceman 140, 141-4; Java Man 22;
    Klasies River Mouth Cave 105;
    Kostenki 39; La Chaussée-Tirancourt
    47; Le Moustier 34; Little Salt
    Spring 139; Murray Valley 66, 67;
    Skateholm 62, 64; Vedbaek 62; Wind-
    over Pond 138; Zhoukoudian 24
Toongimbie (Australia) 67
Torrington, John 170-1
trephination see surgery
Trinil (Java) 22
Trundholm (Denmark) 99
Trupp 59
tumuli, Danish bronze age 96-9;
    Dilmun 100-1; Hochdorf 106-9;
    Macedonian 110-13; Magan 101-2;
    Pazyryk 146-50
Turkana boy 18-19
turquoise 124
Tutankhamen, King 186, 192-6
Tuthmosis I-III, Kings 188, 190
Tuthmosis IV, King 190

U

Uhle, Max 180
Ukok Plateau (Altai Republic) 146, 150-1
Ur (Iraq) 68-71
Ust Ulagan (Altai Republic) 146-51
Utqiagvik (Alaska) 174-7

V

Vaihingen/Enz (Germany) 49
Valley of the Kings (Egypt) 192
Varus 77
Vedbaek (Denmark) 62, 64
Vergina (Macedonia) 110-13
Veronica (Peru) 163
Vértesszöllös (Hungary) 20
Vesonius Primus, house of 156
Vespasian 76
Vesuvius, eruption of 154-8
Villa del Mar (Peru) 181
Visby (Sweden) 52-4
Vix (France) 106

W

Wadi en-Natrun (Egypt) 184
wagons & carts (see also chariots) 71,
    108-9, 150, 156
Wairau Bar (New Zealand) 132-3
Waldemar, King 52
Walker, Alan 16, 18, 19
wall paintings 110
Walpolla Island (Australia) 66
Wamba Yadu (Australia) 67
Wari Kayan (Peru) 79
weapons (see also armour; arrows &
    arrowheads; bows; daggers & knives;
    spears; swords), Chaironeia 77;
    Dilmun 101; Magan 102; Mawangdui 114-
    15; Mycenae 94, 95; Pazyryk 150; Ur
    71
weaving battens 124-5
Webb, Steve 29, 66
Wennersten, Oscar 53
Wheeler, Sir Mortimer 74, 76
White, Tim 17
Wilbour, Charles 188
Willandra Lakes (Australia) 27, 28
Willey, P. 89
Williams, Robert 138
Wilton culture 104-5
Windover Pond (USA) 138-9
Wise, Karen 181
Woodruff Ossuary (USA) 51
Woolley, Sir Leonard 68, 70-1
Wymer, John 105

X

Xenophon 77
Xi'an (China) 114-15

Y

Yasuhira 198
Yekaterinburg (Russia) 56-9
Yeltsin, Boris 58
Yurovsky 57

Z

Zaghunluq (China) 152
Zapotec culture 122-3
Zhoukoudian (China) 22-5
Zimmerman, Larry 50

ACKNOWLEDGEMENTS

Front cover: Sygma
Back cover: E. T. Archive/Cairo Museum
Endpapers: Robert Harding Picture Library
Title page: Ancient Art & Architecture Collection

Page 6 ET; p7 PGB; p8 RHPL; pp12-13 Claude Masset; pp14, 15 Natural History Museum; p16l Transvaal Museum, r Francis Thackeray/Transvaal Museum; p17 AKG; pp18-19 National Museums of Kenya; p20 AKG; p21 Madrid Scientific Films; pp22,23 NHM; p24t AKG,b ET; p25 AKG; pp26-7, 28-9 NHPA; p28tl The Age, Melbourne; p30 A.J.N.W. Prag; p31t AAAC, b Manchester Museum; p32-3 RHPL; p34 ET; p35 NHM; p36l Ralph S. Solecki; p36-7 ET; p38-9 ET; p39t AAAC, b NHM; p40l Novosti, r Dr Klima; p41 ET; p42 AAAC; p 43 Scala; p44-5 AKG; pp46, 47 Claude Masset; pp48, 49 Landesdenkmalamt Baden-Württemberg; pp50, 51 Lawrence Zimmerman; p52, 53,54bl Antikvarisk-topografiska arkivet, Stockholm; p54tr, 55b Museum of London Archaeology Service; p55t Bibliothèque Royale Albert 1er, Brussels; pp56, 57t, 59t Novosti; p57bl,br Sygma; p59b Paul G. Bahn; p60-61, 63, 65 Nationalmuseet, Copenhagen; pp62, 64 Lars Larsson, Lunds Universitet; p66 Australian Museum/Nature Focus; p68 AAAC; p69 Scala; p70 Peter Clayton; p71 Werner Forman Archive; pp72, 73 Charles Higham, University of Otago; pp74-75, 75t English Heritage; p75b Society of Antiquaries of London; pp76-77, 77t AAAC; pp 78, 79 PGB; pp 80, 81, 82 RHPL; p83 PGB; p84-5 WF; pp 86, 87 David W. Phillipson; p88l ET, r Corbis/Bettmann; p89tl, tr Douglas Scott, National Parks Service, br Cynthia McDowell Duke; p90-91 RHPL; pp92, 93t, 95 AAAC; p93b Peter Clayton; p94 C. M. Dixon; pp96, 97, 98b, 99 Nationalmuseet, Copenhagen; p98t AKG; p100 Michael Jenner; pp 101, 102, 103 RHPL; pp104, 105 Johan Binneman; p106-7 Landesdenkmalamt Baden-Württemberg; pp107r, 108, 109 Konrad Theiss Verlag; pp110, 112 Archaeological Museum, Thessaloniki; pp111l, r, 113r Peter Clayton; p113l Manchester Museum; pp114-120, 121b RHPL; p121t Sygma; p122l Connie Cortez; pp122-3, 124-5 RHPL; p1124tl, bl Pictures of Record; p126 RHPL; pp127, 128l WF; p128r Pre-Columbian Art Research Institute; p129 Pictures of Record; p130l painting: Caroline Sassoon/photo: Thurston Shaw; pp130r, 131 WF; pp133-5 José Garanger; p136-7 RHPL; p138 Richard Brunck, Windover Staff Photographer; p139tl Nature/Philip J. Laipis, tr,cr University of Florida; p140 Sygma; p141tl Luigi Capasso, tr and b Frank Spooner Pictures; p142-3 Frank Spooner Pictures; p144-5b Gamma; p145 Sygma; pp146-9, 150br RHPL; p150tl Novosti; p151 Sygma; pp152, 153 Dolkun Kamberi; p154 AAAC; p155 Scala; p156bl Artephot; p156-7 WF; p158 AAAC; p159 Artephot; pp160, 161 Juan Schobinger; pp162, 163 Johan Reinhard; p164 Peter Clayton; p165 RHPL; p166-7 Silkeborg Museum; pp168-9 British Museum; p170 National Maritime Museum, Greenwich; pp171-3 Owen Beattie; pp175-177 WF; p178-9 Artephot; pp180-181 Bernardo Arriaza; p182 WF; p183t AKG, b AAAC; p184-5 BM; pp186, 187r Sygma; p187tl AAAC, bl ET; p188 Egyptian Museum, Cairo; pp189, 190bl Peter Clayton; p190-1 Sygma; p192bl Peter Clayton, r AKG; p 193 Scala; pp194-5, 197 RHPL; p196 Griffith Institute, Oxford; p198 Asahi; p199 Chusonji Temple.

Abbreviations: AAAC = Ancient Art & Architecture Collection, BM = British Museum, ET = E.T. Archive, NHM = Natural History Museum, London, PGB = Paul G Bahn, RHPL = Robert Harding Picture Library, WF = Werner Forman Archive